ALTERNATIV
OF SHARE
HONG KONG

The landscape of shareholder dispute resolution in Hong Kong has changed vastly since the launch of the Civil Justice Reform in 2009. Key initiatives – the voluntary court-connected scheme and reform of the statutory unfair prejudice provisions – were employed to promote the greater use of alternative dispute resolution (ADR) in shareholder disputes. While the Hong Kong government and judiciary introduced such schemes to prove the legitimacy of extrajudicial over court-based litigation processes, their success is still uncertain. In this book, sociolegal theory and sociological institutionalism are used to develop a theoretical framework for analyzing the key stages of institutionalization. The author analyzes how procedural innovations could acquire legitimacy through different types of legal and non-legal inducement mechanisms within the institutionalization process. Recommendations on codifying and innovating ADR policy in Hong Kong shareholder disputes are made, with comparisons to similar policies in the United Kingdom, South Africa and New Zealand.

IDA KWAN LUN MAK has a multidisciplinary academic background, with degrees in law and accountancy. Bilingual in English and Chinese, her research interests are primarily in the fields of company law, dispute resolution, arbitration, mediation and sociolegal studies, with a strong emphasis on empirical work in Hong Kong. Dr Mak is now working as a research assistant in the Department of Law at The University of Hong Kong.

ALTERNATIVE DISPUTE RESOLUTION OF SHAREHOLDER DISPUTES IN HONG KONG

Institutionalizing Its Effective Use

IDA KWAN LUN MAK

The University of Hong Kong

CAMBRIDGE
UNIVERSITY PRESS

CAMBRIDGE
UNIVERSITY PRESS

University Printing House, Cambridge CB2 8BS, United Kingdom

One Liberty Plaza, 20th Floor, New York, NY 10006, USA

477 Williamstown Road, Port Melbourne, VIC 3207, Australia

314-321, 3rd Floor, Plot 3, Splendor Forum, Jasola District Centre, New Delhi - 110025, India

79 Anson Road, #06-04/06, Singapore 079906

Cambridge University Press is part of the University of Cambridge.

It furthers the University's mission by disseminating knowledge in the pursuit of education, learning and research at the highest international levels of excellence.

www.cambridge.org
Information on this title: www.cambridge.org/9781108796118
DOI: 10.1017/9781108151849

First published 2017
First paperback edition 2019

A catalogue record for this publication is available from the British Library

ISBN 978-1-107-19419-9 Hardback
ISBN 978-1-108-79611-8 Paperback

This book is dedicated to my parents,
William Mak Kin-wah and Mary Chan Yuen-han

CONTENTS

FIGURES

TABLES

FOREWORD

The time has been reached when there is a critical need for fundamental rethinking as to the need for alternative forms of dispute resolution (ADR) of shareholder disputes. The burgeoning case load in Hong Kong and other major common law jurisdictions requires research and detailed study, a challenge which Dr Ida Mak Kwan-lun has undertaken with skill and thoughtfulness. *Alternative Dispute Resolution of Shareholder Disputes in Hong Kong: Institutionalizing Its Effective Use* is a totally new work rather than a revised or re-worked edition of an earlier book and Dr Mak has taken the opportunity to survey the field from a fresh perspective, unencumbered by the baggage of the past – and fresh thinking is the hallmark of this book. Dr Mak's work is therefore significant and very timely. The book gives the reader a thorough, stimulating and scholarly treatment of what by any measure has become a very complex corpus of rules. Its excellent analysis will, without doubt, inform the current debate on this important topic. The book deserves to occupy a central place on the bookshelves of practitioners, policymakers and academic commentators.

John Lowry
Professor Emeritus, University College London

ACKNOWLEDGEMENTS

This book is based on my doctoral dissertation, which I completed in the Faculty of Law at the University of Hong Kong during autumn 2014. Substantial modifications and changes have been made to parts of the dissertation for the publication of this book. I would like to take this opportunity to express my sincere thanks and appreciation to the following individuals, without whose encouragement, support and inspiration this book would not have been possible.

First and foremost, I wish to express my gratitude to my fabulous parents, William Mak Kin-wah and Mary Chan Yuen-han, for their enduring love, unselfish support, kindness and sacrifice. In particular, this book would not have been possible without the inspiration of my loving father, who generously shared his knowledge, thoughts and time with me in my long academic journey. The dedication of this book to my parents is a small token of my sincere gratitude to them.

I wish to thank my primary thesis supervisor, Katherine Lynch, for her supervision, valuable guidance and comments on the earlier drafts of my dissertation. I am especially grateful for her generous support, encouragement and valuable insights on the subject that helped me to improve the quality of my work during the dissertation process. I owe a special debt to Professor Richard Walker, the chair professor in the Department of Public Policy of the City University of Hong Kong, for his patience and encouragement and for providing me guidance on how to conduct legal empirical research. I was extremely fortunate to have his generous support in helping me improve the methodological framework in this book. I also wish to express my sincere thanks to Professor Johannes Chan, the former dean of the Faculty of Law at the University of Hong Kong, who provided technical support to launch an online survey through the Faculty of Law's website.

I would also like to extend my profound thanks to Professor John Lowry, the former Chair Professor of Commercial Law in the Faculty of Law at the University of Hong Kong, for his encouragement and valuable suggestions on the publication of this book. I am especially grateful to John for agreeing to write the Foreword to this book despite his busy work schedule.

At Cambridge University Press, I am indebted to my editor, Joe Ng, for his invaluable guidance and suggestions throughout the publication process. I express my heartfelt thanks also to all the anonymous reviewers for their comments and suggestions on my earlier versions of the manuscript. Thanks and gratitude are also to be extended to Bethany Johnson, content manager at Cambridge University Press, and Theresa Kornak for copyediting the manuscript.

I wish to express my heartfelt gratitude to my sister, Ada Mak Chiu-lun, for her constant support, encouragement and love. I am also indebted to Dr Wu Chong-hao, Dr Chan Su Jung, Dr Robert Morris, Dr James Fry, Karen Kong and Michael Wong for offering their kind assistance during my research study. I also want to express my appreciation to all the staff members of the Faculty of Law, Law Library and Main Library at the University of Hong Kong for their timely assistance.

Last but not least, I would like to express my appreciation to all Hong Kong lawyers who agreed to participate in this research study and spent their precious time to complete the questionnaire. Obviously, their opinions about the use of non-adjudicative dispute resolution processes to resolve shareholder disputes have also contributed to making this book a reality.

PART I

Introduction, Overview and Methodology

Introduction

1.1 Resolution of Shareholder Disputes in a Small Private Company

The majority of companies registered in the Hong Kong Company Registry are, in fact, closely held corporations whose shares are not publicly traded.[1] Clearly, these small quasi-partnership types of private limited companies are playing an important role in the Hong Kong economy, as about 60 per cent of the Hong Kong population is employed by these entities.[2] Although the strength of personal and/or family ties offers real benefits for shareholders to work closely together in a privately owned business, minority shareholders in particular are vulnerable to the opportunistic conduct of majority shareholders. Therefore, minority shareholder disputes are of concern primarily to private companies with management ownership concentrated in the hands of a small group of family members.

In general, the family business model can be viewed as the 'powerhouse' that not only generates wealth and economic well-being, but also strengthens the intimacy of family ties that support the ongoing operation of a family business.[3] These blood ties may consequently produce superior performance of a business enterprise.[4] However, the informal organizational structure of small private companies, coupled with the doctrine of majority rules, makes it possible for those who control the majority of shares in the company to employ a variety of squeeze-out techniques

[1] Statistics Relating to the Number of Local Companies Incorporated in Hong Kong. Available at www.cr.gov.hk/en/statistics/statistics_02.htm (Accessed 10 August 2016).
[2] *Corporate Governance Review by the Standard Committee on Company Law Reform: A Consultation Paper made in Phase I of the Review* (Printing Department, 2001) at para. 1.04.
[3] Grant Gordon and Nigel Nicholson, *Family Wars: Classic Conflicts in Family Business and How to Deal with Them* (London: Kogan Page, 2008).
[4] Richard Milne, 'Blood Ties Serve Business Well During the Crisis', *Financial Times*, 28 December 2009, 15 and Benjamin Means, 'NonMarket Values in Family Business', *William & Mary Law Review*, 54 (2013), 1185–1250 at 1230.

(such as exclusion from management, dilution of minority shareholding with an improper motive, excessive remuneration, misapplication of company assets and similar practices), which are unfairly prejudicial to the interests of minority shareholders who hold fewer shares in the company.[5]

Corporate conflicts can be destructive when multiple disputes involving the desire for power and wealth and other personal feelings remain unresolved.[6] In particular, Corporate conflicts involve 'deep-rooted issues which are seen as non-negotiable', whereas shareholder disputes are considered specific disagreements relating to the question of rights or interests in which disputing parties proceed through a range of dispute resolution methods, such as adjudication, mediation, avoidance, self-help and so on.[7] In the corporate environment, the self-interested desire to increase power or wealth could further lead to the breakdown of the personal relationships between shareholders and result in deep-rooted conflicts in which issues are non-negotiable.[8] In general, the most common types of behavioural patterns associated with distinctive characteristics of shareholder disputes in a small, closely held company such as marital discord,[9] sibling rivalry[10] and so on could disrupt the family business.

[5] Sandra K. Miller, 'Minority Shareholder Oppression in the Private Company in the European Community: A Comparative Analysis of the German, United Kingdom, and French "Close Corporation Problem"', *Cornell International Law Journal*, 30 (1997), 381–427 at 391 and John Farrar et al., 'Dispute Resolution in Family Companies', *Canterbury Law Review*, 18 (2012), 155–186 at 159.

[6] Susanna M. Kim, 'The Provisional Director Remedy for Corporate Deadlock: A Proposed Model Statute', *Washington and Lee Law Review*, 60 (2003), 111–181 at 112.

[7] John Burton, *Conflict: Resolution and Provention* (New York: St. Martin's Press, 1993), 2–3 and John Collier and Vaughan Lowe, *The Settlement of Disputes in International Law: Institutions and Procedures*, (Oxford: Oxford University Press, 1999), 1–2.

[8] See generally *A & BC Chewing Gum Ltd* [1975] 1 All ER 1017, *Re Cumana Ltd* [1986] BCLC 430, *RA Noble and Sons (Clothing) Ltd* [1983] BCLC 273 and *North Holdings Ltd v. Southern Tropics Ltd* [1999] 2 BCLC 625. These cases decided by the UK courts reflect that self-interested behaviour led to the breakdown of the personal relationships between shareholders and caused disputes. See also *Russell v. Northern Bank Development Corporation Ltd* [1992] BCLC 1016. This case illustrates that the desire to increase power or wealth led to the breakdown of relationship between shareholders. The term 'deadlock' refers to 'corporate paralysis stemming from disputes between equally powerful shareholder groups'. For details, see Note, 'Mandatory Arbitration as a Remedy for Intra-close Corporate Disputes', *Virginia Law Review*, 56 (1970), 271–294 at 271.

[9] See, for example, *Chu Chung Ming v. Lam Wai Dan* [2014] HKEC 2132 (unreported, HCCW 377/2011, 22 December 2014) (CFI). This case illustrates that marital discord between a husband and wife can further sour their business relationship in a closely held corporation.

[10] See, for example, *Kwok Ping Sheung Walter v. Sun Hung Kai Properties Ltd* [2008] 3 HKC 465, which is another example of shareholder disputes in Hong Kong where siblings are competing for the position of the chief executive officer and chairman.

For instance, disputes can arise over the power to control business activities among members of the second generation after the passing of the founder of a family business.[11] The younger siblings may take an entrenched position with regard to either retaliation against the first-born for receiving preferential treatment or disagreement about the company's strategies. The younger siblings could form an alliance with other senior family members to usurp the first-born's authority by using squeeze-out techniques available under the majority rule to diminish the role or the stake of the first-born in the company. In this scenario, an unresolved dispute among the siblings and other family members within the company escalates into a full-blown crisis that would jeopardize the survival of the family business.

Clearly, there could be various possible underlying factors in shareholder disputes (such as unresolved issues from the past, sibling rivalry, interpersonal relationships, etc.) inviting a general state of hostility between members in a small private company (i.e., corporate conflicts). Corporate conflicts from which shareholder disputes emerge are undesirable, as these could eventually lead to the irretrievable breakdown in relations in a small private company (such as deadlock). To prevent the relational breakdown due to unresolved personal conflicts among shareholders in a small and closely held corporation, both the Hong Kong government and the Judiciary should aspire to developing a sophisticated dispute resolution system that offers a range of formal and informal dispute resolution processes for local businesspersons and their lawyers to choose from.[12] Further, such a system could reinforce Hong Kong's competitiveness and attractiveness as a global financial centre.

Over the past decades, the Hong Kong government has sought to emulate the United Kingdom's corporate legal framework by amending its Companies Ordinance virtually step-by-step tracking many of the

---

[11] See, for example, *Re Mak Shing Yue Tong Commemorative Association Ltd* [2005] 4 HKLRD 328, which is a typical example of how the death of the founder of a family business led to a disruption involving a breakdown of relationships among a number of grandchildren in that company. A winding-up on the just and equitable order was sought under Section 177(1)(f) of the Companies (Winding-Up and Miscellaneous Provisions) Ordinance (Cap. 32).

[12] Linda R. Singer, *Settling Disputes: Conflict Resolution in Business, Families, and the Legal System*, 2nd ed. (New York: Westview Press, 1994), 15–29. According to Singer, there are a variety ways to resolve shareholder disputes, ranging from the base of unassisted negotiation to the apex of traditional court adjudication process. See also John Lande, 'A Guide for Policymaking that Emphasizes Principles, and Public Needs', *Alternatives to High Cost Litigation*, 26:11 (2008), 197–205 at 204.

reforms in the United Kingdom.[13] Court-based shareholder proceedings have been generally regarded as the most appropriate ways of dealing with shareholder disputes where the majority shareholders are exercising abusive power to gain outright control of the company, depriving the company minority of their rights and interests.[14] Minority shareholders submit their disputes for resolution by a third-party judge, thereby surrendering a degree of control over the proceedings under this traditional, litigation-based approach to resolving minority shareholder disputes.[15] An independent neutral judge has the authority to impose an authoritative decision on the parties based on evaluations of the pre-existing legal principles and the legal rights of the disputing parties. Generally speaking, there are three underlying reasons for the attractiveness of court-based shareholder proceedings under the statutory unfair prejudice provisions.

First, the statutory unfair prejudice remedy was initially introduced as an alternative to the just and equitable winding-up remedy in Hong Kong.[16] This provision makes it easier for a minority shareholder to bring an action to the court in a case in which the nature of the complaint is related to the infringement of personal rights rather than a breach of duty to, or other misconducts actionable by, the company.[17]

In Hong Kong, the vast majority of companies are small and medium-sized enterprises.[18] They are often formed on the basis of mutual trust originating from close and personal relationships between members.[19]

---

[13] See, for example, the proposed rules of 4, 5, 6 and 9 of the new Companies (Unfair Prejudice Proceedings) Rules (Cap. 622) formulated with reference to the Companies (Unfair prejudice Applications) Proceedings Rules 2009 of the United Kingdom.

[14] Farrar et al., 'Dispute Resolution in Family Companies', 159–161.

[15] For details, see John H. Farrar and Laurence J. Boulle, 'Minority Shareholders Remedies – Shifting Dispute Resolution Paradigms', *Bond Law Review*, 13 (2001), 1–32 at 7–8.

[16] Hong Kong Companies Law Revision Committee, *Company Law: Second Report of the Companies Law Revision Committee* (Government Printer, 1973) at paras. 5.95–103. In 1973, the Hong Kong Companies Law Revision Committee recommended introducing the statutory protection of minority shareholders. The underlying policy reason behind the introduction of a statutory remedy for minority shareholders is to provide more effective protection to this group. This recommendation was subsequently adopted and Section 168A was inserted by No. 51 of the Companies (Amendment) Ordinance 1978.

[17] Corporate Governance Review by the Standard Committee on Company Law Reform: A Consultation Paper made in Phase I of the Review at para. 16.02. The underlying premise for the statutory remedies for shareholders is 'the member's personal right to be treated fairly'.

[18] Statistics Relating to the Number of Local Companies Incorporated in Hong Kong.

[19] *Ebrahimi v. Westbourne Galleries Ltd* [1973] AC 360 at 379.
    Section 29(1) of the Hong Kong Companies Ordinance states that a private company is defined as a company which by its articles (a) restricts the rights to transfer its shares; and

A member in a small private enterprise typically places great reliance on the understandings that form the basis on which the company was formed to actively participate in the business affairs.[20] These understandings, however, are in fact not truly reflected in the articles or any other written agreements. The character of a quasi-partnership company was reflected in a seminal case, *Ebrahimi v. Westbourne Galleries Ltd*, where Lord Wilberforce stated that[21]

> The words ["just and equitable"] are a recognition of the fact that a limited company is more than a mere judicial entity, with a personality in law of its own: that there is room in company law for recognition in fact that behind it, or amongst it, there are individuals, with rights, expectations and obligations inter se which are not necessarily submerged in the company structure.

On that basis, it is not uncommon that the statutory unfair prejudice remedy is usually sought by aggrieved shareholders in private companies, as the scope for finding expectations which are supplementary to a member's strict legal rights is obviously greater in small quasi-partnership types of private limited companies.[22]

Second, the court's discretionary power in granting relief under the unfair prejudice provisions has been substantially enhanced through the Companies (Amendment) Bill 2004 and more recently the new Companies Ordinance (Cap. 622) which took effect on 3 March 2014.[23] Specifically, Section 725(2)(b) of the new Companies Ordinance expands the court's discretion to grant corporate relief in an unfair prejudice petition.[24] This

---

(b) limits the number of its members to 50, not including persons who are in the employment of the company and persons who, having been formerly in the employment of the company, were while in that employment and have continued after the determination of that employment to be, members of the company; and (c) prohibits any invitation to the public to subscribe for any shares or debentures of the company.

[20] See, for example, *Grace v. Biagioli* [2006] BCC at 104.

[21] AC 360 at 379.

[22] Alan J. Dignam and John Lowry, *Company Law*, 8th ed. (Oxford: Oxford University Press, 2014), 234.

[23] Legislative Council, *Paper on Companies Bill Prepared by the Legislative Council Secretariat* (Background Brief), (2011); Hong Kong Financial Services and the Treasury Bureau, *New Companies Ordinance: Subsidiary Legislation for Implementation of the New Companies Ordinance* (Phase Two Consultation Document) (Hong Kong Financial Services and the Treasury Bureau, 2012), Part 12 and the Hong Kong SAR Government, *Press Releases: Companies* (Unfair Prejudice Petitions) *Proceedings Rules Submitted to LegCo* (15 May 2013).

[24] This provision is consonant with the theme running through English law that members of a company cannot claim for losses which merely reflect the company's loss, i.e., reflective

provision can be viewed as the most remarkable improvement, as it provides greater clarity and certainty with regard to the court's power to grant
damages in the event of unfair prejudice.[25] Also, the provision of Section
168A of the former Companies Ordinance (Cap. 32) is modified to be in
line with the corresponding provisions in the UK Companies Act 2006,
which extend the scope of unfair prejudice remedy to cover 'proposed
acts or omissions'.[26]

Third, the new statutory unfair prejudice remedy has proved to be more
effective than the statutory derivative actions.[27] Remedies under the unfair
prejudice provisions are much wider than both the common law and statutory derivative actions.[28] A list of specific remedies is set out in the unfair
prejudice provision (such as the court's power to grant damages in circumstances of unfair prejudice, or a share purchase order for a buyout of the
minority shareholders, etc.). This provision empowers the court to make
any order that it thinks fit for giving relief. In addition, an unfair prejudice
claim is generally perceived to be more attractive, as shareholders would
not necessarily need to go through the expenses and uncertainties of a leave
application.[29]

However, Hong Kong's corporate legal framework is largely influenced
by its UK counterpart, as it was a former British colony.[30] The English
common law adversarial system maintains its influence over the manner in which evidence is to be adduced by the parties during the course

---

loss (*Prudential Assurance Co Ltd v. Newman Industries Ltd (No 2)* [1982] Ch 204 (CA (Civ.
Div.))). This principle is reflected in Section 725(5) of the new Companies Ordinance. In
Re Lehman Brown Ltd [2013] HKEC 357 (unreported, CACV 272/2011, 13 March 2013)
(CA), the court held that the award of damages under Section 725(2)(b) (formerly Section
168A (2C)) should be set aside if it contravened the principle of reflective loss.

[25] Rita Cheung, 'Corporate Wrongs Litigated in the Context of Unfair Prejudice
Claims: Reforming the Unfair Prejudice Remedy for the Redress of Corporate Wrongs',
Company Lawyer, 29:4 (2008), 98–104 at 101–102.

[26] Section 724(1)(b) of the Companies Ordinance (Cap. 622). A similar provision is found in
Section 994(1)(b) of the UK Companies Act 2006.

[27] The statutory derivative action in the predecessor Sections 168BA to 168BK of the former Companies Ordinance (Cap. 32) is now found in Part 14, Division 4 (Sections 730 to
738) of the new Ordinance.

[28] Section 725(2) to (5) sets out the orders that the court can make upon finding that there
is unfair prejudice following a petition under Section 724. This provision is derived from
Section 168A(2), (2B), (2C) in the former Companies Ordinance (Cap. 32).

[29] Rita Cheung, *Company Law and Shareholders' Rights* (Hong Kong: LexisNexis, 2010), 293.

[30] Article 8 of the Hong Kong Basic Law stipulates that the laws previously in force in Hong
Kong, i.e., the common law, rules of equity, ordinances, subordinate legislation and cus-
tomary law shall be maintained, unless they contravene the Basic Law, and are subject to
any amendment by the Legislative Council.

of unfair prejudice proceedings. Shareholder litigation remains costly, as the complexity of both the evidentiary and procedural rules may eventually lead to a greater reliance on lawyers to represent a lay businessperson who is without any litigation experience in court.[31] Thus, the courts would have to serve as the last resort for minority shareholders whose legal or equitable rights or interests have been violated by those who control the majority of shares in a company.

Indeed, shareholders react to disputes not only through public court adjudicative process for settlement, but also through various techniques, including revenge, self-help, avoidance, negotiation, mediation and similar methods for handling disputes.[32] Shareholder disputes involve both legal and non-legal elements that can influence not only the outcome of the case, but also the choice of a particular process.[33] Every procedure has its own characteristics. Shareholders and their lawyers can decide which dispute resolution methods fit their needs. In general, the basic processes for settling shareholder disputes are listed as follows:

- **Negotiation:** A quasi-partnership company enables shareholders to explore the possibility of early settlement by negotiating the terms of the buyout before trial.[34]
- **Facilitative mediation:** This process opens the channel of communication that encourages the parties to maximize their chances of maintaining a good relationship in the future.[35]
- **Collaboration and collaborative practice:** Like mediation, this process is a 'solution-oriented and interest-based process' that involves identification and selection of options and alternatives maximizing the

---

[31] Alex Lau et al., 'In Search of Good Governance for Asian Family Listed Companies: A Case Study on Hong Kong', *The Company Lawyer*, 28:10 (2007), 306–311 at 310.

[32] William L. F. Felstiner, 'Avoidance as Dispute Processing: An Elaboration', *Source: Law & Society Review*, 9:4 (1975), 695–706 at 695 and Donald Black, 'The Elementary Forms of Conflict Management', *New Directions in the Study of Justice, Law, and Social Control* (New York: Plenum Press, 1990), 43–62.

[33] Carrie Menkel-Meadow, 'From Legal Disputes to Conflict Resolution and Human Problem Solving: Legal Dispute Resolution in a Multidisciplinary Context', *Journal of Legal Education*, 54:1 (2004), 7–29 at 10.

[34] Philip Lawton, 'Modelling the Chinese Family Firm and Minority Shareholer Protection: The Hong Kong Experience 1980–1995', *Managerial Law*, 49:5/6 (2007), 249–271 at 263. According to Lawton, judicial support for an early buyout offer at a fair price is by far the most commonly sought remedy under the statutory unfair prejudice provisions.

[35] Frank E. A. Sander and Lukasz Rozdiczer, 'Matching Cases and Dispute Resolution Procedures: Detailed Analysis Leading to a Mediation-Centered Approach', *Harvard Negotiation Law Review*, 11 (2006), 1–41 at 35.

interests of all parties.[36] However, the most obvious difference between mediation and collaborative approach is 'the dynamics of the process'.[37] The collaborative model enables the parties to work with a team of collaborative lawyers and other experts (such as psychologists, accountants and financial planners) in achieving mutually a satisfactory settlement.[38] The collaborative process could also be used in resolving shareholder disputes as this process offers not only individual support to each client.[39] In addition, the multidisciplinary nature of the collaborative practice offers specialized support from professionals in helping the parties to deal with sensitive and emotional issues.

- **Mini-trial:** Shareholders may strongly prefer a mini-trial if they want to minimize the costs associated with the lengthy investigation of the unfair prejudice conducts during the court litigation process. A mini-trial is generally considered a suitable alternative means of resolving shareholder disputes where shareholders seek to explore the possibility of early settlement. In the mini-trial, a neutral third party can make an early assessment of the strengths and weaknesses of each side's case and the likely outcome of litigation.[40]

- **Expert determination:** Expert determination is a common mode of informal dispute resolution process used to resolve shareholder disputes.[41] In expert determination, a neutral third party is appointed by the parties who possesses sufficient technical expertise in the subject matter of the disputes to bring to bear in the making of decisions. The nature of expert determination makes it particularly suitable to solving unfair prejudice cases where the only outstanding issue is a technical matter such as the valuation of minority's shareholdings in the event of a buyout.[42]

- **Arbitration:** This process has generally been preferred over litigation for resolving cross-border shareholder disputes as the enforcement of arbitration agreements is secured by the most important international

---

[36] P Oswin Chrisman et al., 'Collaborative Practice Mediation: Are We Ready to Serve This Emerging Market', *Pepperdine Dispute Resolution Law Journal*, 6:3 (2006), 451–464 at 453.

[37] Robert Lopich, 'Collaborative Law Overview: Towards Collaborative Problem-solving in Business', *ADR Bulletin*, 10:8 (2009), 161–166 at 163–165.

[38] Ibid.

[39] Ibid. at 165–166.

[40] Catherine Cronin-Harris, 'Mainstreaming: Systematizing Corporate Use of ADR', *Albany Law Review*, 59 (1995), 847–879 at 853.

[41] For details, see Chapter 2.

[42] See, for example, *O'Neill v. Phillips* [1999] BCC.

treaty, namely, the New York Convention on the Recognition and Enforcement of Foreign Arbitral Award (the New York Convention 1958).[43]

- **Adjudication:** A court adjudicative process is particularly suitable where both parties have the desire to discontinue their business relationship and to achieve a clean break.[44]

Obviously, court-based shareholder proceedings are by no mean the most superior settlement procedures. First, the underlying causes of shareholder disputes including misunderstandings, feelings and personality clashes are often overlooked or ignored by either the court or the corporate lawyers. These subjective aspects of shareholder disputes are, in fact, located at the submerged part of the iceberg, and it is not always a straightforward matter for the court or lawyers to identify one factor or a combination of factors which contribute to the breakdown of a quasi-partnership type company (see Figure 1.1).[45]

In general, the role of the court is not to investigate who or what caused the breakdown of personal relationships between shareholders.[46] Instead, the focal point of the court's enquiry in determining whether a shareholder has been prejudiced in an unfair manner is the effect of the opportunistic conduct of the majority and not the nature of the conducts that are the subject of the complaint.[47] Judges often miss the true cause of a dispute (such as personality clashes) as they concentrate on the 'objective aspects' of shareholder disputes and the application of law and equity in determining whether the conduct complained about is unfairly prejudicial to

---

[43] See generally Stavros L Brekoulakis, 'The Notion of the Superiority of Arbitration Agreements Over Jurisdiction Agreements: Time to Abandon It?', *Journal of International Arbitration*, 24:4 (2007), 341–364.

[44] James Carter and Sophie Payton, 'Arbitration and Company Law in England and Wales', *European Company Law*, 12:3 (2015), 138–143 at 143.

[45] Jeremy Lack, 'Appropriate Dispute Resolution (ADR): The Spectrum of Hybrid Techniques Available to the Parties' in Arnold ingen-Housz (ed.), *ADR in Business: Practice and Issues across Countries and Cultures*, Vol. II (The Hague: Kluwer Law International, 2011), 341–342.

[46] *O'Neill v. Phillips* [1999] BCC 600 at 612.

[47] *Re Yung Kee Holdings Ltd* [2012] HKEC 1480 (unreported, HCCW 154/2010, 31 October 2012) (CFI) at para. 116 and *Anthony A Sperandeo v. George Lencsak* [2015] HKEC (unreported, HCMP 1022/2013, 4 December 2015) at para. 11. See also D. D. Prentice, 'The Theory of the Firm: Minority Shareholder Oppression: Sections 459–461 of the Companies Act 1985', *Oxford Journal of Legal Studies*, 8:1 (1988), 55–91 at 78 and David Milman, 'The Rise of the Objective Concept of 'Unfairness' in UK Company Law', *Company Law Newsletter*, 286 (2010), 1–4.

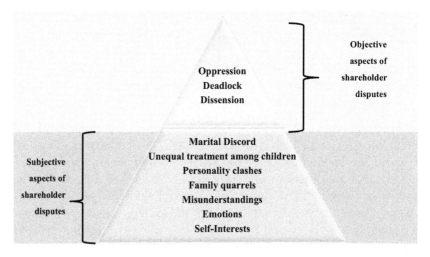

Figure 1.1 The iceberg of disputes between shareholders in a family-owned business.

the interests of minority shareholders. In general, the objective aspects of shareholder disputes can be classified as follows:[48]

• **Dissension:** Disputes between the shareholders inter se may lead to dissension, where a minority shareholder might either dissatisfy or disagree with the corporate policies which management is pursuing.[49]
• **Oppression:** A dissident shareholder may file a petition to the court alleging that the conduct of the majority shareholders was unfairly prejudicial to the interests of the petitioners.[50]
• **Deadlock:** Dissension may subsequently result in serious disagreement in a company, and this may be harmful to the continuation of an ongoing business, as it could lead to the drastic consequence of a winding-up.[51]

---

[48] Note, 'Mandatory Arbitration as a Remedy for Intra-close Corporate Disputes', *Virginia Law Review*, 56 (1970), 271–294.

[49] A. J. Boyle, *Minority Shareholders' Remedies* (Cambridge: Cambridge University Press, 2002), 101, Boyle notes that a distinction has to be made between a breach of duty by a director and a serious and persistent mismanagement when considering proceedings brought under either the statutory derivative action or personal action under Section 994 of the UK Companies Act 2006. This is due to the fact that disagreement between shareholders as to a particular managerial decision is not enough to justify the court's intervention.

[50] Section 724 of the Companies Ordinance (Cap. 622).

[51] Companies (Winding-Up and Miscellaneous Provisions) Ordinance (Cap. 32).

The court's approach to the scope of unfair prejudice provision affects significantly lawyers' approaches towards handling of shareholder disputes. The true causes of shareholder disputes, such as misunderstandings, fears and personal feelings, are rarely discussed between lawyers and their clients.[52] Consequently, court adjudicative process focuses specifically on a faction of disputing issues, regardless of the submerged part of those underlying facts that contribute to shareholder disputes.

Second, Lord Hoffmann's reasoning in *O'Neill v. Phillips* has been expressly adopted and applied by the Hong Kong courts, which recognize only the parties' expectations arising either from formal contractual agreements or informal understandings binding under the general principles of law and equity.[53] An alleged unfairly prejudicial conduct is assessed objectively not only on whether an honest and reasonable man would regard the conduct complained is unfairly prejudicial to the interests of the members generally or of some part of its members in the particular business context.[54] In addition, the content of 'unfairness' is to be judged by reference to established equitable rules (such as the doctrine of good faith) instead of allowing vague notions of unfairness to be used in creating commercial uncertainty as to the costs and length of the proceedings.[55] This approach inevitably limits the concept of unfairness, as the type of the petitioner's legitimate expectations is usually confined within the ambit of the statutory unfair prejudice remedy as delineated in *O'Neill v. Phillips*, on the basis of the recognition either that the expectations formed part of the implied terms of the agreements or understandings when a person becomes a member or that they arise out of the exercise of strict legal rights in a manner which equity would regard as contrary to good faith.[56]

---

[52] Jeremy Lack, 'Appropriate Dispute Resolution (ADR): The Spectrum of Hybrid Techniques Available to the Parties' in Arnold ingen-Housz (ed.), *ADR in Business: Practice and Issues across Countries and Cultures*, Vol. II (The Hague: Kluwer Law International, 2011), 341–342.

[53] *Re Ching Hing Construction Co Ltd* [2001] HKEC 1402 (unreported, HCCW 889/1999, 23 November 2001) (CFI) at para. 34; *Wong Man Yin v. Ricacorp Properties Ltd & Others* [2003] 3 HKLRD 75 at 88–89; *Re Kam Fai Electroplating Factory Ltd* [2004] HKEC 556 (unreported, HCCW 534/2000, 8 December 2003) at para. 82 and *Re Yung Kee Holdings Ltd 3* [2014] 2 HKLRD 313 at 346.

[54] *Re Yung Kee Holdings Ltd 3* [2014] 2 HKLRD 313 at 344.

[55] See supra note 46.

[56] John Lowry, 'Mapping the Boundaries of Unfair Prejudice' in John de Lacy (ed.), *The Reform of United Kingdom Company Law* (London: Cavendish, 2002), 239–240; Robin Hollington, *Hollington on Shareholders' Rights*, 7th (ed.) (London: Sweet & Maxwell,

Although the concept of unfairness has been narrowly construed, the categories of unfairly prejudicial conduct are not closed.[57] This is particularly true as the court is entitled to exercise its discretionary power in the statutory unfair prejudice jurisdiction to elucidate the equitable principles and considerations, including the imposition of equitable constraints to estop the majority from exercising a strict legal right which is unfairly prejudicial to the interests of the members generally or of some part of its members.[58] Unfair prejudice proceedings can still be lengthy and potentially expensive. Specifically, in order to establish a good arguable case that the alleged conduct is unfairly prejudicial, the petitioners still have to produce detailed accounts of the history of the company and show that the parties have come to some other specific arrangements or promises which are not reflected in the articles and the provisions of the Ordinance. On such a basis, it seems appropriate to consider a broad array of innovative dispute resolution techniques that may help to reduce the burgeoning caseload on the court.[59]

Generally speaking, the term alternative dispute resolution (ADR) is used interchangeably with the term 'innovative dispute resolution', and it is defined as an alternative method of settling disputes which are separated from court adjudication.[60] ADR includes a broad range of informal non-litigious forms of dispute resolution processes, including but not limited to arbitration, mediation, expert determination, early neutral evaluation, mini-trial, hybrid processes (such as the combination of mediation and arbitration) and similar.[61] Each of these informal out-of-court processes can be ranked in terms of the degree of formality (flexibility/rigidity) and

---

2013) and Stefan H.C Lo and Charles Z Qu, *Law of Companies in Hong Kong* (HK: Sweet & Maxwell/Thomas Reuters, 2013), 445.

[57] John Lowry, 'The Pursuit of Effective Minority Shareholder Protection: Section 459 of the Companies Act 1985', *Company Lawyer*, 17 (1996), 67–72 and Lo and Qu, 'Law of Companies in Hong Kong', 442.

[58] In *Re Yung Kee Holdings Ltd* 3 [2014] 2 HKLRD 313 at 358, the court felt justified to follow the approach taken by Lord Hoffman in *O'Neill* and acknowledged that the jurisprudential basis for the court to impose equitable constraints over the unfair exercise of strict legal rights rested on the traditional equitable principles instead of the law of partnership. The traditional equitable principles include the doctrines of equitable estoppel, and constructive trust.

[59] Lowry, 'The Pursuit of Effective Minority Shareholder Protection', 72.

[60] Andrew J. Pirie, 'Alternative Dispute Resolution in Thailand and Cambodia: Making Sense on (Un)Common Ground' in Douglas M. Johnston and Gerry Ferguson (eds.), *Asia-Pacific Legal Development* (UBC Press, 1998), 505.

[61] Henry J. Brown and Arthur Marriott, *ADR Principles and Practice*, 2nd ed. (London: Sweet & Maxwell, 2011), 19–24.

the level of control of the processes across the spectrum. These informal out-of-court processes place efficiency, privacy, consent and individual participation above strict observance of legal rules and principles developed either by the court or as legislative enactments. As Hwang indicates, it is generally accepted that arbitration and other non-judicial methods are particularly suitable for the resolution of private company shareholder disputes.[62]

At present, the key initiatives to promote the greater use of ADR to resolve shareholder disputes include the development of a voluntary court-connected ADR scheme for shareholder disputes initiated in 2009[63] and the reform of the statutory unfair prejudice provisions which took effect on 3 March 2014.[64] The new court rules, judicial directives on ADR and a new set of specific procedural rules for unfair prejudice applications have been introduced that confer specific case management powers on the courts to encourage earlier settlement of disputes and to monitor the preparation of cases for trial.[65] Court-connected mediation becomes an integral part of modern case management systems as judges have to carry out their duties to actively promote the greater use of mediation in resolving shareholder disputes.[66] Mediation is now recognized as the primary ADR process used for the reform of the law and procedures relating to unfair prejudice proceedings.[67] Clearly, the Hong Kong Judiciary and the Hong Kong government are considered to be the key role-players in promoting and encouraging the greater use of private extrajudicial processes for resolving shareholder disputes.

The Civil Justice Reform (CJR) in Hong Kong represents a major and innovative shift from the traditional, litigation-centred approach to resolving disputes and to move towards a regime which recognizes the proper

[62] Michael Hwang, 'The Prospects for Arbitration and Alternative Dispute Resolution', in Fianna Jesover (ed.), *Corporate Governance in Emerging Markets Enforcement of Corporate Governance in Asia the Unfinished Agenda* (Paris: OECD, 2007), 87.
[63] Practice Direction 3.3.
[64] Section 727 of the Companies Ordinance (Cap. 622) and Rule 6 of the Companies (Unfair Prejudice Petitions) Rules (Cap. 622L).
[65] Ibid. and Order 1A, Rule 4(2)(e) of the Rules of the High Court (RHC).
[66] Lawrence Boulle, *Mediation: Principles, Process, Practice* (Sydney: Butterworths, 1996), 186–193.
[67] Rimsky Yuen, 'HK a Perfect Partner in Mediation', Conference on *Asia Pacific International Mediation Summit* (India, 15 February 2015). See, for example, that Practice Direction 3.3 sets out the provision for voluntary mediation with respect to the presentation of petitions at any stage of the unfair prejudice proceedings.

use of alternative methods to resolve disputes. However, it is uncertain whether the effects of these ADR initiatives have achieved the intended goals of extrajudicial processes being perceived as more attractive and acceptable approaches to resolving shareholder disputes. In particular, the concern is not only that the widespread use of mediation as the predominant means to resolve shareholder disputes may exacerbate imbalance of power between the majority and minority shareholders in a closely held corporation.[68] An additional consideration is that the majority shareholders may be reluctant to settle or compromise at the mediation stage, as they believe that they would win the case.[69]

Given the limitations of mediation and other alternative processes in resolving shareholder disputes, a balance must be struck between the right of access to the courts and the need for the maintenance of public confidence in using ADR processes to resolve shareholder disputes. This raises deeper questions about the extent to which innovative dispute resolution techniques are introduced as part of the legal framework for the resolution of shareholder disputes, and equally important, about the extent of understanding and awareness of innovative dispute resolution methods among the local legal professions.

Against the background of a new disputing landscape of Hong Kong, this book seeks to develop a theoretical framework in analysing the key stages of institutionalization that enhance the legitimacy of informal out-of-court processes for the resolution of shareholder disputes. In this context, 'institutionalization' refers to a process by which certain practices (such as mediation) have acquired legitimacy through their link to a broader cultural framework of beliefs or a set of rules or norms that most people support and will therefore endorse the practices.[70] Institutionalization is directly linked with legitimacy or acceptance,

---

[68] Owen M. Fiss, 'Against Settlement', *The Yale Law Journal*, 93:6 (1984), 1073–1090 at 1076 and Marc Galanter, 'Litigation and Dispute Processing: Part One', *Law & Society Review*, 9:1 (1974), 95–160 at 99–100.

[69] The facilitative model is adopted as the dominant model of mediation in Hong Kong; see Section 3 of the Hong Kong Mediation Ordinance (Cap. 620). This model 'places decision-making control entirely on the hands of the parties and not the mediator'. For details see Robert A. Baruch Bush and Joseph P. Folger, 'Mediation and Social Justice: Rists and Opportunities', *Ohio State Journal on Dispute Resolution*, 27 (2012), 1–52 at 38.

[70] Walter W. Powell and Paul J. DiMaggio, 'Introduction', in Paul J. DiMaggio and Walter W. Powell (eds.), *The New Institutionalism in Organizational Analysis* (Chicago: University of Chicago Press, 1991), 9 and James E. Westphal, 'The Social Construction of Market Value: Institutionalization and Learning Perspectives on Stock Market Reactions', *American Sociological Review*, 69 (2004), 433–457 at 433.

which provides a social basis in which certain practices are deemed desirable, proper or appropriate within some socially constructed system of norms, rules, values and beliefs.[71] The degree of institutionalization can then be measured in terms of three main types of legitimacy: pragmatic, moral and cultural-cogitative legitimacy.[72] Thus, the implications of the transition from the initial phase of ADR development to a more sophisticated stage in which extrajudicial processes would generally be perceived as preferred vehicles to resolve shareholders disputes can be understood in the conception of a relationship between the types of legitimacy derived from the key stages of institutionalization and the types of institutional pressures exerted by legislative mandates, the court system and the critical role of lawyers in constructing a new paradigm for dispute resolution.

Previous sociolegal academics, however, have not examined the key stages of institutionalization involved in producing legitimacy for the use of ADR for shareholder disputes in Hong Kong. In particular, scholars are less concerned with how the involvement of lawyers and the combined set of policy instruments could support the institutionalization process for ADR development.[73] Others analyse the concept of the institutionalization process in a narrow sense, as only one type of regulative legitimacy (such as court rules and specific legislations) is normally considered the most desirable method of institutionalizing the significant use of

---

[71] Mark C. Suchman, 'Managing Legitimacy: Strategic and Institutional Approaches', *Academy of Management Review*, 20:3 (1995), 571–610 at 574. The typology of legitimacy is listed as follows: (1) Pragmatic legitimacy rests on the self-interested calculation of interests of actor who are more closely linked to a particular organizational field (such as the legal field); (2) moral legitimacy relates to how new practices become justified in highly structured settings (such as the court system); and (3) cogitative legitimacy represents a powerful source of legitimacy. New practices are less likely to be challenged, as they are located within framework based on common principles and rules.

[72] For details, see Chapters 3 and 4.

[73] Paul J. DiMaggio and Walter W. Powell, 'The Iron Cage Revisited: Institutional Isomorphism and Collective Rationality in Organizational Fields', *American Sociological Review*, 48:2 (1983), 147–160 at 150–154. According to DiMaggio and Powell, three types of institutional mechanisms affect the process of institutionalization: (1) coercive pressure that is caused by the formal and informal pressures and influences made by the authoritative institutions, such as the government and the Judiciary; (2) mimetic pressure stems from the need to cope with uncertainty by imitating practices which are perceived to be more legitimate or more successful; and (3) normative pressure stems from professionalization. Professionalization can be conceptualized as 'the collective struggle of members of an occupation to define its conditions and work methods and to establish a cognitive base and occupational legitimacy for it'. For details, see Chapters 3 and 4.

extrajudicial processes to resolve civil disputes.[74] There has been relatively little focus on the specific interest regarding the interaction of a set of legal and non-legal instruments which affect the attitudes of Hong Kong lawyers to promote the greater use of ADR for shareholder disputes. This book makes three contributions towards the development of a theoretical framework for evaluating the current ADR initiatives for shareholder disputes, particularly judicial policy on ADR and the legislative policy on the reform of unfair prejudice provisions in Hong Kong.

First, the literature about Hong Kong lawyers' attitudes towards the use of ADR for shareholder disputes following the implementation of the CJR in April 2009 is neither very big nor particularly rich. This evaluation would aid the Hong Kong Judiciary to refine its policy strategies for achieving the target of greater responsiveness of lawyers to a new disputing climate by endorsing more pragmatic and effective approaches to resolving shareholder disputes.

Second, this book attempts to address the unresolved problem about the degree to which ADR has been institutionalized by the Hong Kong Judiciary as a means of altering lawyers' traditional and litigation-centred approach to resolving shareholder disputes. To date, no prior empirical research has completely examined the relationship between the legitimacy of ADR practices within the legal environment and the spread of ADR practices in the Hong Kong context.

Last but not least, this book provides the first empirical analysis of the potential impact on the reform of the civil process in 2009, which may change Hong Kong lawyers' attitudes towards the use of ADR for shareholder disputes.[75] This analysis helps to determine the spread of ADR practices within the two branches of the Hong Kong legal profession.

The following section applies the theory of sociological institutionalism as a lens through which to analyse how the institutionalization process actually unfolds in a way such that ADR can secure legitimacy through the supportive role of the legal professions and a range of policy instruments developed by the government and the Judiciary.

---

[74] Bruce Monroe, 'Institutionalization of Alternative Dispute Resolution by the State of California', *Pepperdine Law Review*, 14:4 (1987), 945–987 at 946; Sharon Press, 'Institutionalization: Savior or Saboteur of Mediation?', *Florida State University Law Review*, 24 (1997), 903–917 at 904; Bobbi McAdoo et al., 'Institutionalization: What Do Empirical Studies Tell Us about Court Mediation?', *Dispute Resolution Magazine*, 9 (2003), 8–10 at 8; and Penny Brooker, *Mediation Law: Journey through Institutionalism to Juridification*, (Routledge, 2013), 14–15.

[75] See Chapter 6.

1.2 Arguments Development: Institutionalizing and Legitimizing ADR Policy in Shareholder Disputes

The book attempts to build on the work in sociolegal theory and socio-logical institutionalism seeking to establish a theoretical framework to examine the key stages of institutionalization that may secure the legit-imacy of ADR for the resolution of shareholder disputes in Hong Kong. New institutional theory from sociology thus offers a useful model in analysing how ADR practices are evolving through the three sequential stages: (1) pre-institutionalization, (2) semi-institutionalization and (3) full institutionalization.[76] Institutionalization is defined as a process by which procedural innovations acquire legitimacy and ultimately become 'taken-for-granted' dispute resolution processes within the local business and legal professional communities.[77] Institutionalization constitutes a social basis from which legitimacy stems from the rules or other social beliefs.[78] In general, institutionalization involves the integration of pro-cedural innovations into sources of reproduction, usually existing ones such as law, the legal professional codes of conduct and similar.[79] As such, innovative dispute resolution practices (such as mediation) would then be highly institutionalized and perpetuated over time if these practices are reproduced by persons who 'repeatedly (re)mobilize and (re)mobilize in historical processes' (such as law, the professions, identity categories and patterns in the life course).[80] The utility and benefits of using non-litigation

---

[76] Pamela S. Tolbert and Lynne G. Zucker, 'Studying Organization: Theory & Method' in Stewart R. Clegg and Cynthia Hardy (eds.), *The Institutionalization of Institutional Theory* (Thousand Oaks, CA: SAGE, 1999), 59–61.

[77] See supra note 66.

[78] Ibid. and Suchman, 'Managing Legitimacy', 932–933.

[79] The reproduction of practices may to some extent reflect the issues of institutional persis-tence, for details, see Walter W. Powell, 'Expanding the Scope of Institutional Analysis' in Walter W. Powell and Paul J. DiMaggio (eds.), *The New Institutionalism in Organizational Analysis* (Chicago: University of Chicago Press, 1991). Powell suggests that there are four avenues of institutional reproduction: (1) the exercise of power; (2) interdependencies which extend across organizational boundaries to other organizations, particularly in the case of hierarchical relations; (3) taken-for-granted assumptions; and path-dependent development processes. Teubner notes that law could also be understood as 'a self-reproducing system, which since the operations of law are dependent of its internal states, would have to be defined as a "non-trivial" machine. Law is certainly synthetically deter-mined, but not analytically determinable; it is dependent on the past, but not predictable'. For details, see Gunther Teubner, '"And God Laughed..." Indeterminacy, Self-Reference and Paradox in Law', *German Law Journal*, 12:1 (2011), 376–406 at 378.

[80] Ronald L. Jepperson, 'Institutions, Institutional Effects, and Institutionalism', in Walter W. Powell and Paul J. DiMaggio (eds.), *The New Institutionalism in Organizational Analysis*

modes of dispute resolution for shareholder disputes would not be questioned or challenged by the local business and legal professional communities if ADR practices are highly institutionalized.

However, it is uncertain whether mediation and other alternative processes have acquired legitimacy as fair and desirable procedures for resolving shareholder disputes within the local business and professional communities. As the former Secretary for Justice of Hong Kong Wong Yan-lun noted, this is particularly true given that mediation has not yet earned its legitimacy within the local business and legal professional communities as compared with other jurisdictions.[81] Similarly, Ms Elsie Leung Oi-sie noted that there are barriers to the development of mediation in Hong Kong, as the general public has many misconceptions about mediation's function and outcomes when compared with the normal judicial process.[82] One possible reason for this may be attributable to lawyers' scepticism about the procedural fairness in the mediation process. Most notably, the process of mediation may be open to abuse by unscrupulous parties who use mediation as a tactical ploy to discover information about the strengths and weaknesses of the other side's case in subsequent litigation process.[83] Apart from that, it has been suggested that many litigants and their legal representatives seek to avoid an adverse costs order and other consequences of failure to mediate by simply going through the mediation process with no intention to attempt settlement.[84]

Clearly, the company law, civil procedure rules and a set of directives on mediation issued by the Judiciary do not simply perform a symbolic

(Chicago: University of Chicago Press, 1991), 148 and Jeannette A. Colyvas, 'Ubiquity and Legitimacy: Disentangling Diffusion and Institutionalization', Sociological Theory, 29:1 (2011), 27-53 at 44.

[81] Wong Yan-Lung, 'The Use and Development of Mediation in Hong Kong', Asian Dispute Reivew, (2008), 54–56 at 56.

[82] Elsie Leung, 'Mediation: A Cultural Change', Asian Pacific Law Review, 17 (2009), 39–46 at 44–45.

[83] Interim Report and Consultative Paper on Civil Justice Reform at para.636.

[84] SCMP, Mediation Isn't Being Taken Seriously, (29 July 2011) at www.scmp.com/article/ 974803/mediation-isnt-being-taken-seriously (Accessed 10 January 2014).

The chairman of the Joint Mediation Helpline Office, Chan Bing-woon, commented that most people attempted mediation because they were simply trying to avoid being penalized by the court for not entering the mediation process. Recently, the 2015 Survey on the use of mediation in Hong Kong, conducted by Herbert Smith Freehills, revealed that '...many litigants and their lawyers are paying lip service to the [mediation] process purely to avoid the adverse costs and other consequences of not mediating'. For details, see 'ADR in Asia Pacific: Spotlight on Mediation in Hong Kong', ADR in Asia Pacific Guide, (London: Herbert Smith Freehills, 2015), Vol. 1, 18.

function, providing a set of established rules to either encourage or discourage parties to behave in a desired manner.[85] An actor conforms to established practices not because such practices are backed by the coercive force of the state, but because they are recognized as a set of institutionalized and binding rules within the local community.[86] This reveals that laws can be considered as viable 'instruments of social engineering' that affect the attitudes of the people to comply voluntarily with certain practices.[87] On that basis, practice directions, court rules and the new corporate legislation can be considered as effective instruments to shape policy development on ADR for the resolution of shareholder disputes in Hong Kong. In other words, informal out-of-court process has generally been accepted as a legitimate means of resolving shareholder disputes through the court rules, practice directions and the corporate legislation.

In fact, ADR is underused if its potential benefits are not as widely known as they should be among the local businesspeople and legal professions.[88] Previous empirical studies on corporate-related dispute resolution illustrate that business enterprises were generally positive about their experience with out-of-court processes because these processes are generally viewed as flexible techniques for efficiently and effectively settling disputes.[89] It follows that the attitude or motivation of businesspeople to engage in ADR processes can affect the overall likelihood of success of the ADR initiatives for shareholder disputes, as they are the end users of ADR processes.

However, it cannot be ignored that the legal professions are capable of performing special roles in legitimizing the greater use of ADR within the statutory unfair prejudice regime. This argument rests on the

---

[85] John W. Meyer and Brian Rowan, 'Institutionalized Organizations: Formal Structure as Myth and Ceremony', *American Journal of Sociology*, 83:2 (1977), 340–363 at 343–346.

[86] See Lawrence M. Friedman, *Law and Society: An Introduction*, (Englewood Cliffs, NJ: Prentice Hall, 1977), 18.

[87] See Id. at 14.

[88] See Lord Justice Jackson, 'New Approach to Civil Justice: From Woolf to Jackson', Conference on *Civil Justice Reform: What Has It Achieved?* (Hong Kong, 15 April 2010).

[89] See David B. Lipsky and Ronald L. Seeber, 'Patterns of ADR Used in Corporate Disputes', *Dispute Resolution Journal*, 54:1 (1999), 68–71 at 71; John Lande, 'Getting the Faith: Why Business Lawyers and Executives Believe Mediation', *Harvard Negotiation Law Review*, 5 (2000), 137–231 at 176–179; Loukas Mistelis, 'International Arbitration – Corporate Attitudes and Practices – 12 Perceptions Tested: Myths, Data and Analysis Research Report', *The American Review of International Arbitration*, 15 (2004), 527–591 at 550–559 and Thomas J. Stipanowich and J. Ryan Lamare, 'Living with ADR: Evolving Perceptions and Use of Mediation, Arbitration, and Conflict Management in Fortune 1000 Corporations', *Harvard Negotiation Law Review*, 19 (2014), 1–68 at 67–68.

assumption that the legal professions occupy dominant positions in the field to take control over the arrangements in ADR schemes introduced by the Judiciary and to influence the pace of promoting ADR in Hong Kong.[90] The degree to which the legal professions would support the institutionalization process of ADR for the resolution of shareholder disputes depends on how a variety of policy options are transmitted within the legal field.[91] Professional networks are effective for spreading peer influence and reinforcing the wide dissemination of ADR practices.[92] The more the information about the benefits of using ADR to resolve shareholder disputes is transmitted through the legal professional networks, the stronger the degree of institutionalization of ADR practices.[93] This analysis is in parallel to the institutional view that that full institutionalization of a given practice likely depends on the 'conjoint effects of relatively low resistance by opposing groups, continued cultural support and promotion by advocacy groups'.[94] On that basis, institutional theory sheds light on how institutionalization actually unfolds in a way that ADR can secure legitimacy through a range of policy instruments and the role of the legal professions (see Figure 1.2).

As a whole, institutionalization is first triggered by ADR policy in responding to the pressures not only within the local court system, but also those of interstate competition with regard to the relative attractiveness of doing business (such as the costs of conducting litigation, the availability of non-litigation modes of dispute resolution and similar).[95]

[90] Lon L. Fuller, *Morality of Law* (New Haven, CT: Yale University Press, 1977); Pierre Bourdieu, 'The Force of Law: Toward a Sociology of the Judicial Field', *Hastings Law Journal*, 38 (1987), 805–853; Lon L. Fuller, 'The Lawyer as an Architect of Social Structures' in Kenneth I. Winston (ed.), *The Principles of Social Order: Selected Essays of Lon L. Fuller* (Oxford: Hart Publishing, 2001), 286–287; Simon Roberts and Michael Palmer, *Dispute Processes: ADR and the Primary Forms of Decision-Making*, 2nd ed. (Cambridge: Cambridge University Press, 2005), 45; Julie Macfarlane, *The New Lawyer: How Settlement is Transforming the Practice of Law* (Vancouver, B.C.: UBC Press, 2008); and Brooker, 'Mediation Law', 260–264.

[91] Royston Greenwood et al., 'Theorizing Change: The Role of Professional Associations in the Transformation of Institutionalized Fields', *Academy of Management Journal*, 45:1 (2002), 58–80 at 60–61.

[92] DiMaggio and Powell, 'The Iron Cage', 152–153.

[93] Lynne G. Zucker, 'The Role of Institutionalization Cultural Persistence' in Walter W. Powell and Paul J. DiMaggio (eds.), *The New Institutionalism in Organizational Analysis* (Chicago: University of Chicago Press, 1991), 87. According to Zucker, the history of transmission provides a basis that 'the meaning of the act is partly of the inter-subjective common-sense world'.

[94] Tolbert and Zucker, 'Studying Organization', 178.

[95] Hong Kong Judiciary, *Reform of the Civil Justice System in Hong Kong*, Interim Report and Consultative Paper on Civil Justice Reform (Hong Kong Judiciary, 2000) at para. 9.

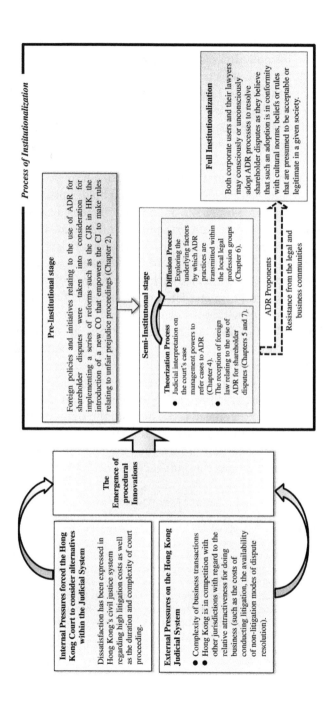

Figure 1.2 Institutionalization of ADR policy for shareholder disputes in Hong Kong.

Note: This model builds on the following literature: Tolbert and Zucker, 'Studying Organization', 173–178 and Greenwood et al., 'Theorizing Change', 59–61

These pressures eventually become burdens on the courts to allocate judicial resources effectively that meet the needs and expectations of the disputants. The introduction of ADR into the Hong Kong courts is partly a response to remove the enormous pressure on the court dockets.[96] Although both the Hong Kong government and the Hong Kong Judiciary have provided supportive and practical steps to institutionalize ADR practices for shareholder disputes in recent years, Hong Kong is now somewhere between the stage of semi-institutionalization and the stage of full institutionalization.

It is certainly true that the utility and benefits of using informal out-of-court processes (such as mediation) to resolve shareholder disputes are more vulnerable to challenge by ADR's opponents. There is an appreciable literature criticizing that private extrajudicial means can (1) reinforce the power imbalance between the parties; (2) promote law without justice; (3) heighten the risks of prejudice when the issue to be adjudicated touches a sensitive or intimate area such as, for example, housing or cultural-based conduct; and (4) neutralize conflicts by setting up mandatory referral of cases to ADR within the court system.[97]

The critique of ADR undermines the assertion made by ADR's proponents that informal out-of-court processes are especially beneficial to those minority shareholders who are either unable to fund the litigation or weary of using adversarial approaches to resolving intra-close corporate disputes.[98] On that basis, it is imperative to consider how the policy objectives of introducing extrajudicial processes into the statutory unfair prejudice regime would be refined and evolve through policy learning and adaption.[99] This raises the question of how the development of a broad range of policy instruments and the influence of the legal professions

[96] Ibid. and Jerold S. Auerbach, *Justice without Law?* (Oxford: Oxford University Press, 1983).

[97] Stephen B. Goldberg et al., 'ADR Problems and Prospects: Looking to the Future', *Judicature*, 69 (1985), 291–299 at 292–293; Richard Delgado et al., 'Fairness and Formality: Minimizing the Risk of Prejudice in Alternative Dispute Resoltuion', *Wisconsin Law Review*, (1985), 1359–1404 at 1391–1399. Delgado and his colleagues provide an excellent analysis on the criticism made by those ADR's opponents.

[98] Robert D. Raven, 'Alternative Dispute Resolution: Expanding Opportunities', *The Arbitration Journal* 43:2 (1988), 44–48 at 45–47 and Francis E. McGovern, 'Beyond Efficiency: A Bevy of ADR Justifications (An Unfootnoted Summary)', *Dispute Resolution Magazine*, 3 (1996), 12–13 at 12–13.

[99] For an excellent discussion of policy learning and adaption, see Richard Rose, 'What Is Lesson Drawing?', *Journal of Public Policy*, 11:1 (1991), 3–30 at 7. Policymakers in a country may have a strong incentive to learn lessons from other country as there might be substantial similarities between cultures and legal families.

could ultimately increase the institutionalization process of ADR for the resolution of shareholder disputes in Hong Kong.[100]

This book, by examining the recent development and growth of ADR for shareholder disputes in Hong Kong, finds that mediation and other alternative processes have not yet been fully institutionalized as preferred approaches to resolving shareholder disputes. On that basis, this book argues that the success of ADR initiatives for shareholder disputes depends not only on the efforts of the Judiciary and the government to devise a broad range of policy instruments in supporting the institutionalization process, but also on the critical role of lawyers in legitimizing the use of ADR.

First, both the court rules and a set of directives on mediation improve the legitimacy of the judicial institutions to promote the greater use of ADR within the local business community and legal professions in Hong Kong. This is particularly true, as the legitimacy of both the civil procedure rules and a set of ADR referral directions issued by the Judiciary derived not only purely from the authority but also from the endorsement of a powerful group of local businessmen.[101] One plausible line of reasoning of this is that both the court rules and case management directions on mediation are designed in conformity with the objectives of the Basic Law of the Hong Kong Special Administrative Region (the Basic Law) in preserving the existing private market-orientated legal system.[102]

Law and society theorists such as Friedman and Cotterrell note that judges are statutorily bound to interpret the rules in light of a set of governing principles which were established or enacted by an authoritative body (such as the legislative body).[103] Clearly, if the law is designed in accordance with the societal necessities that gained support from a group of powerful actors, judges are more willing to follow a legalistic approach to articulating reasons as the law meets the social demands.[104] Hong Kong

---

[100] For further discussion, see Chapter 7.

[101] For detail, see Chapter 4.

[102] Ibid.

[103] Lawrence M. Friedman, 'On Legalistic Reasoning: A Footnote to Weber', *Wisconsin Law Review*, (1966), 148–171 at 153–154 and Roger Cotterrell, *The Politics of Jurisprudence: A Critical Introduction to Legal Philosophy* (London: Butterworths, 1989).

[104] Lawrence M. Friedman, 'Legal Rules and the Process of Social Change', *Stanford Law Review*, 19 (1967), 786–840 at 840. In Lawrence M. Friedman, 'Some Comments on Legal Interpretation', *Poetics Today*, 9:1 (1988), 95–102 at 97, Friedman distinguished between primary and secondary legitimacy. The former means that an authority is somehow considered legitimate in itself because its sources of legitimacy are derived from the highest authority. The latter is generally referred as the process of judicial reasoning or interpretation where judges enjoy certain degrees of discretions and creative powers in interpreting

judges are accordingly more willing to apply rules in a manner which is consistent with ADR goals if these objectives are consistent with social norms underpinning the cultural rules of a given society, which emphasize the importance of safeguarding the free operation of business and the right of access to the courts.[105]

Second, the new statutory unfair prejudice regime being introduced in the 2014 corporate legislation is a 'relatively self-contained social system' that accommodates the existence of ADR for the resolution of shareholder disputes.[106] On the one hand, the statutory unfair prejudice provision remains relatively autonomous from the political sphere, as it captures the interest of private enterprises for safeguarding the free operation of business affairs through contractual mechanisms.[107] On the other hand, the law remains relatively autonomous from the judicial sphere, as ethical considerations are generally taken by the court in articulating public values in the constitution.[108] Thus, the court will not make any order to compel the parties to resort to ADR in lieu of traditional court litigation processes for shareholder disputes.

Third, the legal professions serve as ADR advocates or agents of legitimacy supporting the development of ADR policy in Hong Kong.[109] In particular, judges, the leaders of the legal practitioners, use their intellectual or cognitive capacities to convince all practicing lawyers to assist their clients in using mediation and other alternative processes to resolve shareholder disputes. Lawyers also play a key role in assisting their clients

the law which is passed by the legislative body. According to Friedman, he said: 'In any society, all authority that is not primary is secondary; to put it another way, authority that is not primary has to justify itself and its behaviour; it must somehow derive a sense of rightness from some person or institution that has primary legitimacy. Reasoning or interpretation is thus the process through which a secondary authority links its decisions and acts to an authority of unquestioned or primary legitimacy. ' Clearly, judicial reasoning is the best exemplar of secondary legitimacy.

[105] For details, see Chapter 4.
[106] For details, see Chapter 5.
[107] Ibid.
[108] Ibid.
[109] For details, see Chapter 6. See also Hong Kong Department of Justice, *Report of the Working Group on Mediation* (Hong Kong Department of Justice, 2010) at para. 5.8, which illustrates that the following parties could play very important roles in the promotion of mediation: (1) the Hong Kong Judiciary, (2) the Hong Kong Bar Association, (3) the Hong Kong Law Society, (4) Mediation service providers, (5) frontline conflict resolvers, (6) Chambers of Commerce, (7) Consumer Council and (8) schools and universities. For details, see Fuller, 'The Lawyer as an Architect of Social Structures', 286–287. Fuller notes that lawyers are often viewed as important 'agents' or 'architects' in changing their clients' perceptions of using new dispute resolution techniques to resolve disputes.

to explore the benefits of using ADR to resolve shareholder disputes. The legitimacy of ADR derives from a cognitive process through which ADR promoters employ a symbolic (such as the use of law) or rhetoric (the use of language) device that connects ADR practice to the existing legal culture.[110] The present empirical study provides evidence supporting that law can be viewed as a powerful policy instrument to convey a message to lawyers that ADR was perceived as being compatible with court-based shareholder proceedings.[111] Similarly, the empirical findings of this study also demonstrate that the legitimacy of ADR requires active efforts of ADR promoters to employ non-legal instruments (such as ADR training) encouraging Hong Kong lawyers to adopt ADR on behalf of their clients.[112]

Last but most importantly, much remains to be done in refining Hong Kong's current ADR programme by looking elsewhere for direction towards international expectations for the development of sophisticated ADR programme for shareholder disputes.[113] This book further proposes that two conditions theoretically help ensure that the new corporate law, the amended civil procedure rules and a set of ADR referral directives issued by the Judiciary could achieve their maximum impact on further policy development of ADR in Hong Kong.

First, the inclusion of ADR into the voluntary codes of corporate governance for small and medium-sized private companies in Hong Kong is to be welcomed as it provides additional guidelines for the court to determine the appropriate standard of conduct for directors to behave in a manner which is consistent with ADR goals.[114] Second, the new Companies Ordinance that permits a minimum level of judicial intervention with regard to jurisdictional limits of the arbitral tribunals to grant specific kinds of relief such as a winding-up order should be retained.[115] This approach permits greater freedom for private companies to contract out some of the members' statutory rights to file a petition to the court through an arbitration agreement, while retaining a certain degree of the court to control over the specific kind of remedies that the arbitral tribunals should not be granted.[116]

---

[110] Roy Suddaby and Royston Greenwood, 'Rhetorical Strategies of Legitimacy', *Administrative Science Quarterly*, 50 (2005), 35–67.
[111] For further discussion, see Chapter 6.
[112] Ibid.
[113] For further discussion, see Chapter 7.
[114] Ibid.
[115] Ibid.
[116] Ibid.

1.3 Organization of the Book

This book is organized into three key parts. Part I includes this introductory chapter and Chapters 2 and 3. Chapter 2 provides an overview of the recent development and growth of ADR in the resolution of shareholder disputes in Hong Kong. Chapter 3 then develops a methodological framework for evaluating policy development on ADR in resolving shareholder disputes. It provides a rationale for and description of data collection methods and instruments, as well as for data analysis techniques.

Part II comprises three chapters, with a focus on how mediation and other out-of-court processes can secure legitimacy from corporate law, court rules, judicial directives on mediation and the support of the local legal professions. Chapter 4 analyses the policy reasons for the development of court-connected ADR procedures in Hong Kong. This analysis helps to determine whether the amended court rules together with a set of judicial referral directives have improved the legitimacy of the court to further promote the greater use of ADR in resolving shareholder disputes. Chapter 5 considers how the reform of provisions concerning protection of minority shareholders facilitates the coexistence of both informal out-of-court processes and court-based shareholder proceedings. Chapter 6 seeks to identify the key factors affecting the attitudes of Hong Kong lawyers to choose ADR methods in helping their clients to resolve shareholder disputes.

Part III consists of one chapter, which explores the feasibility of formulating a set of specific company law provisions in relation to the proper use of out-of-court processes for the resolution of shareholder disputes in Hong Kong. Chapter 7 includes the use of comparative sociology of law to develop three testable series of arguments regarding the conditions under which Hong Kong may learn from the experience of the United Kingdom, New Zealand and South Africa by incorporating the use of informal dispute resolution methods into the company legislation.

Finally, a concluding chapter summarizes the findings presented in the earlier chapters. This chapter concludes the study by drawing together the main themes of the book in relation to the process of institutionalizing the greater use of extrajudicial processes for the resolution of shareholder disputes. This analysis provides more detailed recommendations for future research purpose. In particular, it underlines the importance of developing other sophisticated empirical models to examine the unfolding changes of an institutional process that could ultimately lead to the stage of full institutionalization.

Some important limitations to the present study should be acknowledged at the outset. First, this study does not attempt to resolve the broad issues in attempting to expand the scope of ADR applications in derivative actions. Instead, it focuses on shareholder disputes, primarily on disputes between minority and majority shareholders in a private company registered in the Hong Kong Company Registry. Second, this book is concerned primarily with shareholder disputes rather than corporate conflicts. It pays more attention to examining how and why the development of a variety of policy instruments can secure the legitimacy of innovative dispute resolution processes for handling shareholder disputes in Hong Kong. Third, the study does not employ substantive case law analyses together with the historical perspectives in analysing the substantive law development that have impacted on the development of unfair prejudice proceedings. Fourth, the empirical study is limited to analysis of Hong Kong lawyers' attitudes towards the use of mediation instead of other modes of non-litigation dispute resolution processes (such as arbitration and expert determination). This is predicated on the fact that the intentions of the CJR together with the Chief Executive's Policy Address of the Chief Executive of the Hong Kong Special Administrative Region are to encourage the parties and their legal representatives to pursue mediation. Last but not least, this study is limited to the theoretical realm by comparing with those common law jurisdictions including South Africa, the United Kingdom and New Zealand which have developed sophisticated ADR programmes for resolving shareholder disputes.

2

Development and Growth of ADR for
Shareholder Disputes in Hong Kong

An Overview

2.1 Introduction

In Hong Kong, a new dispute resolution culture has emerged since the Civil Justice Reform (CJR) began in 2009. There has been a fundamental shift from an adversarial litigation model of dispute resolution to a more collaborative and less confrontational approach to resolving disputes. Disputants are encouraged to explore alternative solutions using compromise and contractual arrangements through the assistance of a neutral third party during the ADR process instead of accepting a legal determination based on assessments of each party's legal rights.[1] Moreover, the Companies (Unfair Prejudice Petitions) Proceedings Rules (Cap. 622L) have now been introduced that confer on the court discretionary power to make an order about referring matters to ADR, including mediation and other alternative processes. Alternative methods of settling disputes are used in conjunction with, or as alternatives to, court-based shareholder proceedings. Hong Kong is now undergoing a new movement towards a new dispute resolution paradigm which encourages the greater use of mediation and other alternative processes to resolve shareholder disputes.

To set the stage for subsequent theoretical and empirical analysis, this chapter seeks to present an overview of the development and growth of ADR in the resolution of shareholder disputes in Hong Kong. Next, it begins to explain why mediation and arbitration have gained prominence recently for various types of dispute such as construction, commercial and shareholder disputes. It then considers how the government, the Judiciary and the legislative body provide impetus for the growth of

---

[1] Penny Brooker, 'The "Juridification" of Alternative Dispute Resolution', *Anglo-American Law Review*, 28 (1999), 1–36 at 4–5.

ADR for shareholder disputes. Finally, it concludes that the Hong Kong Judiciary continues to play an important role in implementing a comprehensive ADR policy in raising awareness among lawyers, judges and shareholders in Hong Kong on the benefits of using extrajudicial procedures to resolve shareholder disputes.

2.2 Development of ADR in Hong Kong

ADR has been introduced in Hong Kong in numerous ways, ranging from private (or 'contractual') in which parties agree to submit their disputes to private, non-judicial fora of resolution (such as Hong Kong International Arbitration Centre [HKIAC] and Hong Kong Mediation Council [HKMC]),[2] to the public judicial realm in which litigants adopt extrajudicial processes in the court system (court-connected ADR), sometimes at their opinion and sometimes as required by the court rules.[3]

The growing popularity of using mediation to resolve shareholder disputes is most notable in the recent civil procedure reform in Hong Kong. This may be attributable to the fact that a mediation process is far more flexible than an arbitration process even though both involve the participation of a neutral third party to assist in the resolution of disputes. Mediation differs from arbitration in that the mediation process, in itself, is far more flexible than arbitration in which the mediator assists the disputing parties to reach a voluntary outcome that will best satisfy their interests.[4] Generally, the mediator is not expected to be an expert in the subject matter of the dispute.[5] Instead, his or her role is that of a facilitator assisting the parties to explore the interests and needs on each side and to generate solutions which are acceptable to both.

Arbitration, by contrast, involves the use of a neutral third party (the arbitrator) who possesses sophisticated knowledge and skills in the commercial or technical field. An arbitrator can render a decision based on

---

[2] Note, 'ADR, the Judiciary, and Justice: Coming to Terms with the Alternatives', *Harvard Law Review*, 113:7 (2000), 1851–1875 at 1857. HKIAC was established in September, 1985 and it offers arbitration services in commercial, construction, joint venture and shipping areas. In contrast with the HKMC, it was established in January 1994 and is a division of HKIAC. It offers mediation services in building management, construction, commercial, financial, community and family areas.

[3] Ibid.

[4] Susanna M. Kim, 'The Provisional Director Remedy for Corporate Deadlock: A Proposed Model Statute', *Washington and Lee Law Review*, 60 (2003), 111–181 at 130.

[5] Fung, The Honourable Justice, 'Mediator's Qualifications and Skills', Conference on *Mediation Conference* (Hong Kong, 21 March 2014).

the assessment of the claims of the disputing parties.[6] Nonetheless, both mediation and arbitration are generally used and promoted in Hong Kong as viable dispute resolution techniques in a wider range of cases (such as disputes in the financial and construction sectors).[7] The growth of settlement alternatives in both private and public spheres enables the parties to choose the most appropriate forum to resolve disputes.

Originally, the impetus for promoting mediation and arbitration in Hong Kong stemmed primarily from the construction industry.[8] The application of the multitiered dispute resolution process for the Hong Kong Airport Core Programme (ACP) has generally been regarded as a notable landmark of success in using mediation and other hybrid forms of dispute resolution since the early 1990s.[9] Given that the benefits of using mediation at an early stage can lead to a high success rate under the ACP,[10] this has profoundly influenced the future development of arbitration, mediation and other hybrid forms of dispute resolution in both commercial and financial sectors.

Along with the development of mediation and other alternative processes, the Hong Kong government is committed to developing Hong Kong as an ideal hub of dispute resolution services in the Asia Pacific region.[11] First, the Hong Kong government has generously funded the HKIAC despite the fact that it is a totally independent body to deal with

[6] Kim, 'The Provisional Director Remedy for Corporate Deadlock', 128–129.
[7] David Sandborg, 'Dispatch From Hong Kong', *Dispute Resolution Magazine*, (2013), 45–47.
[8] Timothy Hill and Damon So, 'Resolving Construction Claims through Mediation', *Asian Dispute Review* (2010), 58–60 at 58. According to Hill and So, members of the construction industry have played important roles in the founding of Mediation Council in 1994.
[9] David Sandborg, 'Construction ADR: Multistep ADR Gets Creative at Hong Kong's New Airport', *Alternatives to High Cost Litigation*, 17:3 (1999), 41–61 at 60. The multitiered dispute resolution clause of the Airport Core Programme (ACP) was set out in Clause 92 and it comprised four stages: (1) Engineer's Decision, (2) Mediation, (3) Adjudication and (4) Arbitration.
[10] Wong Yan-Lung, 'The Benefits of Mediation', Conference on *Hong Kong Mediation Council Annual Dinner* (Hong Kong, 17 March 2006). Our former Secretary for Justice Wong Yan-Lung notes that the benefits of using mediation at an early stage can lead to a success rate as high as 80 per cent or all ACP disputes were settled at mediation or through negotiation at the mediation stage. Thus, adjudication was rarely used in the end under the programme.
[11] The HKSAR Chief Executive Leung Chun-ying, Hong Kong Chief Executive, *The Policy Address 2014: Support the Needy, Let Youth Flourish, Unleash Hong Kong's Potential* (Printing Department, 2014) at para. 12 and The HKSAR Chief Executive Leung Chun-ying, *The 2016 Policy Address: Innovate for the Economy, Improve Livelihood, Foster Harmony, Share Prosperity* (Printing Department, 2016), para. 58.

local and international disputes.[12] Over the past three decades, the HKIAC has gained international recognition not only because it was ranked as the third best arbitral institution worldwide in 2015.[13] The HKIAC has offered professional and high-quality ADR services, such as mediation and conciliation, in assisting the parties to resolve their disputes. Apart from the development of a range of ADR services, a high quality of ADR services can be assured, as HKIAC not only supervises the quality of the mediator and/or arbitrator but also offers training and accreditation standards.

For instance, HKIAC has issued ADR rules (e.g., the Hong Kong International Arbitration Centre Administered Arbitration Rules, 2013), which aim to supplement the new Hong Kong Arbitration Ordinance (Cap. 609).[14] This is particularly relevant because the existing Hong Kong arbitration law gives no guidance as to various procedural rules in governing the arbitral process. One possible reason for this is that the Hong Kong arbitration law is based on the United Nations Commission on International Trade Law (UNCITRAL) Model Law on International Commercial Arbitration as amended in 2006 (the Model Law), which adheres to the principles of party autonomy and limited court intervention.[15] The Model Law can be characterized as a 'specialized international regime', which provides a model arbitration law for the state to determine whether it is appropriate to copy the model law, or modify it, or to adopt only a few of its provisions, taking into consideration the local circumstances and requirements.[16] It follows that the new Arbitration Ordinance has achieved a proper balance that allows the parties and the arbitral tribunal broad discretion to determine their own procedures, including the possibility of incorporating additional institutional rules, while at the

---

[12] Cheung Sai-On, 'Construction Mediation in Hong Kong', in Penny Brooker and Suzanne Wilkinson (eds.), *Mediation in the Construction Industry: An International Review* (London: Spon Press, 2010), 66.

[13] Karen Tan, HKIAC Tops Prestigious Global Arbitration Survey at www.hkiac.org/news/hkiac-tops-prestigious-global-arbitration-survey (Accessed 4 May 2016).

[14] This set of rules came into force on 1 November 2013.

[15] Renata Brazil-David, 'Harmonization and Delocalization of International Commercial Arbitration', *Journal of International Arbitration*, 28:5 (2011), 445–466 at 450–451.

[16] For an excellent analysis of how the world of arbitration tends to become more independent from states and that it tends to become a global arbitration regime, see Katherine L. Lynch, *The Forces of Economic Globalization: Challenges to the Regime of International Commercial Arbitration* (The Hague: Kluwer Law International, 2003), 84–86, 174–175 and 210–211; Thomas Schultz, 'Secondary Rules of Recognition and Relative Legality in Transnational Regimes', *The American Journal of Jurisprudence*, 56 (2011), 59–88.

same time maintaining the overriding principles of natural justice, impartiality and due process underlying the arbitral process.[17]

Second, a cross-sector Working Group on Mediation was established and financially sponsored by the Hong Kong government in 2008 following the Chief Executive's Policy Address in 2007 calling for plans to utilize mediation more effectively in Hong Kong.[18] The Working Group on Mediation chaired by the Secretary for Justice proposed adoption of various policy instruments to facilitate more effective and extensive application of ADR in both the local business and legal professional communities.[19] This includes the promulgation of Mediation Ordinance, by striking a reasonable balance between providing a proper legal framework for the conduct of mediation and the need to maintain the flexibility of the mediation process.[20]

In addition, other non-legal policy instruments such as the establishment of a single system of accrediting mediators and the promotion of education and publicity for the general public are the key policy strategies to promote the greater use of ADR within the local community.[21] Accordingly, the adoption of both legal and non-legal policy instruments could enhance the legitimacy of mediation for certain types of disputes, including shareholder disputes.

Third, the passage of a new Arbitration Ordinance (Cap. 609) illustrates that Hong Kong intends to take a step further by bringing its arbitration law into conformity with international soft law principles.[22] The new Ordinance unified the arbitration system based on the Model Law. The most important changes brought about by the new arbitration law

---

[17] Lynch, 'The Forces of Economic Globalization', 80–84.

[18] See The HKSAR Chief Executive Donald Tsang, *The 2007 Policy Address: A New Direction for Hong Kong* (Publishing Department, 2007) at para. 85 and Hong Kong Department of Justice, *Report of the Working Group on Mediation* (Hong Kong Department of Justice, 2010) at para. 2.1.

[19] Report of the Working Group on Mediation, para. 2.1.

[20] Ibid., Chapter 7. The Mediation Task Force was set up in 2001 to implement the recommendations made in the Working Group's Report. The Mediation Ordinance (Cap. 620) was enacted in June 2012 and came into force on 1 January 2013.

[21] Ibid., Chapters 5 and 6. A single accreditation body, namely, the Hong Kong Mediation Accreditation Association Limited (HKMAAL) was set up on 28 August 2012. This body provides a single set of standards for training and accreditation of mediators. This enhances public confidence and credibility in mediation services.

[22] Lee Tin-Yan, 'Introductory Note to the New Arbitration Ordinance of the Hong Kong Special Administrative Region', *International Legal Materials*, 51 (2012), 133–197 and Kun Fan, 'The New Arbitration Ordinance in Hong Kong', *Journal of International Arbitration*, 29:6 (2012), 715–722.

in Hong Kong include (1) the incorporation of express provisions dealing with the duty of confidentiality[23] and (2) the introduction of a new
provision that expressly allows an arbitrator to act as a mediator after the
arbitration proceedings have commenced, provided that all parties agree
in writing.[24]

A new provision that facilitates the use of hybrid processes (such as
med-arb) is generally in line with the objectives introduced by the CJR,
which seeks to promote a 'Mediate First culture' for the public to resolve
disputes through mediation before resorting to litigation or arbitration.[25]
Recently, the commitment to further promote the use of mediation within
the framework of international arbitration is illustrated in *Gao Haiyan
v. Keeneye Holdings Ltd*.[26] In this case, the Court of Appeal in Hong Kong
took a pro-enforcement stance by recognizing and enforcing a mainland
Chinese arbitral award, where the same person was used as the mediator
and the arbitrator in med-arb.[27]

While a hybrid form of dispute resolution (such as med-arb) is rarely
used in Hong Kong, some Asian jurisdictions such as Singapore and
Mainland China support the greater use of a hybrid process to resolve
commercial disputes.[28] Likewise, the med-arb process could be considered as a viable cost-effective means to resolve shareholder disputes. In
particular, a hybrid of mediation and arbitration processes could create an
incentive for the parties to optimize the benefits of using mediation to settle the case, while providing them with the certainty of a final decision.[29]
The same neutral third party serving as both mediator and arbitrator may
increase the likelihood of settlement at the mediation phase, as an arbitrator may use information obtained in private caucus sessions against the
parties in the arbitration phase.[30]

---

[23] Section 18 of the Hong Kong Arbitration Ordinance (Cap. 609).
[24] Section 33 of the Hong Kong Arbitration Ordinance (Cap. 609).
[25] Johnson Lam Man-hon, 'The Speech of the Honourable Mr Justice Lam, Justice of Appeal',
Conference on *'Mediation First' Pledge Reception* (Hong Kong 18 July 2013).
[26] [2012] 1 HKLRD 627.
[27] Ibid.
[28] Ibid. and The Singapore International Mediation Centre introduced a new Arb-Med-Arb
Protocol in 2014 which encourages the use of mediation in arbitral process. This protocol represents a departure from the traditional notion of med-arb, as it provides that the
mediator and the arbitrator should be different people.
[29] Susanna M. Kim, 'The Provisional Director Remedy for Corporate Deadlock: A Proposed
Model Statute', *Washington and Lee Law Review*, 60 (2003), 111–181 at 132.
[30] Sections 33(3)(b) and 33(4) of the Arbitration Ordinance (Cap. 609). However, the
appointment of a member of arbitral tribunal to serve as a mediator after the arbitration

Although a combination of mediation and arbitration could raise confidentiality and impartiality concerns associated with the neutral third party serving as both mediator and arbitrator, the HKICA introduced a new mediation rule to safeguard the confidentiality of the mediation process and to maintain the fundamental principles of due process.[31] Parties may simply decide to adopt this rule as part of their dispute resolution clauses or agreement to prevent the same neutral third party serving as both mediator and arbitrator in a hybrid process. Parties could maximize their opportunities to reach a voluntary and mutually acceptable agreement as a different person is appointed for the remaining part of the arbitral proceeding. This would remove concerns of impartiality.[32] From the preceding illustration, parties are encouraged to use a hybrid process within the framework of international arbitration as they retain their powers to determine whether the same person can serve as mediator and arbitrator in the med-arb process.

Last but most importantly, the success of mediation pilot schemes introduced by the Judiciary coupled with the supportive role of the Hong Kong government led to a more expansive use of mediation and other out-of-court processes in a broader range of cases (such as shareholder disputes) in the courts.[33] Since 2009, the CJR was implemented by way of an amendment of the court rules that confers specific case management powers on the court to facilitate the greater use of mediation and other out-of-court processes to resolve disputes.[34] The amended court rules have recognized the court's inherent power to make directives or orders to encourage the use of ADR in conjunction with formal court litigation

has started is subject to the parties' written consent; see Section 33(1) of the Arbitration Ordinance (Cap. 609)

[31] Article 14 of the HKIAC Mediation Rules (effective from 1 August 1999) prohibits mediators from being appointed as arbitrators if the case moves from mediation to arbitration. This provision is broadly in line with international practices on hybrid processes that different persons should serve as mediator and arbitrator in the same disputes. See Article 7.3 of the International Chamber of Commerce ADR Rules and Article 14 of the UNCITRAL Model Law on International Commercial Conciliation.

[32] Emilia Onyema, 'The Use of Med-Arb in International Commercial Dispute Resolution', *American Review of International Arbitration*, 12 (2001), 411–423 at 418.

[33] Report of the Working Group on Mediation, Chapter 4. Before the Civil Justice Reform began in 2009, the Judiciary of Hong Kong had launched a series of pilot schemes for voluntary mediation in four distinctive types of disputes, such as family, construction, building construction and corporate cases. Given that most users in the voluntary mediation pilot schemes were satisfied with the mediation processes, the Judiciary has subsequently issued practice directions in respect of these areas.

[34] Order 1A, Rule 4(b)(e) of the Rules of the High Court (RHC). Six underlying objectives are contained in the amended RHC, one of which is to facilitate the settlement of disputes.

processes in the courts.[35] The court can retain its inherent judicial power to determine in what circumstances an order for ADR is appropriate, while at the same time improving the efficiency of the litigation process.

The interest of the Judiciary in supporting ADR was further evident in the issuance of Practice Direction 31, which provides details supplementary to the law and rules on civil procedure.[36] This directive is applicable to all relevant civil cases in both the Court of First Instance and District Court. The main features of Practice Direction 31 include the filing of the Mediation Certificate, the Mediation Notice and the Mediation Response, which aim to assist the court to determine when a court-ordered mediation referral is appropriate and whether refusal to mediate is reasonable.[37] This judicial directive stipulates the new duties for parties and their legal representatives and the operation of new mediation procedures in the courts.[38] The main objective of this directive is to encourage parties to attempt mediation to resolve disputes at any stage prior to trial.[39]

In sum, both the Hong Kong government policy on ADR and the positive steps taken by the Judiciary to actively promote the greater use of ADR within the court system have laid down a good foundation for the growth of ADR in shareholder disputes.

2.3 The Growth of ADR in Shareholder Disputes

The following sections consider how ADR initiatives of both the Hong Kong government and the Hong Kong Judiciary have provided a strong impetus for the growth of mediation and other out-of-court processes (such as expert determination) in shareholder disputes.

---

[35] Order 1A, Rule 2(1) of the RHC stipulates that : 'The Court shall seek to give effect to the underlying objectives of these rules when it: (a) exercises any of its powers (whether under its inherent jurisdiction or given to it by these rules or otherwise); or (b) interprets any of these rules or a practice direction.'

[36] Practice Direction (PD) 31 on mediation was made effective from January 2010.

[37] PD 31, paras. 4 and 5 provide guidance on when refusal to mediate may attract cost sanctions. In addition, Order 62, Rule 5 provides that the court is required to take into account the conduct of parties when exercising its discretion as to costs.

[38] Under Part B of the PD 31, all parties who are legally represented by lawyers are required to file a Mediation Certificate (attached to Appendix B of the PD 31) at the same time as the Timetabling Questionnaire (i.e., 28 days after the close of pleadings). If a party is not legally represented, the court may consider, at any suitable stage, whether mediation is appropriate with regard to all circumstances of the case (Part C of the PD 31).

[39] The Mediation Certificate must be signed respectively by the solicitors and the party they represent (PD 31, para. 9). The Mediation Certificate will indicate whether a party is willing to engage mediation and if not, why not (PD 31, Part 1 of Appendix B). Accordingly,

2.3.1 Government Policy Promoting the Use of ADR

Government policy on ADR in Hong Kong had a significant impact on raising public acceptance towards the use of ADR for resolving shareholder disputes by three ways. First, the Secretary for Justice of Hong Kong has set up a Mediation Task Force to implement the recommendations in the Working Group on Mediation.[40] One of the core areas of the Mediation Task Force is to promote the greater use of mediation in business sector through a 'Mediation First' campaign. More than seventy companies and forty trade associations or organizations signed the 'Mediation First' pledges and affirmed their commitment to consider the use of mediation to resolve disputes before resorting to other means of dispute resolution since the Mediation First Pledge campaign was launched in 2009.[41] One may infer that the greater the number of Hong Kong corporations that subscribe to the Pledge, the greater is the willingness of the business parties to cooperate and seek out settlement options.

Second, the Hong Kong government continues to uphold the authority of the Basic Law in order to maintain Hong Kong's status as an international financial centre.[42] The Basic Law recognizes not only the principle of freedom of contract, but also the constitutional principle of access to courts.[43] This constitutional document is regarded as the highest source of law in Hong Kong, as it 'has laid a solid foundation for the continued stability and prosperity of Hong Kong'.[44] The Basic Law provides a legitimate framework for legislators to formulate rules (such as the new company legislation and the civil procedure rules) in a manner which is consistent not only with the substantive rule of law, but also with Hong Kong's dominant economic values (i.e., the free-market orientation) which are accepted by a group of leading business and legal professional people in Hong Kong.[45]

---

parties and their legal representatives should consider the possibility of ADR to resolve disputes before the trial begins.

[40] Legislative Council, *Legislative Council Panel on Administration and Legal Services: Mediation* (2013).

[41] Report of the Working Group on Mediation at para. 5.40.

[42] The 2007 Policy Address, para. 115; The HKSAR Chief Executive Leung Chun-yin, *The 2013 Policy Address: Seek Change, Maintain Stability, Serve the People with Pragmatism* (Printing Department, 2013) at para. 10 and The 2014 Policy Address, para. 190.

[43] Article 35 of the Hong Kong Basic Law provides that all Hong Kong citizens have the right of access to courts. Article 110 of the Hong Kong Basic Law provides that the Hong Kong government has to safeguard the free operation of financial business and financial markets.

[44] The 2007 Policy Address, para. 115.

[45] Ma Ngok, 'Electric Corporatism and State Interventions in Post-Colonial Hong Kong' in Chiu Wing-Kai Stephen and Wong Siu-lun (eds.), *Repositioning the Hong Kong Government* (Hong Kong: Hong Kong University Press, 2012), 71. Ma notes that the Basic Law Drafting

Last but most importantly, the Hong Kong government strives to further attract suitable arbitration and mediation institutions to set up offices in Hong Kong.[46] Both the Secretariat of the International Court of Arbitration of the International Chamber of Commerce and the China International Economic and Trade Arbitration Commission have chosen Hong Kong as the first location to establish their presence outside their home jurisdictions.[47] The establishment of privately run ADR centres in Hong Kong could be viewed as a way to respond to an increasing demand for court-connected ADR.[48] In sum, the Hong Kong government has laid down a solid foundation (especially publication of the government-funded cross-sector Working Group on Mediation) for the Hong Kong Judiciary to further develop the greater use of informal dispute resolution processes for resolving shareholder disputes.

2.3.2 Judicial Support for Early and Informal Resolution of Shareholder Disputes

The court has wide powers by virtue of Section 724 of the Companies Ordinance to carry out factual investigations with regard to shareholders' unfairly prejudicial conduct of the company's affairs. The breadth of the court's discretion tends to generate complex and sensitive issues which require investigation, full discovery and detailed evidence to be adduced by the parties.[49] This makes unfair prejudice proceedings lengthy and costly. The Hong Kong Judiciary played an important role in exercising its case management power to facilitate the early settlement of shareholder disputes prior to the implementation of the CJR in 2009.[50] It was evident from the fact that Lord Hoffman's guidance (*obiter dicta*) in *O'Neill* on what constitutes a reasonable buyout offer as a means of negotiating shareholder disputes at an early stage of unfair prejudice proceedings was applied in the Hong Kong case of *Re Prudential Enterprise Ltd*.[51]

Committee was composed of a large number of influential local businessmen and profession to write the 'Hong Kong blend of capitalism' into the Basic Law.

[46] The 2013 Policy Address, para. 39.

[47] Rimsky Yuen, 'Secretary Justice's Speech', Conference on *19th International Congress of Maritime Arbitration* (11 May 2015).

[48] Edward Brunet, 'Questing the Quality of Alternative Dispute Resolution', *Tulane Law Review*, 62 (1987), 1–56 at 48–51.

[49] English Law Commission, *Shareholder Remedies Consultation* (Law Commission Consultation Paper, No 142, 1996), 140.

[50] *Re Prudential Enterprise Ltd [2002]* 1 HKLRD 267.

[51] Ibid. at 273–74 and this decision was subsequently followed in *Re Ranson Motor Manufacturing Co Ltd* [2007] 1 HKLRD 751 at 759–760. In *O'Neill v. Phillips* [1999] BCC,

In addition, there is also a strong tendency of the Hong Kong courts to exercise their case management powers to encourage the early settlement of minority shareholder disputes before the CJR came into effect in 2009. In *Re Prudential Enterprise Ltd*, Cheung JA made the point that[52]

> ...there is a public interest to be served in the due administration of justice. It is important to reduce costs and delay in civil litigation, not only to the parties but also those who are waiting in the queue to have their cases tried. It is the duty of the judge to identify the crucial issues and to ensure that these issues are tried as expeditiously and inexpensively as possible.... In terms of exercising case management, which is a task for the trial judge...

Obviously, judicial case management of unfair prejudice proceedings is one of the most important parts of the CJR, as the pace of the litigation process is controlled by the court instead of the litigants and their lawyers. Under the new case management procedures as set out in Practice Direction 3.4, the parties must comply with various duties in accordance with a default timetable. This may speed up the litigation process as the courts now control the progress of the proceeding, such as the scope and manner of making discovery and adducing evidence to the court.

In addition, judicial promotion of ADR has become the cardinal feature of unfair prejudice proceedings in the Hong Kong courts after the CJR came into effect in 2009.[53] The central aim of this reform was to shift the emphasis away from the traditional, litigation-centred approach to resolving disputes, and to move towards a regime which recognizes the proper use of alternative modes of dispute resolution at any stage of unfair prejudice proceedings.[54] In order to fulfil the objectives underlying the CJR, the Judiciary took a step further by promulgating two sets of practice directions which extend the court's case management powers to refer certain matters to mediation and other out-of-court processes with the consent of the parties. These can be illustrated as follows.

Lord Hoffman set out guidelines regarding the basic requirement of a reasonable offer to buyout: (1) The offer must be to purchase the shares at a fair value. (2) The offer should provide for the value, if not agreed, to be determined by a competent expert. (3) The offer should have the value determined by the expert as an expert. (4) The offer should provide for the equality of arms between the parties. (5) The offer should make suitable provisions for the question of costs.

[52] [2002] 1 HKLRD 267 at 267.

[53] See, for example, the issuance of Practice Direction 3.3.

[54] Hong Kong Judiciary, *Reform of the Civil Justice System in Hong Kong*, Final Report of the Working Party on Civil Justice Reform (Hong Kong Judiciary, 2004), para. 16.

Practice Direction 3.1: The Use of Expert Determination on Valuation of Shares at the Stage of Petition

The popularity of using expert determination to resolve shareholder disputes can be reflected in Practice Direction 3.1.[55] Expert determination is a common mode of informal dispute resolution used to resolve shareholder disputes. In expert determination, a neutral third party is appointed by the parties who possesses sufficient technical expertise in the subject matter of the disputes to bring to bear in the making of decisions.[56] The nature of expert determination is quite different from arbitration. In particular, the process of expert determination is more flexible than the arbitration process, as the parties can determine whether the expert's decision will be binding or non-binding.[57] Apparently, the nature of expert determination makes it particularly suitable to solving unfair prejudice cases where the only outstanding issue is a technical matter such as the valuation of minority's shareholdings in the event of a buyout. The interest of the courts in supporting the greater use of expert determination for share valuation issues was evident in *O'Neill v. Phillips*, as Lord Hoffman stated that the share value, if not agreed on, should be determined by a competent expert, with the costs of the expert to be shared by the parties.[58] This approach was taken by the Hong Kong court in *Re Prudential Enterprise*.[59]

Practice Direction 3.3: Voluntary Use of Mediation and Other Alternative Processes for Unfair Prejudice Petition

Mediation is generally perceived as a preferred means to resolve shareholder disputes, as private squabbles can be dealt with in a fashion which is more responsive to the needs of the parties than traditional court-based litigation process.[60] The informality of the mediation process encourages the parties to communicate and exchange sensitive information concerning the company. The interest of the courts in encouraging the greater use of mediation and other alternative processes was reflected in Practice Direction 3.3, which provides a scheme for voluntary mediation in petitions presented under the Unfair Prejudice provisions. This

---

[55] PD 3.1, Part II, para. 5.66

[56] Henry J. Brown and Arthur Marriott, *ADR Principles and Practice*, 2nd ed. (London: Sweet & Maxwell, 2011), 21.

[57] See Id.

[58] [1999] BCC 600 P 614.

[59] [2002] HKLRD 267at 273.

[60] Rita Cheung, 'ADR and Shareholder Disputes: The Anglo-American Experience and Hong Kong Challenges', *Asian Dispute Review* (2008), 118–121 at 120.

judicial direction provides details supplementary to the Companies (Unfair Prejudice Petitions) Proceedings Rules for the companies judge to issue directions with regard to the appropriateness of ADR for the resolution of shareholder disputes. The main features of Practice Direction 3.3 include the filing of the Mediation Notice, which aims to send a clear message about early settlement by way of mediation and other cost-effective alternatives to court-based shareholder proceedings (see Figure 2.1).

In sum, the Hong Kong Judiciary has played a substantial role in promoting the use of mediation and expert determination to resolve shareholder disputes. The recent reform of civil procedures in Hong Kong has had a significant impact on creating a robust corporate law model that provides cost-effective alternatives to court-based shareholder proceedings.

2.3.3 The Reform of Section 168A of the Companies Ordinance to Increase the Use of ADR

The new corporate legislation was enacted on 3 March 2014 and it recognized that court-connected ADR can be viewed as an alternative, informal dispute resolution method supplementing an effective court system.[61] The C (UPP) PR was made in pursuant to Section 727 of the new company law, which expands the court's power to make an order that it thinks fit for referring matters to ADR during unfair prejudice proceedings.[62] The inclusion of an express reference into the unfair prejudice petition rules provides greater certainty as to the extent to which the court can exercise its case management powers to refer cases to ADR at the stage of presenting an unfair prejudice petition.[63] The court may, either on application by one of the parties or of its own motion, grant a stay of legal proceeding to allow parties to make effective use of extrajudicial mechanisms for disposing of the case or any issues relating to it.[64]

It seems that the new company law has achieved noteworthy success in respect of recognition of the role of the judge as the case manager to encourage the parties to explore the possibility of extrajudicial processes to resolve shareholder disputes. Clearly, recent corporate law reform

---

[61] Section 727 of the Companies Ordinance (Cap. 622) and the Companies (Unfair Prejudice Petitions) Proceedings Rules (Cap. 622L).

[62] Section 727 of the Companies Ordinance empowers the Chief Justice (CJ) to make subsidiary legislation for regulating the conduct of unfair prejudice proceedings.

[63] Rule 6(f) of the Companies (Unfair Prejudice Petitions) Proceedings Rules (Cap. 622L) (C (UPP) PR).

[64] Ibid.

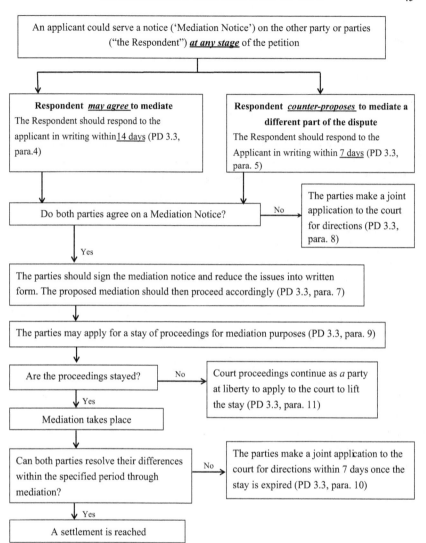

Figure 2.1 An illustration of how Practice Direction 3.3 operates.

initiatives of the minority protection are broadly in line with the reform objectives of CJR in Hong Kong.[65] Such changes represent that there is a paradigm shift in the development of Hong Kong corporate law which

---

[65] Order 1B, Rule 1(2)(e) of the Rules of the High Court (Cap. 4A) confers specific case management powers on the court to make an order to stay the whole or part of proceedings

recognizes ADR as a cost-effective approach to resolving shareholder disputes, while at the same time retaining the jurisdiction of the court to exercise its power to balance the conflicting interests of each member of the company generally.

2.4 Conclusion

As a whole, the Hong Kong government has formulated well-developed directions for the Hong Kong Judiciary on how mediation and other non-litigation modes of dispute resolution can be further developed in the future. The steps taken by the Hong Kong Judiciary to promote the use of extralegal processes to resolve shareholder disputes has been rather far behind government policy on ADR. This can be seen in the Hong Kong Judiciary's promulgation of a specific set of directions on mediation for judges, parties and their lawyers regarding the application of extrajudicial processes to resolve shareholder disputes.[66]

Recent reform of the legislative provisions concerning the protection of minority shareholders also recognizes the important role of the judges to exercise their case management powers to encourage the litigants and their lawyers to consider alternative options to resolve shareholder disputes. The new unfair prejudice petitions rules give judges explicit authority to adjourn the proceedings for the purpose of using media-tion and other types of informal dispute resolution processes to resolve shareholder disputes.[67] Clearly, mediation and other private extrajudicial dispute resolution processes have been institutionalized, as these prac-tices are incorporated within the corporate legislation, the civil procedure rules and the directives issued by the Judiciary.

---

in accordance with the underlying objectives in Order 1A, Rule 1. Moreover, the Hong Kong courts are required to exercise their case management power to order a stay of the proceedings in accordance with the provisions of relevant PDs (e.g., PD 3.3 on voluntary mediation in petitions presented under Sections 168A and 177(1)(f) of the CO).

[66] PD 3.3 This direction provides a framework within which the court can actively exercise its case management power to facilitate the greater use of ADR and for the parties to make use of extralegal procedures at any stage of unfair prejudice proceedings.

[67] Rule 6(f) of the Companies (Unfair Prejudice Petitions) Proceedings Rules (Cap. 622L).

Key Methodology and Methods for Evaluation of Policy Development on ADR in Shareholder Disputes

3.1 Introduction

The disputing landscape for the resolution of shareholder disputes has undergone significant changes since the Civil Justice Reform (CJR) began in 2009. In addition, a separate set of procedural rules were introduced under Section 727 of the new Companies Ordinance, which empowers the courts to exercise their discretionary powers, to make an order about referring matters to mediation or other alternative dispute resolution (ADR).[1] A new set of procedural rules applying to unfair prejudice petitions is broadly in line with the reform objectives of the CJR in Hong Kong.[2] These changes represent a paradigm shift in the approach to the resolution of shareholder disputes in Hong Kong which recognizes ADR as a cost-effective approach to resolving shareholder disputes, while at the same time retaining the jurisdiction of the court to exercise its power to protect minority shareholders' interests from unfairly prejudicial conduct by majority shareholders in privately owned businesses.[3]

Clearly, the objectives of these ADR initiatives (i.e., judicial policy on ADR and the legislative policy on the reform of unfair prejudice provisions in Hong Kong) are consistent with the aim of raising the general public's awareness and promoting the greater use of mediation and other out-of-court processes to resolve shareholder disputes.

---

[1] Rule 6(f) of the Companies (Unfair Prejudice Petitions) Proceedings Rules (Cap. 622L).
[2] Order 1B, Rule 1(2)(e) of the Rules of the High Court (Cap. 4A) confers specific case management powers on the court to make an order to stay the whole or part of proceedings in accordance with the underlying objectives in Order 1A, Rule 1. Moreover, the Hong Kong courts are required to exercise their case management power to order a stay of the proceedings in accordance with the provisions of relevant practice directions (e.g., Practice Direction 3.3 on voluntary mediation in petitions presented under Sections 168A and 177(1)(f) of the CO).
[3] Section 727 of the Companies Ordinance (Cap. 622). There are equivalent procedural rules for unfair prejudice applications in the Companies (Unfair Prejudice Applications) Proceedings Rules 2009 of the United Kingdom.

This book seeks to evaluate the outcomes of ADR initiatives, particularly related to the legitimacy of ADR for shareholder disputes, by examining how the actions of specific types of mechanisms (such as both legal
and non-legal policy instruments) are triggered in the context of a new
disputing landscape of Hong Kong since 2009. The design of this research
study is based on a methodical approach to the evaluation of ADR initiatives for shareholder disputes considering the context, mechanisms and
outcomes, as defined in realistic evaluation.[4] Realistic evaluation is therefore the key methodology employed within this study.

Realistic evaluation methodology was undertaken for the following
reasons. First, the 'theory-based' realistic approach to evaluation of the
current ADR initiatives for shareholder disputes is perceived to be better
than the experimental model as applied to evaluations. This is due to the
fact that experimental research design is based mainly on anecdote or
personal understandings of social actions within a certain context.[5]
By contrast, the 'theory-based' realistic approach focuses on the use of
relevant knowledge and theories to construct a justified model for programme evaluation.[6] For that reason, the realistic evaluation framework
provides a theoretical foundation for developing steps to solve research
issues on how a mix of legal and non-legal policy instruments could be
viewed as specific 'triggering mechanisms' to facilitate the more extensive use of ADR in resolving shareholder disputes within a context in
which there has been a fundamental cultural change in dispute resolution since 2009.[7]

Second, the realistic evaluation framework embraces the use of pluralist research methods, including qualitative and quantitative approaches to
the understanding of the phenomena being studied.[8] Similarly, sociolegal
theorists such as McCrudden advocate a 'pluralism of methodological
approaches', including doctrinal analysis of law, sociolegal research,

---

[4] Ray Pawson and Nick Tilley, *Realistic Evaluation* (London: SAGE, 1997).
[5] The realistic evaluation framework employed in this research study is based on the 'theory-
driven' approach to evaluation developed by Chen and Rossi. For details, see Chen Huey-
Tsyh and Peter H. Rossi, 'Evaluating with Sense the Theory-Driven Approach', *Evaluation
Review*, 7:3 (1983), 283–302 at 285. See also Martin Partington, 'Empirical Legal Research
and Policy-Making', in Peter Cane and Herbert M. Kritzer (eds.), *The Oxford Handbook of
Empirical Legal Research* (Oxford: Oxford University Press, 2010), 1004. Partington argues
that '"evidence-based" policy-making is likely to be better than policy-making shaped by
anecdote or personal preferences.'
[6] Ibid.
[7] See Section 3.2.1 B.
[8] Pawson and Tilley, 'Realistic Evaluation', 85.

and so forth, to examine the relationship between law and social change.[9] Extending this position would suggest that the adoption of different types of research methods, including doctrinal analysis of law, comparative study of law and empirical legal research on lawyers' attitudes towards the use of ADR for shareholder disputes, enriches the understanding of how informal out-of-court processes within shareholder disputes evolved since the CJR began in 2009.[10]

This chapter begins to identify the overriding objectives of this research by proposing the recommended methodology. It then moves to the discussion of research techniques used for conducting this research. The discussion will also consider the empirical research and how to design the questionnaire to measure the attitudes of lawyers towards the use of ADR in Hong Kong.

3.2 Methodology Development for Evaluation of Policy Development on ADR in Shareholder Disputes

This section begins the discussion of the research methodology used to analyse the core research questions in a systematic manner and provides theoretical foundation for the arguments advanced. It then explores the various types of research methods employed in this study.

3.2.1 Focus of Research: Institutionalizing and Legitimizing of ADR

This research study seeks to evaluate the critical stages of institutionalization that secures the legitimacy of ADR for the resolution of shareholder disputes in Hong Kong. Consideration will also be given to how procedural innovations could acquire legitimacy through various types of legal and non-legal inducement mechanisms within the institutionalization process. The question as to what methodology is involved becomes of key importance, as it entails fundamental assumptions of research that guide the direction of collection and analysis of data through the mixture of research methods (such as qualitative and quantitative techniques) in every stage of the research process.[11]

---

[9] Christopher McCrudden, 'Legal Research and the Social Sciences', *Law Quarterly Review*, 122 (2006), 632–650 at 642.

[10] See Sections 3.3.1–3.3.3.

[11] John W. Creswell and Vicki L. Plano Clark, *Designing and Conducting Mixed Methods Research* (Thousand Oaks, CA: SAGE, 2007), 4–5.

3.2.2 Using Realistic Evaluation Methodology to Understand the Process of Institutionalizing the Effective Use of ADR for Shareholder Disputes

The experimental evaluation approach has been widely used by many researchers, from the early literature of dispute resolution until the present time.[12] Although the experimental evaluation approach has dominated the impact assessment of ADR policy for civil disputes in the past decades, experimentalists are interested in the question of 'whether' a programme works and not in 'how or why' it works.[13] As a result, it is not uncommon that the findings of an experimental research on the impact or outcome of a particular ADR programme (such as a court-connected ADR programme) have little or no relevance.[14] The problem of little or no effect on the outcome may be attributed to the inadequacy of the experimental evaluation methodology.[15] This includes the lack of validity of the information generated from the random assignment of cases into the experimental and the control groups as well as the lack of a theoretical framework to identify causal mechanisms.[16]

Apparently, the theoretical underpinning of 'how' ADR initiatives work in a certain context is of paramount importance in designing and carrying out the research. Careful consideration should be given to the theoretical assumptions underlying ADR initiatives for shareholder disputes in Hong Kong. The 'theory-based' realistic approach to evaluation is particularly relevant in the present study. This is attributed mainly to the fact that the realistic evaluation helps to explore the key question of 'how' legitimacy produced through a combined set of legal and non-legal instruments supports the process of institutionalizing the effective use of informal out-of-court processes for shareholder dispute resolution. This

---

[12] See, for example, Hazel Genn, Department for Constitutional Affairs, *Central London Pilot Mediation Scheme, Evaluation Report* (1998); Hazel Genn, *Paths to Justice: What People Think and Do About Going to Law* (Oxford: Hart Publishing, 1999); Hazel Genn, *Court Based ADR initiatives for Non-Family Civil Cases* (Department for Constitutional Affairs, Research Series1/02, 2002) and Hazel Genn et al., *Twisting Arms: Court Referred and Court Linked Mediation Under Judicial Pressure* (Ministry of Justice Research Series, Series 1/07, 2007).

[13] Chen Huey-Tsyh and Peter H. Rossi, 'The Multi-Goal, Theory-Driven Approach to Evaluation: A Model Linking Basic and Applied Social Science', *Social Forces*, 59:1 (1980), 106–122 at 110 and Pawson and Tilley, 'Realistic Evaluation', xv.

[14] Chen and Rossi, 'The Multi-Goal, Theory-Driven Approach to Evaluation', 106–107.

[15] Ibid.

[16] Ibid.

core question can then be addressed through the development of a theoretical model which is based mainly on the work in sociolegal theory and sociological institutionalism.[17]

Apart from that, the 'context-mechanisms-outcome' (CMO) pattern configurations developed by Pawson and Tilley provide a theoretical foundation for developing steps for analysing the extent to which ADR is generally accepted or legitimated through a combine set of legal and non-legal policy instruments within the institutionalization processes.[18] The CMO configurations outline the following three areas that are required to be investigated during the research process.

Conditions for the Development of ADR Methods for Shareholder Disputes in Hong Kong

This involves an investigation of the 'context', which describes the conditions in which ADR has gained its legitimacy as an alternative means of court-based unfair prejudice proceedings.[19] On that basis, it is necessary to review the resolution of shareholder disputes in the new disputing landscape since the CJR began in 2009.

Arguably, ADR could be considered as complementing unfair prejudice proceedings if the court-based shareholder litigation process is proved to be costly and ineffective.[20] However, an established culture of early settlement in the statutory unfair prejudice provision emphasizes that the appropriate use of expert determination and bilateral negotiation between the parties at an early stage may have either a small positive impact or no impact on lawyers' enthusiasm for ADR.[21] One possible reason for this may be attributed to the current Section 725 of the Companies Ordinance that the court is empowered to make an order in requiring the majority shareholders or the company to purchase the shares of the dissenting members at an early stage. Thus, it is not surprising that the court ordered

---

[17] For details, see Chapter 1.

[18] Pawson and Tilley, 'Realistic Evaluation', 83–88. Pawson and Tilley proposed that the 'context-mechanism-outcome' pattern configurations encompass models indicating how a programme triggers mechanisms, among whom and in what conditions to bring about the behavioural changes of individual actors.

[19] Ibid., 69–70.

[20] See Chapter 6.

[21] See, for example, *Re Prudential Enterprise Ltd* [2006] 1 HKLRD 267 at 277. More recently, the issuance of Practice Direction 3.1: Bankruptcy and Winding-Up Proceedings improves the court's power to make directions regarding expert evidence on valuation. See also Chapter 6, this generates a testable hypothesis statistical analysis.

buyout relief is by far the most commonly sought remedy under the statutory unfair prejudice provision.[22] Given that the court plays an important role in promoting early settlement through a buyout order, the new court rules and the practice directions give the court explicit powers to actively exercise its case management powers to refer shareholder dispute to ADR processes.[23]

Recently, the new Companies Ordinance has taken a step further to include a provision that empowers the Chief Justice (CJ) to make rules in encouraging the litigants to attempt mediation and other alternative out-of-court methods to resolve shareholder disputes before or shortly after the start of proceedings.[24] For this reason, it is necessary to consider whether the new company law, the court rules and referral practices on ADR issued by the CJ match with the new disputing environment in Hong Kong which may lead to the achievement of the desired ADR goals.[25]

Establishing Appropriate Mechanisms to Improve the Understanding and Awareness of ADR

The second area that needs to be considered is the establishment of the appropriate mechanisms to improve the understanding and awareness of informal out-of-court processes for shareholder disputes. This refers to the ways in which the development of a variety of policy instruments could result in the creation of a new paradigm of dispute resolution which embraces the complementary benefits of various dispute settlement procedures for settling shareholder disputes, including but not limited to public court adjudication.[26]

ADR is characterized as an 'emerging field', as its structure field is under-organized and it does not specify its organizational norms and practices (logic) precisely.[27] Institutional theory suggests that for a

---

[22] Philip Lawton, 'Modelling the Chinese Family Firm and Minority Shareholer Protection: The Hong Kong Experience 1980–1995', *Managerial Law*, 49:5/6 (2007), 249–271 at 263.

[23] Order 1A, Rule 4(2)(e) of the RHC.

[24] The new procedure rules in governing the conduct of unfair prejudice proceedings, namely the Companies (Unfair Prejudice Petitions) Proceedings Rules, is made pursuant to Section 727 of the new companies legislation. This section stipulates that, subject to the approval of the Legislative Council, the Chief Justice may make rules for regulating the proceedings on unfair prejudice petitions.

[25] For details, see Chapter 4.

[26] Pawson and Tilley, 'Realistic Evaluation', 65–66.

[27] Jill M. Purdy and Barbara Gary, 'Conflicting Logics, Mechanisms of Diffusion, and Multilevel Dynamics in Emerging Institutional Fields', *Academy of Management Journal*, 52:2 (2009), 355–380 at 357. Purdy and Gray said: 'Established fields are hierarchically

particular emerging practice or norm (such as ADR) to be sustained or legitimate, three supportive mechanisms which are located within the institutional processes have to be identified: coercive, normative and mimetic.[28] On that basis, it is necessary to analyse whether the combined set of policy instruments comprised of 'coercive, normative, and mimetic elements' provide a legitimate basis for the general acceptance of using ADR to resolve shareholder disputes in Hong Kong. These can be ana- lysed as follows:

- **Coercive mechanism**: This refers to force or pressure which stems from an actor who has the capacity to establish rules or mandates, inspect others' conformity to these, and, as necessary, manipulate sanctions in the form of either rewards or punishment.[29] This type of mechanism can further be divided into two categories according to the type of incen- tives provided.[30] The first type exhibits a stringent approach regarding the use of legislative mandates to restrict certain behaviours through sanctions.[31] For example, a costs rule is applicable to parties and their legal representatives who failed to act reasonably to comply with the Practice Direction on mediation.[32] Thus, laws relating to ADR, such as the Companies Ordinance, the civil procedure rules and a set of direc- tives on mediation issued by the Hong Kong Judiciary provide legisla- tive frameworks to support the application of out-of-court processes for the resolution of shareholder disputes. The ultimate effect of these rules and practice directions provide incentives for the parties and their lawyers to use out-of-court settlement processes in settling share- holder disputes.[33] Informal out-of-court processes can be considered as

distributed, with some actors exercising influence over norms governing legitimate behav- ior; by contrast, in emerging fields "structures of domination" have not yet been established.'

[28] Paul J. DiMaggio and Walter W. Powell, 'The Iron Cage Revisited: Institutional Isomorphism and Collective Rationality in Organizational Fields', *American Sociological Review*, 48:2 (1983), 147–160 at 150–151.

[29] Ibid.

[30] P. Devereaux Jennings and Paul A. Zandbergen, 'Ecologically Sustainable Organizations: An Institutional Approach', *Academy of Management Review*, 20:4 (1995), 1015–1052 at 1029 and Klaus J. Hopt and Felix Steffek, 'Mediation: Comparison of Laws, Regulatory Models, Fundamental Issues' in Klaus J. Hopt and Felix Steffek (eds.), *Mediation: Principles and Regulation in Comparative Perspective* (Oxford: Oxford University Press, 2013), 32.

[31] Hopt and Felix, 'Mediation', 32.

[32] Order 62, Rule 5 of the Rules of the High Court (RHC) empowers the court to exercise its discretion as to costs. Order 62, Rule 8 of the RHC empowers the court to make a wasted costs order against a legal representative. See Chapter 4.

[33] Hazel Genn, *Judging Civil Justice*, The Hamlyn Lectures 59th Series (Cambridge University Press, 2010), 95. Genn took an opposite view on this point. Genn notes that 'the effect of

legitimate modes for resolving shareholder disputes, as these processes have been integrated within the court system and legal mandates.[34]

- The second type exhibits a lenient approach regarding the use of market-based incentives to encourage the party to attempt ADR.[35] For example, Italy has introduced tax advantages for mediation, such as exempting mediation agreements from the stamp tax and granting a tax credit towards the full mediation fee if the mediation is successful.[36] However, there is no equivalent provision in Hong Kong.

- **Normative mechanism**: This stems primarily from a taken-for-granted system of values, beliefs and habits.[37] Unlike the coercive mechanism, it does not have a direct financial incentive or sanction which would affect the attitudes of local business and legal professional communities to adopt ADR in resolving shareholder disputes. Instead, corporate users and their lawyers may consciously or unconsciously adopt ADR processes as they believe that such an adoption is in conformity with cultural norms, beliefs or rules that are presumed to be acceptable or legitimate in a given society. This type of mechanism is associated with the professionalization of the occupational group which seeks to create a new resolution paradigm for shareholder disputes by establishing its autonomy from other fields.[38] The legal professions could serve as agents of legitimacy in supporting the development of ADR for shareholder disputes.[39] This is due to the fact that they are professional dispute handlers who develop cognitive models of dispute resolution (such as mediation and adjudication models) and institutionalize them into their everyday practice.[40] Similarly, the legal professional bodies (including the Law Society of Hong Kong and the Hong

---

the rules in relation to ADR is not to provide a direct incentive for parties to settle disputes by mediation but to impose a further threat of financial penalty on a party who might be deemed to have unreasonably refused an offer of mediation.'

[34] For further discussion, see Chapter 4.

[35] Hopt and Felix, 'Mediation', 33.

[36] Ibid.

[37] DiMaggio and Powell, 'The Iron Cage Revisited', 152–153.

[38] Ibid. and Yves Dezalay and Bryant Garth, 'Fussing about the Forum: Categories and Definitions as Stakes in a Professional Competition', *Law and Social Inquiry*, 21 (1996), 285–312.

[39] See Chapter 6.

[40] John Lande, 'The Diffusion of a Process Pluralist Ideology of Disputing: Factors Affecting Opinions of Business Lawyers and Executives', Ph.D thesis, University of Wisconsin-Madison, (1995), 25 and Penny Brooker, *Mediation Law: Journey through Institutionalism to Juridification* (London: Routledge, 2013), 243–246 and 251.

Kong Bar Association) and the universities must compromise with non-professional clients, regulators and public opinion to define the methods and conditions of their work in raising the awareness of using ADR to resolve shareholder disputes among all practicing members of the Hong Kong's legal profession.[41] This could be done by introducing ADR courses as part of either continuing education programme for practicing lawyers or the university law school curriculum at both the undergraduate and postgraduate levels.[42]

- **Mimetic mechanism:** This stems from the need to cope with uncertainty by the imitation of foreign models which are perceived to be more legitimate or more successful.[43] For example, Hong Kong may draw lessons from the development of a mixture of approaches to the codification of ADR devices for shareholder disputes in the United Kingdom, New Zealand and South Africa, particularly against the background of the closer affinity with the legal systems of these common law countries.[44]

Thus, institutional theory provides a useful conceptual framework for understanding how the three types of institutional mechanisms – coercive, normative and mimetic – support the development and operation of extrajudicial processes for shareholder disputes in Hong Kong.[45]

Outcome Patterns of the Acceptance of Using ADR to Resolve Shareholder Disputes

The final and most important area that needs to be examined is the outcome patterns of the acceptance of using ADR to resolve shareholder disputes within the local business and legal professional communities. The outcome patterns can be measured in terms of legitimacy, which is the product of institutionalization processes.[46]

Basically, there are three types of legitimacy – pragmatic, moral and cognitive – which can be viewed as the generalized perception that certain actions or practices are deemed 'desirable, proper, or appropriate within some socially constructed system of norms, values, beliefs, and

---

[41] DiMaggio and Powell, 'The Iron Cage Revisited', 152. See also Chapter 6.
[42] See Chapter 6.
[43] DiMaggio and Powell, 'The Iron Cage Revisited', 151–152.
[44] See Chapters 5 and 7.
[45] See Chapters 4 to 7.
[46] Ronald L. Jepperson, 'Institutions, Institutional Effects, and Institutionalism' in Walter W. Powell and Paul J. DiMaggio (eds.), *The New Institutionalism in Organizational Analysis* (Chicago: University of Chicago Press, 1991), 149.

definitions.'[47] Accordingly, the following typology of legitimacy proposed by Suchman can be used to analyse how ADR practices are evolving through the three sequential stages: (1) pre-institutionalization, (2) semi-institutionalization stage and (3) full institutionalization.[48]

- **Pragmatic legitimacy**: This type of legitimacy rests on the self-interested calculation of interests of actors who are more closely linked to a particular organizational field (such as the legal field).[49] Most often, this type of legitimacy might arise when there is a growing number of litigation lawyers who believe that ADR practice such as mediation or other modes of out-of-court ADR processes would be considered as the most profitable practice within the legal professional field.[50]
- **Moral legitimacy:** This type of legitimacy relates to how new practices become justified in highly structured settings (such as the court system).[51] In this context, the inclusion of ADR practices within the court's case management powers would become legitimate if the court interprets the court rules in a manner which is in line with the dominant economic and social values of Hong Kong.[52] Similarly, the reception of foreign law, notably, legislative enactment of a set of procedural rules for unfair prejudice applications based on the UK model, is perceived to be effective in generating legitimacy among the local business and professional communities.[53]
- **Cultural-cognitive legitimacy**: This type of legitimacy can be described as 'for things to be otherwise is literally unthinkable'.[54] This means that certain types of practices become 'taken-for-granted'

[47] Mark C. Suchman, 'Managing Legitimacy: Strategic and Institutional Approaches', *Academy of Management Review*, 20:3 (1995), 571–610 at 574.
[48] Pamela S. Tolbert and Lynne G. Zucker, 'Studying Organization: Theory & Method' in Stewart R. Clegg and Cynthia Hardy (eds.), *The Institutionalization of Institutional Theory* (Thousand Oaks, CA: SAGE, 1999), pp. 175–178 and Royston Greenwood, Royston Greenwood et al., 'Theorizing Change: The Role of Professional Associations in the Transformation of Institutionalized Fields', *Academy of Management Journal*, 45:1 (2002), 58–80 at 59–61.
[49] Suchman, 'Managing Legitimacy', 578–579.
[50] Yves Dezalay and Bryant Garth, 'Fussing about the Forum: Categories and Definitions as Stakes in a Professional Competition', *Law and Social Inquiry*, 21 (1996), 285–312 at 290–291. For further discussion, see also Chapter 6.
[51] Suchman, 'Managing Legitimacy', 579–582.
[52] For further discussion, see Chapter 4.
[53] For further discussion, see Chapters 5 and 7.
[54] Suchman, 'Managing Legitimacy', 583 (citing Lynne G. Zucker, 'Organizations as Institutions' in Samuel B. Bacharach (ed.), *Research in the Sociology of Organizations: A Research Annual* (Greenwich, CT: JAI Press, 1983), 25).

notions with a 'rule-like status in social thought and action'.[55] The notion of taken-for-grantedness represents the most powerful source of legitimacy, as a new, innovative, yet-to-be established practice can be substituted by a prior established practice.[56] For example, this may happen under a circumstance (i.e., the stage of full institutionalization) that the continuing popular dissatisfaction with the public court system (such as problems associated with costly and lengthy court litigation) may affect the general public's acceptance towards the use of ADR to resolve shareholder disputes. Informal ADR processes (such as mediation) would be considered as substitutes for shareholder litigation. ADR processes have gained their legitimacy as fair and appropriate modes of dispute resolution within the local legal professions and the general public.[57]

In sum, the inclusion of relevant theory (such as institutional theory) into the realistic evaluation framework enlarges the knowledge base about the problems of the excessive length and costs of unfair prejudice proceedings and consideration of a wide range of policy instruments for the development of ADR for shareholder disputes. The realistic evaluation methodology provides a framework for linking research questions or hypotheses to specific research methods for an analysis of how legitimacy produced through a combined set of legal and non-legal instruments supports the process of institutionalizing the effective use of innovative dispute resolution methods for shareholder disputes resolution.[58] The following section explains why the use of pluralist research

---

[55] Walter W. Powell and Paul J. DiMaggio, 'Introduction' in Paul J. DiMaggio and Walter W. Powell (eds.), *The New Institutionalism in Organizational Analysis* (Chicago: University of Chicago Press, 1991), 1, 7–9.

[56] Suchman, 'Managing Legitimacy', 583.

[57] For further discussion, see the concluding chapter.

[58] It should be noted that there is a conceptual difference between 'research question' and 'hypothesis'. The former allows the researcher to develop a set of questions based on a problem or phenomenon where limited knowledge is known. Thus, it allows for a wide range of answers by making a discovery instead of proving an assumption. On that basis, research questions can further be used to explore the relationships between variables that may lead to a hypothesis. In contrast, hypothesis is generally referred as a 'statement that has a specific prediction that is believed to occur as a result of conducting a study.' Thus, hypotheses can be empirically tested by examining the relationships between variables. For more detail, see Linda Cooley and Jo Lewkowicz, *Dissertation Writing in Practice: Turning Ideas into Text* (Hong Kong University Press, 2003), 31–33 and Carrie A. Picardi and Kevin D. Masick, *Research Methods: Designing and Conducting Research with a Real-World Focus* (Thousand Oaks, CA: SAGE, 2014), 20.

methods is suitable in addressing research questions within a realistic evaluation framework.

3.2.3 The Acceptance of Mixed Research Methods for Conducting a Realistic Evaluation

A further supporting reason for the use of realistic evaluation methodology is that it values the use of various research methods (such as qualitative or quantitative approaches) rather than seeking to promote or rely on a specific method for studying research problems.[59] Broadly speaking, the advantage of using pluralist research methods including a doctrinal approach to the study of law, comparative study and empirical legal research on lawyers' attitudes towards the use of ADR for shareholder disputes is that they provide a more complete picture of the extent to which ADR is generally accepted or legitimated through a combined set of legal and non-legal policy instruments.

In particular, one of the main purposes of this research design is either discovery (inductive or qualitative analysis) or testing (deductive or quantitative analysis).[60] In doctrinal research, the process of reviewing and analysing both the primary (a body of case law and legislation) and secondary (journal articles or other written commentaries on the case law and legislation) sources can be viewed as an inductive approach to legal research.[61] This approach helps to explore the question of what are the key policy instruments and contextual factors that allow the Hong Kong government and the Judiciary to promote the greater use of ADR for shareholder disputes in Hong Kong.[62]

However, the deductive approach is also appropriate for the present study, as it measures the attitudes of Hong Kong lawyers towards the use of ADR for shareholder disputes since the CJR began in 2009. Inferences will then be drawn by using a range of statistical tools (such as logistic regression) to verify a set of hypotheses developed in Chapter 6. The following sections illustrate how the realistic evaluation methodology is implemented with the following types of research methods.

---

[59] Pawson and Tilley, 'Realistic Evaluation', 85.

[60] Janice M. Morse, 'Principles of Mixed Methods and Multi-method Research Design' in Abbas Tashakkori and Charles Teddle (eds.), *Handbook of Mixed Methods in Social & Behavioral Research* (Thousand Oaks, CA: SAGE, 2003), 196.

[61] Ian Dobinson and Francis Johns, 'Qualitative Legal Research', in Mike McConville and Chui Wing-Hong (eds.), *Research Methods for Law* (Edinburgh: Edinburgh University Press, 2007), 31–32.

[62] Morse, 'Principles of Mixed Methods and Multi-method Research Design', 196.

3.3 Key Research Methods Used in This Book

This section seeks to introduce the different types of research methods used within the present research study: (1) the traditional approach to the study of law, (2) comparative study and (3) empirical legal research. The adoption of pluralistic research methods is preferred, as it provides a better understanding of how procedural innovations can acquire legitimacy through various types of legal and non-legal inducement mechanisms within the institutionalization process.

3.3.1 Doctrinal Approach to the Study of Law

The first method employed is the doctrinal approach to the study of law. There are three major reasons to explain why the doctrinal approach to the study of law is appropriate here. First, it seeks to uncover the original policy reasons behind the promotion of negotiated settlement either through the courts to manage cases at earlier stage of the proceedings or by court referral to ADR at any stage of the litigation process. An analysis of relevant case law, civil procedure rules and the companies legislation in the post-CJR era helps to determine whether the rules of court and referral practices on ADR issued by the CJ coincide with the new disputing environment in Hong Kong which may lead to the achievement of the desired ADR goals.

However, the study of relevant case law reports published before the CJR began in 2009 should not be ignored, as they can serve as a benchmark for comparison with the existing case law developments on ADR for shareholder disputes. In addition, this analysis helps determine whether it is appropriate to introduce statutory provisions for enforcement of mediation agreements in any future reform of the Mediation Ordinance. The alternative is to maintain the status quo and allow judges to apply contract law principles in determining the enforceability of mediation agreement on a case-by-case basis.

Prior to the start of the CJR in 2009, Hong Kong courts adopted different interpretative approaches with regard to the enforcement of mediation agreements.[63] In *Hyundai Engineering & Construction Co. Ltd v. Vigour,*

---

[63] Zhao Yun, 'Revisiting the Issue of Enforceability of Mediation Agreements in Hong Kong', *China-EU Law Journal* 1 (2013), 115–133, 116. Professor Zhao distinguishes between 'enforcement of mediation agreements' and 'mediated settlements'. The former refers to 'agreements or clauses in contracts where the contracting parties agree to participate in mediation before resorting to arbitration or litigation in the event of disputes.' The latter refers to 'agreements that are reached after or as a result of mediation'.

the decision of the Court of First Instance reflected the pro-mediation stance by recognizing that the mediation agreement is enforceable despite the fact that the agreement failed to stipulate the mediation procedure or a time frame.[64] However, this decision was reversed by the Court of Appeal and it was held that the mediation agreement reached by the parties was imprecise and therefore unenforceable.[65]

By contrast, the Court of Appeal in *iRiver Hong Kong Ltd v. Thakral Corp (HK) Ltd* adopted a robust approach in promoting the benefits of using ADR for early settlement.[66] Although the subjects of the disputes are different in these two respective cases, no clear policy objectives were spelled out with regard to the approaches taken by the courts towards ADR. It appears that the reported case law prior to the CJR begun in 2009 failed to achieve consistency between the decisions of different judges with regard to enforcement of mediation agreements. It remains to be seen what impact the reported case law decided prior to the introduction of CJR and the passage of the Mediation Ordinance in 2012 will have in practice, in particular, to what extent Hong Kong lawyers are more willing to adopt informal out-of-court processes in assisting their clients to resolve shareholder disputes since the CJR began in 2009.[67]

As a whole, an analysis of case law decided prior to the CJR began is useful. First, it provides a benchmark for determining whether the objectives of the reforms are clearly set out in the post-CJR era so that Hong Kong judges are more likely to produce a result that is consistent with the policy objective of promoting ADR. Moreover, this analysis helps to determine the extent to which court decisions regarding the enforceability of mediation agreements made before 2009 affect Hong Kong lawyers' attitudes towards the use of ADR for shareholder disputes.[68]

Second, an analysis of the available judgements from the Hong Kong courts delivering shareholder disputes and mediation cases, from 2009 onward after CJR seems relevant to this study as well. This analysis helps to explore the judicial attitudes towards ADR since the CJR began in 2009. This is certainly true, as law and society theorists such as Manning points out that a legal decision cannot be isolated from the analysis of social and economic factors influencing the decision-making power of a

---

[64] [2004] 3 HKLRD 1.
[65] [2005] 3 HKLRD 723 at 724.
[66] [2008] 4 HKLRD 1000 at 1015–1016.
[67] For further discussion, see Chapters 6 and 7.
[68] For further discussion, see Chapter 6.

judge despite the fact that the legitimacy source of law derives primarily from authoritative source.[69]

From this perspective, the law is better conceived as a set of acceptable social beliefs or values that most people endorse rather than treating law as authoritative.[70] This is due to the fact that many laws are sufficiently ambiguous, as they do not provide a clear set of guidelines for certain actions.[71] Judges perform their important role by providing a workable meaning of the law that most people support that action or order.[72] On that basis, the study of the reported case law regarding the judicial attitudes towards ADR from 2009 to 2016 helps to identify a mix of legal and other cultural factors affecting the judicial acceptance of the use of informal out-of-court processes for shareholder disputes.

Third, this research also seeks to provide a strong and compelling reason to expand the scope of ADR in dealing with shareholder disputes. A study of the majority of Section 168A reported cases, from 2004 when the shareholder remedies provisions were substantial revised by the Companies (Amendment) Ordinance 2004, up to the present, was conducted. Consideration will also be given on evaluating the new legislative reform of the statutory unfair prejudice provision which came into force in March 2014.

3.3.2 Comparative Approaches in the Study of Law

Broadly speaking, a comparative study of law is a good research method to study the relationship between systems of law through analysing the history of the systems or of the rules.[73] Two comparative approaches are relevant to the present study.[74]

First, the traditional approach to a comparative study of law focuses on the effects of legal transplants. Alan Watson advocates the study of legal transplants in comparative law, as this approach helps to understand how

---

[69] Peter K. Manning, "'Big-Bang' Decisions: Notes on a Naturalistic Approach' in Keith Hawkins (ed.), *The Uses of Discretion* (Oxford: Clarendon Press, 1992), 249.

[70] Ibid.

[71] Ibid.

[72] Ibid. and Manning, "'Big-Bang' Decisions: Notes on a Naturalistic Approach', 249.

[73] Alan Watson, *Legal Transplants: An Approach to Comparative Law*, (Lake Mary, FL: Vandeplas, 1974), 6–7.

[74] Konrad Zweigert and Hein Käotz, *Introduction to Comparative Law*, 3rd rev (ed.) (Oxford: Clarendon Press, 1998), 6–12 (1998). Zweigert and Käotz identifies two approaches to the study of comparative law: (1) traditional approach to comparative study of law and (2) comparative sociology of law.

the complex dynamics of cross-jurisdictional legal transfers brings legal systems into contact and eventually causes them to change.[75] He characterizes law as relatively autonomous, and law develops by transplanting, not because of exogenous aspects such as social, economic and cultural factors influencing the changes in the law.[76] Instead, the effects of legal transplant could be attributable to imitation of foreign practices, as laws of these countries originated from the same legal families or traditions, and thus they share similarities in terms of their structural reforms.[77]

Institutional theorists such as DiMaggio and Powell have shared a similar view on the reason for imitating foreign practices.[78] They point out that the imitation of foreign practices is extremely effective in generating legitimacy of a new practice among members of the local community.[79] This is particularly true as there remains uncertainty about the impact of Civil Justice Reform on ADR introduced by the Hong Kong Judiciary in 2009, which encouraged litigants to consider the possibility of extrajudicial processes to resolve shareholder dispute.

The traditional approach to comparative study of law can then be applied in this study by examining whether Hong Kong courts and legislators blindly copy one policy programme about the use of ADR from another jurisdiction, without tailoring it to fit the local environment. In particular, it would be unwise for Hong Kong to blindly follow the foreign law without considering its local corporate law context despite the fact it is ideal for Hong Kong to learn from their experience. Hence, an examination of the policy reasons in the United Kingdom, New Zealand and South Africa for the developments of ADR provisions within their corporate law framework is beneficial. In particular, Hong Kong may draw lessons from the development of a mixture of approaches to the codification of ADR devices for shareholder disputes in the United Kingdom, New Zealand and South Africa, particularly against the background of the closer affinity with the legal system of these common law countries.[80]

---

[75] Watson, 'Legal Transplants: An Approach to Comparative Law', 6–7.
[76] William Ewald, 'Comparative Jurisprudence (II): The Logic of Legal Transplants', *The American Journal of Comparative Law*, 43:4 (1995), 489–510 at 498–500.
[77] William Twining, 'Social Science and Diffusion of Law', *Journal of Law and Society*, 32:2 (2005), 203–240 at 211–212.
[78] DiMaggio and Powell, 'The Iron Cage Revisited', 151.
[79] Ibid.
[80] John C. Reitz, 'How to Do Comparative Law', *American Journal of Comparative Law* 46:4 (1998), 617–636 at 625. This analysis is in line with the orthodox position of the traditional approach to comparative study of law as comparatists are expected to search for those

However, comparative sociology of law is particularly relevant to this study as well because Friedman notes that countries whose laws originate in the same legal family or tradition (such as a common law system) might 'move along separate paths' in designing their legislations 'as their societies diverge'.[81] Thus, comparative sociology of law can be applied in this study by developing three testable series of arguments regarding the conditions under which Hong Kong may learn from the experience of the United Kingdom, New Zealand and South Africa by incorporating the use of informal dispute resolution methods into the company legislation.[82] Undoubtedly, the reception of foreign models, notably through a blend or approaches to the codification of ADR for shareholder disputes, is nonetheless extremely effective in generating legitimacy. This is due to the fact that the source of this type of legitimacy stems from the need of the Hong Kong government to cope with uncertainty about the future codification of ADR mechanisms for shareholder disputes, by adopting foreign models which are perceived to be more legitimate or more successful.[83]

3.3.3 Empirical Legal Research on Lawyers' Attitudes Towards the Use of ADR for Shareholder Disputes: Questionnaire Design and Implementation

Empirical legal research is applied to evaluate the impact of procedural changes in court rules since 2009 regarding Hong Kong lawyers' attitudes towards the use of ADR for shareholder disputes. Empirical legal research was used in this study as it seeks to identify the underlying factors affecting lawyers' attitudes towards the use of ADR for shareholder disputes in Hong Kong. This empirical study is particularly relevant to the discussion of how lawyers play crucial roles in legitimizing new ideas on ADR and in mediating the new non-adversarial approaches to resolving legal problems between their clients.[84]

This research adopts an ex post facto design to evaluate how ADR initiatives affect lawyers' attitudes towards the use of ADR for shareholder

aspects of law in one legal system (e.g., Hong Kong) which is functionally equivalent (such as better protection on minority interests in most common law countries, the origins of legal system, etc.) to the other legal system or systems (e.g., the United Kingdom) under comparison.

[81] Lawrence M. Friedman, 'Legal Culture and Social Development', *Law & Society Review*, 4 (1969), 29–44 at 34–35.

[82] For further discussion, see Chapter 7.

[83] Ibid.

[84] For further discussion, see Chapter 6.

disputes since 2009. The author collected the programme data on the target legal professions after 2009 when judicial policy on ADR was started. This research study was carried out between late April and early August 2012. Respondents were asked to complete the questionnaire by themselves.[85] The following subsections describe the key research instruments which were used to carry out this quantitative, cross-sectional research for data collection and subsequent statistical analysis.

Unit of Analysis and the Sampling Frame

The units of analysis in this study are qualified barristers and solicitors who are currently working in private practice in Hong Kong.[86] As at the end of April 2012, the said population size of all the Hong Kong legal practitioners who were engaged in private practice was about 6,697. Clearly, it is impractical to obtain data from every unit of the population by constructing a sampling frame that includes all practicing lawyers in Hong Kong. In addition, a large sample size alone does not guarantee a representative sample.[87] This is particularly true as statistical results are valid if and only if a researcher provides a representative sample for making inferences about a population. Given that the representativeness of the sample of this study is crucial, the samples of this research study were chosen from a specific list of subset of members in a given population, which included most of the practicing barristers and solicitors in Hong Kong.[88] Briefly, practicing barristers were included in this survey for the following reasons.

First, the actual population size of those practicing barristers in Hong Kong is identifiable. The Hong Kong Bar Association provides information relating to its members' personal contact details and the types of services provided, which is available to the public. On that basis, the sample size could then be calculated based on the actual population size of those practicing barristers in Hong Kong.

Second, like solicitors, practicing barristers in Hong Kong on average devoted more time to commercial and company cases[89] Moreover, both

[85] Earl R. Babbie, *The Practice of Social Research*, 12th (ed.) (Thomas Wadsworth, 2007), 257.
[86] Babbie, 'The Practice of Social Research', 94 and Carol H. Weiss, *Evaluation: Methods for Studying Programs and Policies*, 2nd ed. (Prentice Hall, 1998), 185. Unit of analysis is defined as 'the unit that the evaluation measures and enters into statistical analyses.'
[87] William Lawrence Neuman, *Basic of Social Research: Qualitative and Quantitative Approaches*, 3rd ed. (Pearson, 2012), 167.
[88] Rebecca M. Warner, *Applied Statistics: From Bivariate Through Multivariate Techniques* (Thousand Oaks, CA:: SAGE, 2008), 3. Warner notes that it is ideal for a researcher to select a sample from an actual population size which can be identifiable.
[89] Hong Kong Department of Justice, *Consultancy Study on the Demand for and Supply of Legal and Related Services* (Hong Kong Department of Justice, 2008), 10–11 and 36–37.

the practicing barristers and solicitors in Hong Kong are equally involved in ADR processes to assist their clients to resolve shareholder disputes.[90] Therefore, a representative sample for this research could then be drawn from these groups.

Third, the barristers' monopoly of higher-court advocacy is threatened since an amendment to the Legal Practitioners Ordinance (Cap. 159) has extended the rights of audience to solicitors.[91] Barristers might respond to this threat by offering ADR services directly to lay clients without the need for solicitors to act as intermediaries.[92] Given that Hong Kong barristers are also permitted to act for a client in ADR processes,[93] ADR services could then be viewed as an alternative strategy for stimulating barristers' services. In addition, the Hong Kong CJR, together with various court-connected mediation programmes introduced by the Hong Kong Judiciary, have provided incentives for local practicing barristers either to rush to train as dispute resolvers (such as mediators and/or arbitrators), or to incorporate skills of conflict management into their practices.

Last but most importantly, the services provided by in-house lawyers are not available to the public.[94] If in-house lawyers were included in this survey, the author might take additional efforts by requesting referrals of

---

The Supply Report illustrates that a larger proportion of solicitors were providing services for landlord and tenant (accounting for 94 per cent of solicitor firms) and commercial and company matters (accounting 85 per cent of solicitor firms). Similarly, barristers devoted more time to provide services for commercial and company matters (accounting for 68 per cent of barristers).

[90] A t-test was adopted to determine whether the sample means of the two branches of the legal profession involving ADR services to assist their clients to resolve shareholder disputes is significant or insignificant., The samples of the two branches of the legal profession were compared with a test variable 'the number of shareholder disputes that Hong Kong lawyers are involved in ADR processes in resolving shareholder disputes. The results of t-test generated by SPSS showed that the difference in means between the two branches of the legal profession involving ADR services to assist their clients to resolve shareholder disputes were not statistically significant ($F = 12.159$, df = 30.232, n.s.). Hence, the findings suggest that both the practicing barristers and solicitors in Hong Kong are equally involved in ADR processes to assist their clients to resolve shareholder disputes.

[91] Section 39H of the LPO gives the solicitors higher rights of audience if they satisfied the requirements of the Higher Rights Assessment Board.

[92] Traditionally, the symbiotic relationship between the two branches means that barristers and solicitors have performed a complementary role in the litigation proceedings. Barristers, who are generally instructed by the solicitors, act as intermediaries with lay clients. On that basis, barristers can be approached by a member of the public only on the instructions of a solicitor. For details, see para. 50(a) of the Code of Conduct issued by the Hong Kong Bar Association.

[93] See Appendix 4 para. 23 of the Code of Conduct issued by the Hong Kong Bar Association.

[94] Consultancy Study on the Demand for and Supply of Legal and Related Services, 2.

additional individuals to contact in-house lawyers. More importantly, this type of sampling method is another kind of convenient, non-sampling method, rendering the sample less useful, as the data collector might approach the respondents who seem friendliest or most approachable.[95] One of the major drawbacks for a researcher to make generalizations from this sample is that the survey is not representative of the entire population. For these reasons, the two branches of the Hong Kong's legal profession who offer either arbitration/litigation services or commercial and corporate-related matters to the general public will be the target groups under this survey.[96]

Mode of Sampling Processes

The legal practitioner respondents were drawn mainly from the Law Society of Hong Kong and the Hong Kong Bar Association, accredited as mediators and/or arbitrators in the Hong Kong International Arbitration Centre (HKIAC) and specializing in either commercial or corporate-related matters. A proportionate stratified random sampling method was used in this research as this ensures adequate representation of each stratum. A stratified random sample was obtained by dividing the population into two groups of the Hong Kong's legal profession: barristers and solicitors. A random sample would then be drawn from each stratum. The present research study has achieved a relatively high response rate (see Table 3.1). It is justifiable for the author to draw conclusions (inferences) about the population from which the sample was obtained.

Mode of Data Collection

The methods involved in data collection are (1) paper questionnaires distributed through e-mail or by hand and (2) web-based questionnaires through the internet. The questionnaires were uniquely coded for tracking purposes, the responses from the questionnaires were analysed anonymously and individual questionnaire responses were kept confidential.

[95] Picardi and Masick, 'Research Methods', 156.
[96] Consultancy Study on the Demand for and Supply of Legal and Related Services, 10. The Supply Study Report identifies that most Hong Kong legal practitioners generally specialize in one or two specific area(s) of practice, namely, civil law and criminal law. Hong Kong lawyers who specialize in criminal cases are excluded from the present study, as the inclusion of those Hong Kong legal practitioners who specialize in criminal law in the present research study may confound the results and inevitably lead to a low response rate.

Table 3.1 *Number of Respondents and Response Rates*

Professional Title	Number of Issues	Number of Return			Response Rate[a]
		The number of incomplete survey questionnaires[b]	The number of completed survey questionnaires	Total	Completed (Excluded incomplete survey questionnaires) (%)
Barrister	53	1	25	26	49
Solicitor	67	2	42	44	63
Total	120	3	67	70	56

[a] Response rate is calculated as the total number of completed survey questionnaires divided by the number selected in the sample, in the form of a percentage.
[b] Incomplete survey questionnaires are those with more than half of the questions not answered.

Measuring Hong Kong Lawyers' Attitudes Towards the Use of ADR

The purpose of this research is to measure the attitudes of Hong Kong lawyers towards the use of ADR for the resolution of shareholder disputes. The use of five-point Likert rating scales is appropriate, as respondents could establish what they think is desirable by indicating their degree of agreement or disagreement with the statement.[97]

Developing Analytical Techniques to Evaluate the Attitudes of Hong Kong Lawyers Towards the Use of ADR for Resolving Shareholder Disputes

The data collected from the questionnaires were analysed not only by descriptive statistics in summarizing and explaining the data set through graphical representations of data, the measures of central tendency (such as mean, mode and median) and the measures of variability (such as standard deviation).[98] In addition to the basic descriptive statistics, three analytical techniques were used in this research.

[97] Ian Brace, *Questionnaire Design: How to Plan, Structure and Write Survey Material for Effective Market Research* (London: Kogan Page, 2008), 128.
[98] For further discussion, see Chapter 7.

First, a *t*-test was adopted to explore whether the sample means of the two branches of the legal profession are either significant or insignificant with regard to the adoption of foreign legislation and practices in using ADR to deal with shareholder disputes in Hong Kong.[99] This analysis helps to examine the extent to which foreign laws and practices regarding the use of ADR to deal with shareholder disputes could be adopted in Hong Kong with respect to the perspectives of the local legal professional community.[100]

Second, two additional analytical methods were employed to evaluate Hong Kong lawyers' attitudes towards the use of informal out-of-court processes for shareholder disputes since the CJR began in 2009.[101] The first analytical tool was factor analysis. This technique helped to classify the groups, which comprised a set of behavioural aspects of lawyers' decisions in relation to the use of ADR for shareholder disputes, into factor groups according to their inter-correlated relationship.[102]

Following the factor analysis, a multiple binary logistic regression model was used to estimate the propensity of Hong Kong lawyers to adopt mediation and other informal out-of-court processes in assisting their clients to resolve shareholder disputes.[103] Logistic regression analysis is a sophisticated multivariate statistical technique that was used to predict a binary dependent variable (i e , a dichotomous yes–no answer for ADR adoption among Hong Kong lawyers) from a set of categorical independent variables, which were generated from the factor analysis, i.e., the probability that an event will occur.[104]

3.4 Conclusion

In sum, a realistic evaluation approach was used as the key methodology in this study. This approach provides a theoretical foundation for developing steps to solve research issues on how a mix of legal and non-legal policy instruments could be viewed as specific 'triggering mechanisms' to facilitate the more extensive use of ADR for shareholder disputes since the CJR began in 2009. In addition, realistic evaluation methodology values

---

[99] For further discussion, see Chapter 7.
[100] Ibid.
[101] For further discussion, see Chapter 6.
[102] See Section 6.3.1 of Chapter 6.
[103] See Section 6.4 of Chapter 6.
[104] For further discussion, see Chapter 6.

the use of various research methods, including doctrinal approach to the study of law, comparative study and legal empirical research, rather than seeking to promote or rely on a specific method for studying research problems. This helps address research issues from different dimensions and thus enriches the understanding of how informal out-of-court processes within shareholder disputes evolved since Hong Kong's civil process began in 2009.

PART II

Institutionalizing and Legitimizing ADR Policy in Shareholder Disputes: The Role of the Court, the Reforms and Legal Professions

4

The Role of the Court

Securing the Legitimacy of Court-Connected ADR Initiatives for Shareholder Disputes

4.1 Introduction

The problems of lengthy and costly shareholder litigation can be attributed to the traditional civil justice system, which is too adversarial in nature, allowing the parties and their legal advisers rather than the courts to control the pace of the proceeding.[1] The complexity of the law might create some room for unscrupulous litigants or lawyers to indulge in procedural manoeuvres to delay proceedings for the purpose of forcing the opposite side either to write off a claim or settle on unfavourable terms.[2] Is it likely that simplification of court procedural rules will bring about a significant change in the attitudes of those parties (such as judges, lawyers and litigants) involved in the litigation process?

Professor Watson notes that the goals of reducing costs and delays associated with the civil justice system may be hard to accomplish if policymakers place too much emphasis on changing the rules without a full analysis of the legal and social context in which the rules form part of this environment.[3] Similarly, the Civil Justice's Working Party in its Interim Report acknowledges that changing the rules alone cannot be a sufficient response in curing the defects in Hong Kong's civil justice system.[4] This emphasizes that the civil justice reform in Hong Kong might be achieved if the rules of court operate within an institutional, professional and cultural framework can support and complement the

---

[1] Hong Kong Judiciary, *Reform of the Civil Justice System in Hong Kong*, Interim Report and Consultative Paper on Civil Justice Reform (Hong Kong Judiciary, 2000), para. 24.
[2] Ibid.
[3] Garry D. Watson, 'From an Adversarial to a Managed System of Litigation: A Comparative Critique of Law Woolf's Interim Report', in Roger Smith (ed.), *Achieving Civil Justice: Appropriate Dispute Resolution for the 1990s* (London: Legal Action Group, 1996), 77.
[4] Interim Report and Consultative Paper on Civil Justice Reform, para. 190.

proposed changes.[5] A brief analysis of the recent changes in the rules of the court and practice directions provides further insights into the development of court-connected ADR initiatives, such as the use of ADR in conjunction with active judicial case management powers for the resolution of shareholder disputes in Hong Kong. The primary purpose of this chapter is to consider how ADR can be used in conjunction with active judicial case management powers can improve both the quality and efficiency of the court process in dealing with shareholder disputes expeditiously and in a just manner.

The Civil Justice Reform ('CJR') came into effect on 2 April 2009, and was a response to 'social change and technological advances which had resulted in a sharp increase in civil litigation.[6] It is hoped that the introduction of a new set of civil procedure rules accompanying a set of directives on mediation issued by the Hong Kong Judiciary could radically change the way in which the litigation process is managed.[7] The court undertakes a wide range of functions, including not only the traditional role of settling disputes but also the promotion of ADR through the court's new case management powers.[8] Mediation was recognized as a viable and the key means of dispute resolution in civil disputes. Given that both the court rules and case management directions give the court power to encourage litigants to search for more expeditious and cost-effective alternatives to court-based proceedings, mediation and other extrajudicial dispute resolution methods are attached to and under the oversight of the court system.[9] As such, any situation in which the parties to a dispute are ordered, encouraged or voluntarily referred to ADR processes either at the stage of presenting an unfair prejudice petition or during the course of proceedings is typically considered as 'court-connected ADR.[10]

---

[5] Ibid.

[6] Ibid., para. 4.

[7] Ibid., para. 188. See also generally Adrian Zuckerman, 'The Challenge of Civil Justice Reform: Effective Court Management of Litigation', *City University of Hong Kong Law Review*, 1:1 (2009), 49–71.

[8] Order 1A, Rule 4(e) of the RHC provides that the court shall further the underlying objectives of these rules by actively encouraging the parties to use an ADR procedure in resolving civil disputes.

[9] Ibid. and Practice Direction 3.1 on mediation aims to assist the courts as part of their case management powers to facilitate the settlement of disputes by encouraging parties to use mediation during the course of proceedings. Practice Direction 3.3 is specifically designed for unfair prejudice petitions presented under Sections 723–724 of the new Companies Ordinance (Cap. 622) (formerly Section 168A of Companies Ordinance (Cap. 32)).

[10] Ibid.

The court derives its legitimate authority to promote out-of-court pro-cesses from rules of court as they provide that the court should actively exercise its case management powers to encourage the litigants to explore the possibility of extrajudicial processes in resolving their disputes.[11] Legislation on informal out-of-court processes is indeed an indication of government and legislative approval to the process and thus advances the acceptance of ADR among members of the local business community and legal profession.[12] However, the court also plays an important role in legitimizing the use of ADR, as the common law judges bear the bur-den of statutory interpretation. Judicial reasoning or interpretation of the court's case management powers to refer cases to some alternative forms of non-litigious dispute resolution processes can also be considered as a 'secondary means' in which ADR practice is generally accepted by the local business community and legal professions.[13]

Apart from that, the Chief Justice (CJ) of Hong Kong has the power to issue a set of directives to regulate the practice and procedures of the civil courts.[14] Although the new court rules conferred on the courts greater discretionary powers to refer unfair prejudice cases to mediation or other out-of-court processes, this does not necessarily mean that the courts have unlimited powers to coerce the parties to settle through mediation or by other alternative methods of dispute resolution.[15] In fact, these directives do not have statutory force and they provide guidance to the judges, legal professions and local business people by fleshing out details regarding the manner in which the proceedings should go forward. Thus, the informal dispute resolution process becomes meaningful to the local community when the courts make case management decisions in light of established principles and guidelines developed by the courts in the earlier reported cases.[16]

---

[11] Ibid.

[12] Lawrence M. Friedman, 'Some Comments on Legal Interpretation', *Poetics Today*, 9:1 (1988), 95–102 at 97. Friedman notes that an enacted rule can be considered as the pri-mary means to secure legitimacy from the legislative bodies (e.g., the Parliament).

[13] Ibid., 97.

[14] Gary Meggitt and Farzana Aslam, 'Civil Justice Reform in Hong Kong – A Critical Appraisal', *Civil Justice Quarterly*, 28:1 (2009), 111–131 at 112.

[15] Order 1A, Rule 2(2) of the Rules of the High Court (Cap. 4A) stipulates that: 'In giving effect to the underlying objectives of these rules, the Court shall always recognize that the primary aim in exercising the powers of the Court is to secure the just resolution of disputes in accordance with the substantive rights of the parties.' See also Adrian A. S. Zuckerman, *Civil Procedure* (London: LexisNexis UK, 2003), 15.

[16] Lawrence M. Friedman, 'Legal Rules and the Process of Social Change', *Stanford Law Review*, 19 (1967), 786–840 at 824. Friedman points out that: '...rules empty of content

A brief analysis of the reciprocal relationship between the role of court to promote ADR and the nature of court rules and practice directions helps to identify the following issues with regard to the possible ways to improve the court's legitimacy to promote the greater use of ADR for the resolution of shareholder disputes in Hong Kong. First, what are the underlying policy objectives of a court-connected ADR programme for shareholder disputes? Second, where does the legitimacy of a court-connected ADR programme for shareholder disputes come from? Lastly, to what extent can the key objectives of a court-connected ADR programme for shareholder disputes be achieved through the new court rules and case management directives?

This chapter argues that the degree of institutionalization of mediation and other out-of-court practices depends on how court-connected ADR initiatives for shareholder disputes can be considered as legitimate within the system of rules and the dominant economic values, which are inherent in the Hong Kong Basic Law. First, the objectives of a court-connected ADR programme should be designed in accordance with society's dominant social and economic values, and are subsequently embodied in the court rules and practice directions.[17] The local businesspeople and members of the legal profession might thereby fully appreciate the value and benefits of out-of-court processes. This is due to the fact that court-connected ADR initiatives have effectively reached the public through the judicial ruling on an unreasonable refusal to attempt out-of-court processes for shareholder disputes.[18]

Second, the objectives of a court-connected ADR programme should be formulated with the goal of striking a proper balance between improving the efficiency of the court process for dealing with shareholder disputes and enhancing the quality of the court process in preventing misuse of litigation process and expanding a catalogue of options for the resolution of shareholder disputes.[19] Ultimately, this may enhance the legitimacy of

---

except as courts fill them with content, rules capable of expansion by small degrees, discretionary rules concealing the reality of change'. It highlights that the rules can be changed incrementally with the assistance of the court to interpret them in light of governing principles and present demands.

[17] See Section 4.3.

[18] Lawrence M. Friedman, 'The Law and Society Movement', *Stanford Law Review*, 38 (1986), 763–780 at 772 and Lawrence M. Friedman, 'Law, Lawyers, and Popular Culture', *The Yale Law Journal*, 98 (1989), 1579–1606 at 1592–1593. Friedman gave an example by using *Tarasoff v. Regents of the University of California* (1976) to illustrate that law affects the behaviour of citizens unless it reaches some audience.

[19] See Section 4.4.

the court's case management powers to promote the greater use of ADR for shareholder disputes.

Section 4.2 begins with identifying the underlying policy objectives of court-connected ADR programme for shareholder disputes. Section 4.3 shows that the legitimacy of ADR policy objectives derives not purely from its substantive legal provision of the Basic Law, but also from economic and social values (such as free market ideology) which are generally accepted by most of the business community in Hong Kong.[20] Section 4.4 examines the judicial acceptances towards the use of informal out-of-court processes for shareholder disputes in Hong Kong. Section 4.5 concludes with some recommendations to improve existing court-connected ADR programme for shareholder disputes in Hong Kong.

4.2 Policy Objectives of a Court-Connected ADR Programme for Shareholder Disputes

The objectives of a court-connected ADR programme for shareholder disputes can broadly be classified as efficiency objectives and qualitative objectives.[21] The former places great emphasis on the overall cost-effectiveness of out-of-court processes, whereas the latter claims that informal dispute resolution processes offer some degree of party control over the proceedings and solutions are responsive to party needs.[22]

---

[20] Ma Ngok, 'Electric Corporatism and State Interventions in Post-Colonial Hong Kong' in Chiu Wing-Kai Stephen and Wong Siu-lun (eds.), *Repositioning the Hong Kong Government* (Hong Kong: Hong Kong University Press, 2012), 64 and 71. According to Ma, local business persons and profession had ample representation in the Basic Law Drafting Committee. These groups of people tried to exert their influences over the drafting of the Basic Law for the sake of preserving a neo-liberal economic status quo in Hong Kong. See also Wilson Wong and Raymond Yuen, 'Economic Policy' in Lam Wai-man, et al. (eds.), *Contemporary Hong Kong Government and Politics* (Hong Kong: Hong Kong University Press, 2012), 264. Wong and Yuen note that the governance system in Hong Kong is better characterized as 'businessman-ruling Hong Kong model' or 'business-dominated corporatist government' as the political system in Hong Kong is over-represented by the business sector.

[21] Carrie Menkel-Meadow, 'When Dispute Resolution Begets Disputes of Its Own: Conflicts Among Dispute Profssionals', *UCLA Law Review*, 44 (1997), 1871–1933 and Nadja Alexander, 'Global Trends in Mediation: Riding the Third Wave' in Nadja Alexander (ed.), *Global Trends in Mediation* (The Hague: Kluwer Law International, 2006), 9–13.

[22] Ibid. and Robert A. Baruch Bush, 'Defining Quality in Dispute Resolution: Taxonomies and Anti-Taxonomies of Quality Arguments', *Denver University Law Review* 66 (1989), 335–380 at 338–339 and 358–360.

The Hong Kong Judiciary has given proper consideration to different modes of court-institutionalized ADR programmes that have been implemented in other common law jurisdictions, such as the United States and United Kingdom.[23] The objectives of court-connected ADR programmes for shareholder disputes were formulated with the goal of striking a balance between the importance of safeguarding the fundamental rights of a minority shareholder to bring action to the court and at the same time supporting the use of out-of-court processes to reduce cost and time involved in resolving shareholder disputes.[24] Thus, the objectives of a court-connected ADR programme for shareholder disputes can be divided into two groups.

The first group fulfils the efficiency objective as the perceived advantages of out-of-court processes are speedy and less costly.[25] The use of extrajudicial processes in conjunction with active judicial case management could be viewed as an effective instrument to reduce the expenditure on court administration of cases and the time of disposition of shareholder disputes.[26]

The second group fulfils the qualitative objective, as the adoption of mediation and other informal and out-of-court processes improves the quality of the court process, as extrajudicial processes can be used as a means to prevent unscrupulous minority shareholders from misusing the court process for shareholder disputes.[27] The court has an inherent jurisdiction to prevent abuses of court processes.[28] Case management directions made the court's powers to prevent misuse of the adversarial process more apparent.[29] This is partly attributable to the fact that the court may, on the application of one or more of the parties or of its own motion, stay the whole or part of the proceedings for the purpose of narrowing the points of differences between the parties during the ADR session.[30] Moreover, the application of mediation is extended to provide

---

[23] Hong Kong Judiciary, *Reform of the Civil Justice System in Hong Kong*, Final Report of the Working Party on Civil Justice Reform (Hong Kong Judiciary, 2004), para. 787–792.

[24] See Section 4.4.2(a) and (b) .

[25] See supra note 21.

[26] Order 1A, Rule 4(e) of the RHC.

[27] Bush, 'Defining Quality in Dispute Resolution', 359. Bush notes that the qualitative standard of 'individual satisfaction' rest on the belief that the parties can define the good, in his or her own terms by choosing the most appropriate dispute resolution processes in settling their disputes.

[28] Hong Kong Civil Procedure, *The White Book* (Sweet & Maxwell, 2013), Vol. 1, para. 18.19.12.

[29] Practice Directions 3.3 and 31.

[30] Ibid.

for shareholders' claims covered by the legal aided schemes.[31] Court-connected ADR programme thus could be seen as a way to offer greater opportunities for ordinary citizens to access various types of dispute resolution forums, such as mediation to resolve shareholder disputes that meet their needs.

Indeed, the goal of designing a cost-effective Judiciary ADR programme has great constitutional significance for Hong Kong.[32] The inclusion of an ADR process within the court system not only enhances Hong Kong's role as a centre for international and regional business, but also has quantitative benefits, such as reducing the enormous expenses and delays posed by shareholder litigation.[33] Ultimately, courts can deploy their resources proportionately and effectively.

Apart from the cost-effectiveness of ADR, the Hong Kong Judiciary places great emphasis on the use of ADR to improve the qualitative aspects of resolution processes as well.[34] The qualitative objectives of a court-connected ADR programme for shareholder dispute was formulated with the goal of striking a balance between the importance of maintaining the consensual nature of out-of-court processes and the needs to secure the public values of the court to improve the ability of shareholders to seek judicial enforcement of their rights.[35] As such, a court-connected ADR programme for shareholder disputes has fulfilled both the qualitative and quantitative objectives in improving the resolution of shareholder disputes. The next issue concerns the sources of the legitimacy of these ADR policy objectives.

4.3 Legitimizing a Judiciary ADR Programme for Shareholder Disputes: Alignment with the Constitutional Values of the Hong Kong Basic Law

This part seeks to examine whether the objectives of a court-connected ADR programme are broadly aligned with the values underlying the Basic

---

[31] Hong Kong Legal Aid Department, *Litigation vs. Mediation: An Alternative Way to Settle Disputes* (2010).

[32] Article 109 of the Hong Kong Basic Law stipulates that the Government of the Hong Kong Special Administrative Region shall provide an appropriate economic and legal environment for the maintenance of the status of Hong Kong as an international financial centre under. Also, Article 110 of the Hong Kong Basic Law states that the Government of the Hong Kong Special Administrative Region shall safeguard the free operation of financial business and financial market.

[33] See Section 4.4.1.

[34] See Section 4.4.2(a) and (b).

[35] Article 35 of the Hong Kong Basic Law.

Law, which include the maintenance of shareholders' contractual freedom to tailor their own rules in resolving shareholder disputes, and guarantee the fundamental right of access to court.[36] It begins to identify the sources of legitimacy from which the Basic Law derives by applying the typology of legitimacy proposed by Suchman.[37] It then explores the key sources of legitimacy that support a sustainable court-connected ADR programme for the resolution of shareholder disputes in Hong Kong. Consideration is given to the legitimate basis of the Basic Law. Finally, this part argues that ADR practice can acquire both the regulative and cultural-cognitive legitimacy if the objectives of court-connected ADR programme for shareholder disputes are consistent with the constitutional values inherent in the Basic Law.

One of the major purposes of the Basic Law is to maintain the capitalist system of Hong Kong.[38] The reason behind the introduction of the Basic Law was to ensure a smooth political transition in 1997.[39] The law helps to maintain a stable political environment so that business activities can continue to thrive after the handover of Hong Kong from Britain to China in 1997. The Basic Law provides a legitimate framework for the continued success of a capitalist market in Hong Kong. It not only recognizes fundamental rights, but also ensures that fundamental rights, such as property rights, are protected.[40] The maintenance of Hong Kong's market-orientated legal system safeguards the free operation of companies. The notion of the freedom of contract remains the paramount principle in the economic system of Hong Kong.[41] Thus, the freedom of companies to tailor their own contractual provisions in anticipating shareholder disputes that might arise in the future and the fundamental right of a minority

---

[36] Article 35 of the Basic Law stipulates that Hong Kong residents shall have the right of access to the courts. Article 110 of the Basic Law provides that the Hong Kong SAR government shall safeguard the free operation of financial businesses and financial markets, and regulate and supervise them in accordance with law.

[37] Mark C. Suchman, 'Managing Legitimacy: Strategic and Institutional Approaches', *Academy of Management Review*, 20:3 (1995), 571–610 at 574.

[38] Yash Ghai, 'The Rule of Law and Capitalism: Reflections on the Basic Law' in Raymond Wacks (ed.), *Hong Kong, China and 1997: Essays in Legal Theory* (Hong Kong: Hong Kong University Press, 1997), 345.

[39] The Hong Kong Basic Law Promotion Sterring Committee, *Introduction to the Basic Law of the Hong Kong Special Administrative Region* (Hong Kong: Law Press/Joint Publishing, 2000).

[40] Ghai, 'The Rule of Law and Capitalism', 347. Article 6 of the Hong Kong Basic Law stipulates that the Hong Kong government shall protect the right of private ownership of property in accordance with law.

[41] Ibid., 349.

shareholder to bring action to the court are the foundation stone of Hong Kong's society.

Indeed, the sources of the Basic Law originated not only purely from a set of regulatory rules promulgated by a regulatory authority. In addition, the Basic Law acquires cultural-cognitive legitimacy as its provisions originate from the free-market ideology, which is in accord with shared beliefs among the powerful group of elite businesspersons and professionals in Hong Kong. Clearly, the legitimacy of the Basic Law 'derived not from constitutional values or substantive rule of law but from the success of the capitalist market system'.[42] Unsurprisingly, the Basic Law Drafting Committee comprised a large contingent of local Chinese businessmen and professionals.[43] This ensures that local businessmen and professionals will continue to exert a considerable degree of their influences over the economic policymaking and law reform after 1997.[44] This also prevents Hong Kong from turning into a welfare state by redistributing wealth from a high-income group to a low-income group through a set of welfare provisions after 1997.[45]

Clearly, the Basic Law is generally perceived as legitimate because its legitimacy derives not only from the legislative mandates issued by the government, but also from other cultural-cognitive factors (such as the free market principles inherent in the Basic Law).[46] The basic framework laid down by the Basic Law was shaped by legal, social and historical factors.[47] These can be characterized as cultural-cognitive factors, as they can be viewed as norms, values and beliefs, which are presumably accepted by most members of the local business and legal professional community.[48] These cultural factors, which include the continuation of capitalist way of doing business and protection of individual freedoms, are, in fact, rooted

---

[42] Ibid., 344.

[43] Ma, 'Electric Corporatism and State Interventions in Post-Colonial Hong Kong', 71.

[44] Ibid. and Wong and Yuen, 'Economic Policy', p. 262. Wong and Yuen provide an illustration on how the Hong Kong government has maintained a strong relationship with the local business community, particularly in economic policymaking and law reform after 1997.

[45] See Ma, 'Electric Corporatism and State Interventions in Post-Colonial Hong Kong', 71 and Wong Hung, 'Changes in Social Policy in Hong Kong since 1997: Old Wine in New Bottles?', in Lam Wai-man, et al. (eds.), *Contemporary Hong Kong Government and Politics* (Hong Kong: Hong Kong University Press, 2012).

[46] Ghai, 'The Rule of Law and Capitalism', 344.

[47] Ibid.

[48] Cathryn Johnson et al., 'Legitimacy as a Social Process', *Annual Review of Sociology*, 32 (2006), 53–78 at 55.

in British colonial policy.[49] Ultimately, they can be viewed as the constitutional values underpinning the economic provisions of the Basic Law.

Given that the legitimacy of the Basic Law derived from a substantive rule of law as well as the endorsement of a powerful group of local businessmen, the court is more likely to recognize the principle of freedom of contract, as this is the core economic value of Hong Kong society. This is certainly true as the Hong Kong courts have endorsed and applied the approach taken by Lord Hoffman in *O'Neill v. Philips*, which focuses narrowly on the contractual nature of the parties' reasonable expectations for a complaint in unfair prejudice proceedings.[50] It follows that the success of a court-connected ADR programme for shareholder disputes depends on whether ADR policy objectives were formulated in accordance with the constitutional values inherent in the Basic Law.

In general, the economic provisions of the Basic Law embrace both quantitative and qualitative values. The Basic Law not only recognizes the efficiency or qualitative objective of maintaining shareholders' contractual freedom to engage in an effective operation of companies.[51] In addition, the Basic Law embraces qualitative goals by placing emphasis on the needs to safeguard the fundamental right of a shareholder of access to court.[52] Extending this position would suggest that a court-connected ADR programme for shareholder disputes should embrace both qualitative and quantitative values of the Basic Law by providing a cost-effective dispute resolution framework for the resolution of shareholder disputes,[53] by preventing misuse of the court litigation process, and by expanding a catalogue of dispute resolution processes for shareholders to obtain effective redress for grievances.[54]

This analysis has important implications with regard to the legitimacy of the court's case management power to encourage the local business

---

[49] Angus Young, 'Reforming Directors' Duties in Hong Kong: The Journey, Stakeholders and Oversights', *International Company and Commercial Law Review*, 23:4 (2012), 142–154 at 144.

[50] *Re Ching Hing Construction Co Ltd* [2001] HKEC 1402 (unreported, HCCW 889/1999, 23 November 2001) (CFI) at paras. 34; *Wong Man Yin v. Ricacorp Properties Ltd & Others* [2003] 3 HKLRD 75 at 88–89; *Re Kam Fai Electroplating Factory Ltd* [2004] HKEC 556 (unreported, HCCW 534/2000, 8 December 2003) at para. 82 and *Re Yung Kee Holdings Ltd 3* [2014] 2 HKLRD 313 at 346.

[51] Article 110 of the Basic Law stipulates that the Hong Kong government has to 'safeguard the free operation of financial business and financial markets'.

[52] Article 35 of the Hong Kong Basic Law.

[53] See Section 4.4.1(b)

[54] See Section 4.4.2(a) and (b).

people and legal profession to appreciate the benefits of informal out-of-court processes for the resolution of shareholder disputes in Hong Kong. If the policy objectives of a court-connected scheme are consistent with the constitutional values inherent in the Basic Law, court-connected ADR procedures may acquire both regulative and cultural-cognitive legitimacy. Consequently, key actors within the judicial field such as judges would then be willing to validate these policy goals through the judicial interpretation of the court rules, as the legitimacy of these goals derives from two specific sources – cultural-cognitive and instrumental factors – which are inherent in the Basic Law. The next part considers how the courts interpret the rules of courts and judicial practice directions in a manner which is consistent with ADR objectives.

4.4 Evaluating ADR Policy for Shareholder Disputes in Hong Kong: Judicial Acceptance

It is clear that even if a court-connected ADR programme for shareholder disputes has acquired both regulative and cultural-cognitive legitimacy flowing from the Basic Law, to what extent will the court interpret the rules of court and practice direction in a manner which is consistent with ADR goals?[55] The answer to this question to a large extent depends on how judges prioritize a range of ADR policy objectives, namely, efficiency and qualitative objectives of a court-connected ADR programme, in light of the seriousness of problems associated with unfair prejudice proceedings. For example, if the court already had powers to improve the pace and costs of shareholder litigation before the CJR began in 2009, the purpose of introducing court-connected ADR procedures as a way to reduce the costs and delays of unfair prejudice proceedings will become less obvious, and vice versa.

Indeed, a court-connected ADR programme for shareholder dispute can acquire legitimacy even though judicial policymakers prioritize certain interests over others.[56] It will not be surprising that some countries,

---

[55] These goals can be classified into two groups. The first group fulfils the efficiency objective, as the perceived advantages of out-of-court processes are speedy and less costly. The second group opined that alternatives to court-based shareholder proceedings improve the quality of the court process as out-of-court process can be used as means to prevent unscrupulous minority shareholders from misuse of court process for shareholder disputes.

[56] Francis Regan, 'Dispute Resolution in Australia: Theory, Evidence and Dilemmas' in Gongyi Wang and Roman Tomasic (eds.), *Alternative Dispute Resolution and the Modern Rule of Law: Papers from the Sino-Australian* (Seminar, Beijing: Law Press), 50.

such as the United Kingdom, have placed great emphasis on efficiency concerns rather than on the quality of processes in designing its court-connected ADR programme.[57] Their court-connected ADR programmes have acquired legitimacy, as mediation and other out-of-court processes have been institutionalized within the local community through the legislative mandates.[58] Similarly, out-of-court processes can be considered as legitimate and proper methods for resolving shareholder disputes, as the ADR policy objectives were formulated in line with the constitutional values of the Basic Law.[59]

However, academics such as Menkel-Meadow raise concerns that the economic and efficiency considerations which dominate the design of court-institutionalized ADR programmes may blur the boundaries between adjudication and ADR.[60] This poses a serious threat to the constitutional right of a party to obtain redress from the court, as judges might take a strong policy approach to promoting out-of-court processes with the real threat of punishing a party in costs for failing to consider the possibility of private dispute resolution methods to resolve their disputes.[61] It is true that the extent to which the court may exercise its case management power in directing the parties to participate in ADR processes remains uncertain.[62] Thus, the following discussion examines how Hong Kong judges exercise their case management powers by considering

---

[57] Sally Lloyd-Bostock, 'Alternative Dispute Resolution and Civil Justice Reform: Is ADR Being Used to Paper Over Cracks?: Reactions to Judge Jack Weinstein's Article', *Ohio State Journal on Dispute Resolution*, 11 (1996), 397–402.

[58] The legislative provisions of the RHC similar to The Civil Justice Procedure Rules 1998 (enacted in England and Wales).

[59] See, for example, Article 110 of the Basic Law stipulates that the Hong Kong government has to 'safeguard the free operation of financial business and financial markets'.

[60] Carrie Menkel-Meadow, 'Pursuing Settlement in an Adversary Culture: A Tale of Innovation Co-opted or 'The Law of ADR'', *Florida State University Law Review*, 19 (1991), 1–46 at 16, 34–39. Professor Menkel-Meadow identifies some 'dilemmas', which arose particularly in the court-institutionalized ADR programme. She contends that the underlying cause of the dilemmas which exist in the court-institutionalized ADR programme contributed to the clash of ADR and adversarial cultures (i.e., 'settlement within an adversary system'). See also Simon Roberts and Michael Palmer, *Dispute Processes: ADR and the Primary Forms of Decision-Making*, 2nd ed. (Cambridge: Cambridge University Press, 2005), 58–59.

[61] Masood Ahmed, 'Implied Compulsory Mediation', *Civil Justice Quarterly*, 31:2 (2012), 151–175 at 156.

[62] David Sugarman, 'Reconceptualising Company Law: Reflections on the Law Commission's Consultation Paper on Shareholder Remedies: Part 2', *Company Lawyer*, 18:9 (1997), 274–282 at 276.

a range of ADR policy objectives (i.e., both efficiency and qualitative objectives).

4.4.1 Improving the Efficiency of Resolving Shareholder Disputes: Judicial Case Management

It is fair to say that the efficiency principle should dictate the design of court-institutionalized ADR programme. This can be explained by the fact that court proceedings in dealing with shareholder disputes 'can, and frequently do, involve a substantial number of allegations and counter-allegations, substantial costs and a lot of court time, not to mention the strain and emotion on the parties involved'.[63] On such a basis, there are three reasons justifying the court exercising its case management power to encourage litigants to attempt ADR, particularly in dealing with unfair prejudice proceedings.

First, the breadth of the discretion conferred on the court to grant relief under Section 724 of the new Companies Ordinance might lead to a full investigation, lengthy discovery and detailed evidence, all of which can add further costs to the litigants. The practice of discovery in court proceedings, particularly in unfair prejudice proceedings, might give rise to the possibility of abuse and delay, as the evidence to call, the questions to ask in cross-examination, the use of expert evidence and so forth rest on legal professionals instead of the parties.[64] This might erode the concept of 'proportionality' if the court allowed petitioners to establish unfair prejudice by the number of allegations instead of real issues that are worth pursuing.[65]

Indeed, it is not a simple and straightforward task for the lawyers to assist their clients to exclude issues which are generally regarded as unimportant or irrelevant from the petition. Rather, the parties can control

---

[63] *Re Rotadata Ltd* [2000] 1 BCC 686 P 686. This judgement stated that the petition ran 'to over 30 closely typed pages with 121 paragraphs and a total of 21 separate allegations'. See also English Law Commission, *Shareholder Remedies* (London: The Stationary Office, Law Commission Report No 246, Cm 3769, 1997), para. 1.7.

[64] See, for example, *Guinness Peat Group plc v. British Land Co plc* [1999] 2 BCLC 243.

[65] Final Report of the Working Party on Civil Justice Reform, paras. 101–106. The Chief Justice's Working Party suggested that the concept of 'proportionality' must connote a 'common sense notions of reasonableness and a sense of proportion' that the court should exercise its judicial discretion in promoting a sense of reasonableness and resources proportionality. In *Re Rotadata Ltd* [2000] 1 BCC 686 P 692, the Neuberger Justice reiterates the importance of the court should exercise its judicial control over case presentation and investigation as this idea was contemplated in the Lord Woolf's Report.

the amount of evidence to be adduced through alternatives to formal discovery.[66] For instance, a private process of neutral fact-finding enables the parties to conduct their discovery according to their own rules.[67] The facilitative nature of the mediation process is also well suited in cases where the parties remain in ultimate control over the terms of resolution including the scale of discovery.[68] The court should provide effective ADR mechanisms that allow parties to eliminate their misunderstandings and to focus on their future relationship. This may help the parties to reach a possibly effective solution.

Second, it is necessary for the court to avoid unproductive prolongation of unfair prejudice proceedings. This is certainly true that some petitioners would like to use it as a powerful tactic in persuading the respondents to compromise proceedings.[69] There is a public policy consideration for the court to control the conduct of vexatious petitioners, particularly in the context of shareholder disputes. The financial position of a private company may be in peril if a vexatious petitioner uses the adjudicative process with ulterior motives such as damaging a company's reputation or exhaustion of finance corporate resources for the funding of unfair prejudice proceedings. If a director fails to sustain his or her business on a going-concern status, the company would eventually go bust. The company would then be subject to insolvency, which places its assets under the control of a liquidator.[70]

Third, the court should encourage the parties to take possible steps in settling their claims during the course of unfair prejudice proceedings as this notion was contemplated in the House of Lords decision in *O'Neil v. Phillips.*[71] A relief sought for the buyout of petitioners' shares by the majority shareholder(s) was the common remedy awarded by judges.[72]

---

[66] Frank E. A. Sander and Lukasz Rozdiczer, 'Matching Cases and Dispute Resolution Procedures: Detailed Analysis Leading to a Mediation-Centered Approach', *Harvard Negotiation Law Review*, 11 (2006), 1–41 at 23.

[67] Ibid.

[68] Ibid.

[69] See *Re Unisoft Group Ltd* (No. 3) [1994] 1 BCLC 609 at 638, Harman Justice observed that '[Unfair prejudice petitions] have become notorious to the judges of this court – and I think also to the Bar – for their length, their unpredictability of management, and the enormous and appalling costs which are incurred upon them particularly by reason of the volume of documents liable to be produced.'

[70] Section 190 of the Companies (Winding-Up and Miscellaneous Provisions) Ordinance (Cap. 32).

[71] *O'Neill v. Phillips* Lord Hoffman [1999] BCC 600 at 613.

[72] Philip Lawton, 'Modeling the Chinese Family Firm and Minority Shareholer Protection: The Hong Kong Experience 1980–1995', *Managerial Law*, 49:5/6 (2007), 249–271.

Respondents remain free to tender their offer to the petitioners to settle their differences through an appropriate informal out-of-court processes, such as mediation. The advantage of using mediation becomes more visible if parties engage sincerely through the proper function of the mediator. The mediator helps parties to 'achieve a new and shared perception of their relationship, a perception that will redirect their attitudes and dispositions toward one another'.[73] If parties reorient towards each other through the mediation process, a minority shareholder is more willing to stay in the same company and work together with majority shareholders.

In general, an efficient dispute resolution system to resolve shareholder disputes is normally paired with a sophisticated judicial institution which provides not only effective case management policies. In particular, the establishment of a specialized court in handling shareholder disputes and the collaboration between the court and privately run ADR centres in developing schemes to refer suitable cases to external ADR providers are essential for achieving greater efficiency in the country's court's processes.[74] At present, the Hong Kong courts offer no in-house ADR programmes with regard to the court's referral of shareholder disputes to privately run ADR service providers.[75] Parties are free to select a neutral third party (of whatever qualifications or accreditation) from among a number of different privately run ADR service providers. In the absence of a specific statutory scheme that empowers the courts to refer suitable shareholder disputes to privately run ADR service providers and a specialized court

[73] Lon L. Fuller, 'Mediation – Its Forms and Functions', *Southern California Law Review*, 44 (1970), 305–339 at 325.
[74] World Bank Group, *Doing Business 2016: Measuring Regulatory Quality and Efficiency* at www.doingbusiness.org (Accessed 10 September 2016), 153–154. The Doing Business 2016 report includes a new indicator, namely, the quality of judicial processes index, focusing on a country's court structure and proceedings, case management, court automation and alternative dispute resolution. The quality of judicial processes index of the Doing Business 2016 report illustrates that there may remain room for the Hong Kong Judiciary to make further improvements in the promotion of greater use of ADR within the court system, as the quality of judicial processes in Hong Kong is comparatively lower than in other common law countries such as the United Kingdom, the United States, Singapore, Australia and New Zealand. Hong Kong has earned 11 points out of 18 with respect to the new quality of judicial processes index.
[75] At present, several government institutions, such as Small Claims Tribunal, Hong Kong Housing Society and Estate Agents Authority, are now in the process of making cooperation arrangements with Hong Kong Mediation and Arbitration Centre for mediation referral. There are no ADR schemes designed specifically for shareholder disputes working with the court and external ADR providers in Hong Kong. For details, see Hong Kong Mediation and Arbitration Centre, Pro Bono Mediation Services at www.hkmaac.org/mediation/pro_bono.php (Accessed 19 September 2016).

in handling shareholder disputes, it is hard for the court to promote an expeditious shareholder dispute resolution.[76] So it is perhaps unsurprising that the introduction of judicial case management powers has had a moderate impact on the operation of unfair prejudice proceedings under the new Hong Kong Companies Ordinance.

Obviously, a judicial ADR programme which places great emphasis on efficiency concerns can reduce court-docket congestion.[77] The inclusion of an extrajudicial process within judicial management can assist the parties to focus on the critical aspects of the dispute, reducing unproductive efforts such as excessive and unfocused discovery. However, it would be unjustified for judicial policymakers to sacrifice the qualities of the dispute resolution process for the sake of promoting efficiency. In particular, if the law fails to clarify the scope of case management power in operating ADR mechanisms for the resolution of shareholder disputes, the court might exercise very wide discretionary power to adjourn proceedings at any stages and force the parties to attempt ADR.

Against the backdrop of Order 1A, Rule 2(2) of the Rules of the High Court (RHC), it is unlikely for the Hong Kong courts to sacrifice the substantive rights of the parties for the sake of disposing cases in a timely manner through mediation and other alternative processes. More specifically, Practice Direction 31 on mediation provides guidance on when refusal to mediate may attract costs sanctions.[78] This direction stipulates that sanctions will not apply if 'the party has engaged in mediation to the minimum level of participation agreed to by the parties or as directed by the Court prior to the mediation in accordance with paragraph 1 of the Practice Direction 31'.[79]

---

[76] The report illustrates that Singapore has earned 15.5 points out of 18 with respect to the new quality of judicial processes index. One might infer that the courts have the power to refer certain cases to different categories of external ADR providers. For details, see Carol Liew, 'Recent Developments in Mediation in East Asia', in Arnold Ingen-Housz (ed.), *ADR in Business: Practice and Issues across Countries and Cultures*, Vol. II (The Hague: Kluwer Law International, 2011), 526. The United States has earned 13.8 points out of 18 with respect to the new quality of judicial processes index. One might argue that the Delaware has created specialized business courts in handling corporate governance disputes. See Jack B. Jacobs, 'The Role of Specialized Courts in Resolving Corporate Governance Disputes in the United States and in the EU: An American Judge's Perspective', in Louis Bouchez, et al. (eds.), *Topics in Corporate Finance: The Quality of Corporate Law and the Role of Corporate Law Judges* (Amsterdam: Amsterdam Center for Corporate Finance, 2006).

[77] CEDR, CEDR Solve Commercial Mediation Statistics 2001/02 (May 2002) at www.cedr.co.uk (Accessed 4 December 2012).

[78] Practice Direction 31, paras. 4 and 5.

[79] Practice Direction 31 does not specify a 'minimum level of participation' in mediation process. Rather, Appendix C, footnote 4 of the Practice Direction 31 provides examples which

On top of that, an adverse costs order for non-compliance with judicial direction on mediation would not be made by the court if a party has provided a reasonable explanation for not engaging in mediation.[80] This effectively limits the court's case management powers to force parties to use mediation against their will and preserves the voluntary nature of the mediation process. Clearly, Practice Direction 31 could assist the court to make proper assessments on the suitability of dispute resolution processes, including mediation and other informal out-of-court processes but not limited to formal court proceedings.

Although the discretionary power bestowed upon the court to impose a costs sanction for unreasonable refusal to mediate in Practice Direction 31 are expressed in an open-ended language, the flexibility of such direction enables the court to take either a robust or a moderate policy approach in promoting ADR before trial. This can be illustrated as follows. For example, in *Golden Eagle International (Group) Ltd v. GR Investment Holdings*, Justice Lam rejected the *Halsey* approach of placing the burden on the unsuccessful party to show that there was a reasonable prospect that mediation would have been successful.[81] Instead, the Hong Kong court in *Golden Eagle International* adopted a strong policy approach in promoting ADR with the real threat of punishing the refusing party in costs for failing to not to consider ADR.[82] This approach significantly strengthens the costs sanction by providing a strong disincentive against parties who unreasonably refuse to engage in mediation, as it would trigger the costs sanction under the Practice Direction on Mediation.[83] This is certainly true, as the burden is on the refusing party to provide a reasonable explanation for his or her failure to engage in private extrajudicial processes, such as mediation.[84]

Justice Lam's reasoning in *Golden Eagle International (Group) Ltd* was subsequently followed in *Ansar Mohammad v. Global Legend Transportation Ltd*, and Master Levy in the Court of First Instance stated

---

are deemed to be classified as a specified minimum level of participation in mediation. Also in *Hak Tung Alfred Tang v. Bloomberg LP* [2010] HKEC 1227 (unreported, HCA 198/2010, 16 July 2010) (CFI) at paras. 11–12, Registrar Lung accepted that the minimum level of participation should be left to the discretion of the mediator. See also *Upplan Co Ltd v. Li Ho Ming* [2010] HKEC 1257 (unreported, HCA 1915/2009, 5 August 2010) (CFI) at paras. 25–26.

[80] Practice Direction 31, para. 5(2).

[81] HKLRD 3 [2010] 273 at 280–284.

[82] Ibid.

[83] [2010] 3 HKLRD 273 at 280–285.

[84] Gavin Denton and Fan Kun, 'Hong Kong' in Carlos Esplugues and Silvia Barona (eds.), *Global Perspectives on ADR* (Intersentia, 2014), 156.

that the court should take the strongest form of encouragement by advising litigants to consider informal dispute resolution processes for resolving disputes.[85] The reasoning of the judge on this point was based on the fact that the Hong Kong Judiciary has repeatedly sent out a strong message that mediation has become an integral part of the CJR.[86]

On the other hand, the decision in *Pacific Long Distance Telephone v. New World Telecommunications Ltd* has displayed a considerable reluctance to take the strongest form of judicial encouragement of the use of ADR.[87] The learned Deputy Judge Houghton in *Pacific Long Distance Telephone* took a moderate policy approach in promoting mediation by placing the burden on the unsuccessful party to show that the successful party had acted unreasonably in refusing to attempt to informal out-of-court processes.[88] This approach has significantly reduced the pressure on parties to adopt informal out-of-court processes for resolving disputes, as the burden is placed on the unsuccessful party to demonstrate that the successful party had unreasonably refused to try ADR or behaved unreasonably in the course of ADR.

However, the concern about imposition of a requirement on the unsuccessful party to establish unreasonableness of refusal to mediate is tantamount to an unacceptable obstruction on an unwilling party's right to access to the court is overstated. This ignores the fact that Order 1A, Rule (2)(2) of the RHC prevents the court from exercising its active case management powers to compel the parties to engage in mediation. In particular, this rule was designed specifically to ensure that the court should exercise its case management powers to direct cases to ADR in accordance with the substantive rights of the parties.[89]

Arguably, it might well be appropriate for the Hong Kong court to adopt a strong policy approach towards mediation, as informal out-of-court processes have become an integral part of the litigation culture since the CJR began in 2009. This approach ultimately strengthens the costs sanctions against unreasonable refusal to mediation, as the burden is on the part of the unwilling party to provide a reasonable explanation.[90]

---

[85] [2010] HKEC 645 (unreported, HCPI 1057/2007, 23 November 2010) (CFI) at paras. 51 to 55. It should be noted that this is a personal injury case.

[86] Ibid.

[87] [2012] HKEC 732 (unreported, HCA 1688/2006, 10 February 2012) (CFI) at para. 18.

[88] Ibid.

[89] Order 1A, Rule (2)(2) of the RHC.

[90] Kun Fan, 'Mediation and Civil Justice Reform in Hong Kong', *International Litigation Quarterly*, 27:2 (2011), 11–14 at 13.

The court may impose cost sanctions if a party acted unreasonably by refusing to attempt mediation as provided in para. 4 of the case management direction on mediation.[91]

Although the concept of 'encouragement' of ADR by the court is unclear under the court rules, the court is under a duty to discourage unjustified refusal to mediate. This is particularly true, as the court has a duty to further the underlying objective by actively exercising its case management powers to encourage and facilitate the greater use of ADR if appropriate.[92] This approach also reinforces the consensual nature of mediation despite the fact that unwilling parties are required to engage in mediation. Professor Genn and her colleagues make a similar point by contending that referral to mediation does not exclude unwilling parties' right to go to the court; instead, it can be treated only as a procedural step along the way to a court hearing if the case does not settle at mediation.[93] In sum, case management directions on mediation enable the court to further the 'underlying objective' of the court rules by encouraging parties to attempt out-of-court processes voluntarily, especially before the trial begins.[94] Clearly, the goal of designing a cost-effective Judiciary ADR programme is consistent with the constitutional values of the Basic Law by providing a simple and cost-effective framework for the companies in which to operate their affairs.[95]

4.4.2 Enhancing the Quality of Shareholder Dispute Resolution: Proportionality and Freedom to Choose Various Types of Dispute Resolution Processes

This section contends that incorporation of informal out-of-court processes into case management techniques improves the quality of

---

[91] Ibid.
[92] Order 1A, Rule 4(2)(e) of the RHC.
[93] Hazel Genn et al., *Twisting Arms: Court Referred and Court Linked Mediation Under Judicial Pressure* (Ministry of Justice Research Series, Series 1/07, 2007) at 15.
[94] Order 1A, Rule 4 of the Rules of the High Court (Cap. 4A). See also Final Report of the Working Party on Civil Justice Reform, paras. 23, 88, 91–100. The Working Party in the Final Report describes the objectives as 'underlying' rather than adopting the equivalent terminology of the UK counterpart which refers them as 'overriding'. This can be explained by the fact that the reform of the Hong Kong civil justice system should be implemented by an amendment of RHC rather than by introducing a new set of procedural rules. The policy reason behind this is to avoid encouraging over-elaborate and misguided reliance being placed on it.
[95] Articles 109 and 110 of the Hong Kong Basic Law.

shareholder dispute resolution as the court's active case management powers are exercised in accordance with the two qualitative objectives of a court-connected ADR programme. The first objective found in court-connected ADR programme is that sanctions for non-compliance with the court's order to try and resolve disputes through extrajudicial processes will be proportionate to the procedural needs of disputes/disputants and nature of individual cases.[96] The second objective found in a court-connected ADR programme is that it respects individual rights to choose a range of formal and informal out-of-court processes in resolving shareholder disputes.[97] The following discussion examines how the Hong Kong courts strike a fine balance between the consensual nature of private informal ADR and the values inherent in the public courts regarding the objective of promoting proportionality of both the procedure for referring cases to ADR and the assessment of costs for failure to attempt ADR.

a. Proportionality between the Consensual Nature of Private ADR Processes and the Values Inherent in the Public Courts

This subsection considers how the court deals with cases in ways which are proportionate to the substantive rights of shareholders to seek judicial relief and consensual participation of ADR processes. Courts play a crucial role in promoting a range of moral values about 'justice, rights and social cohesion' that the state should maintain.[98] The courts have recognized a list of fundamental rights of shareholders, such as the right to vote under the constitution of the company, the right to seek enforcement of, and redress for breach of expressed agreements or legal rules, or of equitable rules which are unfairly prejudicial to the interests of shareholders.[99] In this regard, a successful enforcement of the fundamental rights of shareholders depends not only on the substantive legal rules

---

[96] Final Report of the Working Party on Civil Justice Reform, paras. 101–111 and subsection (a)(i) to (ii).

[97] Ibid., paras. 801–804 and subsection 4.4.2(b).

[98] Cohen, 'Revisiting Against Settlement', 1144 (citing Owen M. Fiss, 'The Social and Political Foundations of Adjudication', Law and Human Behaviour, 6:2 (1982), 121–128 at 121, 128).

[99] K. W. Wedderburn, 'Shareholders' Rights and the Rule in Foss v Harbottle', Cambridge Law Journal, (1957), 194–215. Lord Wedderburn set out a list of personal rights which allow the shareholders to sue. In Corporate Governance Review by The Standard Committee on Company Law Reform: A Consultation Paper made in Phase I of the Review (Printing Department, 2001), para. 17.01. According to the SCCLR, members' personal rights can be identified through the following sources: (1) memorandum and articles of association, (2) the provisions of statute law, (3) personal contracts and (4) the law. More recently,

that shareholders are entitled to sue in the event of a breach of their rights, but also on the effectiveness of procedures and practices used in the civil litigation process.[100]

However, it is questionable whether public court adjudication can be viewed as a viable tool for shareholders to enforce their rights if a country's civil justice system suffers the problems of excessive length and costs. In particular, the misuse of a traditional, court-litigation process can adversely affect the quality of the judicial process and the prospect of its dealing with cases in a just manner.[101] Shareholders, in turn, are dissatisfied with the court proceedings. This begs the question of whether the inclusion of ADR processes into the court improves the quality of shareholder dispute resolution.

Many informal out-of-court processes such as mediation are based on the principle of party autonomy. Consensual/voluntary participation is a necessary element for ADR success.[102] It is a widely held view that there is a willingness of the parties to attempt extrajudicial processes if the parties feel confident with the mediation process in exchanging information and documents relevant to the dispute.[103] In Hong Kong, judicial policymakers display considerable willingness to uphold individual freedoms that allow the parties to negotiate their contractual arrangements through informal out-of-court processes.[104] The justification underpinning the voluntary ADR scheme in Hong Kong courts resides in the fact that Article 35 of the Basic Law secures litigants' rights to access the court. The Final Report of the Civil Justice Reform reasserted the orthodox position in the civil justice of Hong Kong by stating that '... mediation must be voluntary in the sense that no attempt should be made to force anyone to settle a case'.[105] This approach acknowledges the consensual nature of

---

Velasco identifies that there are four types of shareholder rights that are recognized under existing law. They include (1) economic rights, (2) control rights, (3) information rights and (4) litigation rights. For details, see Julian Velasco, 'The Fundamental Rights of the Shareholder', *University of California, Davis*, 40:2 (2006), 407–467 at 413–423.

[100] Aron Balas et al., 'The Divergence of Legal Procedures', *American Economic Journal: Economic Policy*, 1:2 (2009), 138–162.

[101] Michael Wilkinson, 'Introduction' in Michael Wilkinson and Janet Burton (eds.), *Reform of the Civil Process in Hong Kong* (Hong Kong: Butterworths Asia, 2000), 32–35.

[102] Kathy Mack, *Court Referral to ADR: Criteria and Research* (2003) at www.aija.org.au (Accessed 8 August 2011), para. 6.6.

[103] Ibid.

[104] Final Report of the Working Party on Civil Justice Reform, paras. 814 to 826.

[105] Ibid. In contrast with UK position, the UK courts could exercise their powers in compelling parties to engage ADR process despite the fact that the UK government and its

the mediation process, as there will be no express rules in requiring the parties to attempt out-of-court processes up to a definite stage as a conditional precedent to the use of court proceedings.[106]

The current civil procedure rules were broadly formulated in line with the objectives of the CJR. The court should exercise its case management powers to facilitate the greater use of ADR not only in accordance with the parties' substantive rights, but also by the use of proportionate use of resources and with reasonable expedition.[107] This allows the courts to exercise their discretionary power to refer cases to ADR which are not tied to the rigid language of Hong Kong's civil procedure rules. The court will exercise a balancing and weighting of all the relevant legal principles instead of giving an undue weight to a particular objective as listed in the civil procedure rules. This gives the court more flexibility to decide what order (if any) to make with regard to the judicial encouragement of ADR. The next section considers how the court refers cases to ADR is proportionate to the nature of individual cases in the context of shareholder disputes.

i. Court Referral of Shareholder Disputes to ADR Is Proportionate to the Nature of Individual Cases

The recent decision in *Re Sun Light Elastic Ltd* embraces the qualitative value of the Basic Law by recognizing the fundamental right of a minority shareholder to litigate.[108] This decision reflects that the Hong Kong courts are more willing to accept the use of a private dispute resolution method as a means to improve the quality of shareholder dispute resolution, as evidenced by the fact that the court issued a summons to stay the proceedings pending the conclusion of mediation.[109] If the parties could find a solution that is mutually acceptable through mediation, the remedy of a winding-up order would not be considered as effective and reasonable. This is certainly true, as the winding-up remedy is a drastic one and should necessarily be a remedy of

---

Judiciary did expressly reject the concept of mandatory court-institutionalized ADR programme.

[106] Ibid., paras. 828–831. Ahmed, 'Implied Compulsory Mediation', 164–169. Ahmed points out that the UK courts exercise their powers in compelling parties to engage ADR process despite the fact that the UK government and its Judiciary did expressly reject the concept of a mandatory court-institutionalized ADR programme.

[107] Order 1A, Rule 2(2) of the RHC provides that 'In giving effect to the underlying objectives of these rules, the Court shall always recognize that the primary aim in exercising the powers of the Court is to secure the just resolution of disputes in accordance with the substantive rights of the parties.'

[108] [2013] 5 HKLRD 1 and Article 35 of the Basic Law.

[109] *Re Sun Light Elastic Ltd* [2013] 5 HKLRD 1.

last resort. In general, the court might conclude that there is no real possibility of a winding-up order being made where alternative remedies are available to the plaintiff.[110] For example, the court is less willing to make a winding-up order where the petitioner either would obtain a buyout relief order by the court or an open buyout offer has already been made by the company.[111]

Notably, the Hong Kong courts are more willing to strike out unfair prejudice petitions if the respondents have made a reasonable offer to buyout the interest of a petitioner.[112] This facilitates early settlement, as it empowers the parties to exercise control over the proceedings. This improves the quality of shareholder dispute resolution as it enables parties to use ADR, such as mediation, negotiation or other out-of-court processes to generate solutions that are more flexible and responsive to their needs.[113] This might provide better outcomes than traditional court adjudicative processes, as certain types of parties' reasonable expectations which go beyond strict contractual rights under the articles and traditional equitable principles (such as family values) might be acknowledged in a mediation process. However, it is not uncommon for the petitioner to issue an unfair prejudice petition seeking a buyout order and alternative relief of winding-up because quite often the petitioner will exhaust all possible venues to redress his grievances.[114] Although the respondents

---

[110] Section 180(1A) of the Companies Ordinance (Cap. 32) sets out that where a petition for winding-up is presented by members on the just and equitable grounds, the court is not to refuse to make a winding-up order on the ground only that some other remedy is available unless the petitioners are acting unreasonably in seeking to have the company wound up instead of pursuing the other remedy. See, for example, Re Sam Imperial Corp Ltd [1980] HKLR 649; Re Wong To Yick Wood Lock Ointment Ltd [2003] 1 HKC 484; Re Ranson Motor Manufacturing Co. Ltd [2007] HKLRD 751; and Re Sai Kung PLB (Maxicab) (No.1 &2) Co Ltd [2009] 4 HKLRD 523.

[111] Ibid.

[112] See, for example, Re Prudential Enterprise Ltd [2002] 1 HKLRD 267. This case followed the approach taken by Lord Hoffmann in O'Neill v. Phillips by recognizing that there are five essential elements which constitute a reasonable offer: (1) The offer must allow the shares to be purchased at a fair value; (2) the value, if not agreed, is to be determined by a competent expert; (3) the value should be determined by the expert as an expert – the objectives are economy and expedition; (4) an offer must provide for the equality of arms between the parties; and (5) the issue of costs should be addressed and often the payment of costs would be included in the offer.

[113] Carrie Menkel-Meadow, 'When Dispute Resolution Begets Disputes of Its Own: Conflicts Among Dispute Profssionals', UCLA Law Review, 44 (1997), 1871–1933 at 1872. Menkel-Meadow notes that ADR embraces one of the quantitative goal by providing better outcomes through communication between disputing parties.

[114] Re Sun Light Elastic Ltd [2013] 5 HKLRD 1 citing Re Fides Bros Ltd [1970] 1 WLR 592.

could alternatively apply for a court order to strike out the petition for winding-up relief, the respondents might feel undue pressure on the litigation process.[115]

Recent reform of the civil procedural rules empowers the court to actively exercise its case management powers to promote the greater use of out-of-court processes for the resolution of shareholder disputes.[116] The courts are more willing to exercise their case management powers by striking a proper balance between safeguarding minority shareholders' rights of access to courts, and at the same time preventing litigation that adversely affects the proper operation of a business enterprise.[117] In the judgement of *Re Sun Light Elastic Ltd*,[118] Justice Harris of the Court of First Instance followed the decision in *Re Mahr China Ltd*[119] by stating that the correct approach is to stay rather than strike out the claim for a winding-up.[120] This decision recognized the fundamental right of a minority shareholder to pursue a winding-up remedy in the court. On the other hand, the courts prevent a vexatious shareholder from using litigation as a tactical ploy to push the respondent to settle on unfavourable terms by stating that the court would exercise its power to strike out a winding-up petition sparingly, unless it was 'plain and obvious' that the petition for winding-up would fail.[121]

Moreover, the issuance of Practice Direction 3.3 by the Judiciary empowers the court to exercise its discretionary power to adjourn unfair prejudice proceeding which allows the parties to consider whether mediation and other out-of-court dispute resolution methods are appropriate

---

[115] The principles governing an application to strike out a winding-up petition in the post-CJR era were summarized by Ma CJ in *Wing Fai Construction Co Ltd v. Yip Kwong Robert* [2012] 1 HKLRD 589. The applicable principles on striking out a winding-up petition are as follows: (1) The burden is on the plaintiff to show that it was plain and obvious that the winding-up petition would fail; (2) an application for the winding-up petition is tantamount to an abuse of the process of the court; and (3) when considering the aspect of delay, mere delay would not be sufficient to justify an order to strike out unless a delay which is inordinate and inexcusable causes a substantial risk that a fair trial is not possible.

[116] Order 1A, rule 4(e) of the RHC.

[117] Legislative Council, *Legislative Council Brief: Companies Ordinance (Ord. No. 28 of 2012)*, (2013).

[118] [2013] 5 HKLRD 1 at 5–6.

[119] [2008] 4 HKLRD 141.

[120] *Re Sun Light Elastic Ltd* [2013] 5 HKLRD 1–8.

[121] The test for a strike-out application in *Re Copeland & Craddock Ltd* [1997] BCC 294 P 300 was applied in the Hong Kong courts. See, for example, *Re Sun Light Elastic Ltd* [2013] 5 HKLRD 1 at 8, *Re Mahr China Ltd* [2008] 4 HKLRD 141 and *Re Ranson Motor Manufacturing Co. Ltd* [2007] HKLRD 751 at 758.

for them.[122] Consequently, the new Practice Direction 3.3 streamlines the court proceedings for shareholder disputes in three ways.

First, it saves substantial amounts of time, as parties are required to reduce the issues relating to unfair prejudice petitions to written form.[123] This assists the parties in clarifying the issues in disputes.

Second, the new Practice Direction 3.3 was published by the Judiciary to supplement the law and rule on the procedures for an unfair prejudice petition. This directive was drafted to give detailed guidance to the courts to make directions with regard to the appropriateness of using ADR to resolve the whole or part of the petitioner's claims under the Companies (Unfair Prejudice Petitions) Proceedings Rules. This provides greater certainty as to the extent to which the courts utilize their active case management powers to encourage parties to attempt to resolve shareholder disputes through mediation and other alternative processes before turning to litigation.

Third, Practice Direction 3.3 does not impose a permanent stay on proceedings.[124] Instead, it simply provides parties with an alternative route to avoid court interference regarding the affairs of the company overall. It is clear that disclosure of confidential information such as a company's commercial activity, share price, or its ability to raise financing during the court proceedings may have a divesting effect on the company's affairs. This judicial direction on mediation is particularly useful, as it allows the disputing parties to apply a stay of proceedings for mediation to exchange and discuss sensitive documents.

However, mediation and other alternative processes often have been used as a fishing expedition to discover weaknesses of the other side's case or to cause unnecessary delays by exhausting the financial resources of less wealthy opponents, making it difficult to continue further actions against the wealthier party.[125] ADR further exacerbates the imbalance of power between the majority and minority shareholders in the pursuit of a fair sentiment through informal out-of-court processes. To ensure public confidence with regard to the protection of the weaker party who might otherwise be disadvantaged in the mediation process, the court takes

[122] Practice Direction 3.3, paras. 8–11.
[123] Practice Direction 3.3, para. 7.
[124] Practice Direction 3.3, para. 9, where parties may apply for a stay of proceedings for mediation purposes. A party is at liberty to apply to lift the stay under Practice Direction 3.3., para. 11.
[125] Hazel Genn, *Judging Civil Justice*, The Hamlyn Lectures 59th Series (Cambridge: Cambridge University Press, 2010), 113.

further effort to prevent mediation from being used as a delaying tactic. For instance, the decision in *Chu Chung Ming v. Lam Wai Dan* illustrates that the court maintains a delicate balance between safeguarding the rights of minority shareholders to access relevant 'inside' corporate information for resolving the disputes and the need to ensure that disclosure of the relevant evidence (such as communications made in the mediation) is kept within the proper boundaries of the common law principle in protecting mediation communications.[126]

More recently, Hong Kong moved a step further in enacting rules (i.e., the Mediation Ordinance) on the issue of confidentiality for mediators, parties and non-parties participating in the mediation process.[127] The law protects the confidentiality of the mediation process by stipulating that any information relating to it might not be published or disclosed unless otherwise agreed by the parties or under any exceptions provided for the Ordinance.[128] Thus, the Mediation Ordinance was formulated with the goal of striking a delicate balance between safeguarding confidentiality in mediation and the need to disclose confidential mediation communications which are prepared for and used in the arbitration or court proceedings.

ll. Imposing Cost Penalties Are Proportionate to the Issues Involved for Unreasonable Refusals to Mediate   A court-connected ADR pro gramme embraces the qualitative values of the Basic Law, as it safeguards the fundamental right of a shareholder to bring an action to the court.[129] In general, the traditional rule that the costs follow the event (i.e., the unsuccessful party in litigation will be ordered to compensate the legal costs of the successful party, and this rule is also known as the 'cost indemnity rule') should not be departed from unless the parties had unreasonably refused

---

[126] [2012] 4 HKLRD 897 at 903–904. This judgement applied the common law principles to analyse the concept of confidentiality in mediation, namely: (1) contractual or implied obligations of confidentiality and (2) the without prejudice rule. The court declined to permit the admissibility of communication made in the mediation process, as the respondents failed to prove that there are other public interests (such as economic duress) which justify his disclosure of confidential mediation communications.

[127] Section 8(2) of the Mediation Ordinance (Cap. 620) relates to the issue of confidentiality of mediation communications. This section provides that in general, a person must not disclose mediation communication except as provided by subsection (2) or (3). Thus, the rule of confidentiality is not absolute. Evidence covered by such a duty of confidentiality may be given if the court considers that it is in the interest of justice to do so; see Sections 9 to 10 of the Mediation Ordinance.

[128] Ibid.

[129] Article 35 of the Hong Kong Basic Law.

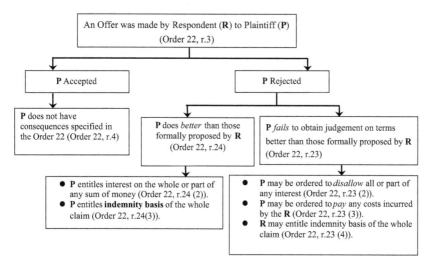

Figure 4.1 An illustration of sanction offer or sanction payment made under Sanction 22 of the Rules of the High Court.

to attempt informal out-of-court processes.[130] In some circumstances, the court may exercise its power to take a strong policy approach regarding the rejection of extrajudicial processes, if necessary, by imposing indemnity costs orders upon a party who had failed to obtain a judgement that is more advantageous than the sanctioned payment under Order 22 of the RHC.[131] Order 22 of Sanctioned Offer or Sanctioned Payment can be viewed as a new innovative procedure that encourages early settlements in shareholder disputes (see Figure 4.1).[132]

This type of sanctions offer creates incentives to settle by allowing proposals to be made without prejudice except as to costs.[133] One of the advantages of Order 22 is that it allows plaintiffs or defendants to concede confidentially that they may not win wholly and protect them from liability for the cost of prolonging litigation unreasonably.[134] Clearly, a cost sanction offer can be viewed as an effective tool to facilitate early settlement

---

[130] Order 62, Rule 3(2) of the Rules of the High Court (Cap. 4A) and Practice Direction 31, paras. 4 and 5.

[131] Order 22, Rule 23 of the RHC.

[132] Order 22, Rules 23 and 24.

[133] Karl Mackie et al., *The ADR Practice Guide: Commercial Dispute Resolution* (Tottel, 2007), 142.

[134] Order 22 creates incentives to settle by allowing proposals to be made by the offerer made without prejudice except as to costs. If the offeree refused to accept the offer made by the offerer, costs can shift or increase liability for the costs of the claim.

through extrajudicial processes as the court may exercise its discretionary power to penalize a party who had failed or refused to attempt ADR process.[135] Therefore, costs sanctions can be viewed as an effective weapon to encourage the successful party to explore the scope and advantages of settlement through mediation and other alternative processes.

However, there are recent court decisions by the Hong Kong courts which seem to display its reluctance to hand out indemnity costs orders if a party had refused to mediate.[136] One possible reason for this is that Rule 22 of the RHC does not lay down any specific guidelines for the court in determining what is 'unjust' with respect to the assessment of costs on the indemnity basis under Rule 22 of the RHC. This may result in satellite litigation.[137] For example, in *Kwan Wing Leung v. Fung Chi Leung*, the learned deputy judge Anthony Chow attempted to enhance legal certainty regarding the scope of the discretionary powers of the court to impose a costs sanction on the party who had failed to attempt informal out-of-court processes.[138] The court noted that using failure to mediate as an unjust reason not to apply the costs sanction in Order 22, Rule 23 of the RHC would result in restricting the court's discretion powers to impose costs sanction upon the party who had failed to attempt private extrajudicial process under the case management directions.[139] Thus, the proper approach taken by the learned judge in *Kwan Wing Leung* was that the costs sanctions stipulated under Order 22 and the case management directions for mediation should be adopted separately and independently of each other.[140]

Generally, the court would also sparingly exercise its discretionary power under the case management directions to impose costs on a party who had refused to engage in extrajudicial processes.[141] In *Re NTK Technology (HK) Ltd*, the defendants had acted unreasonably by refusing to attempt to mediate their differences with the petitioner despite the

---

[135]   *Golden Eagle International (Group) Ltd v. GR Investment Holdings* HKLRD 3 [2010] 273.

[136]   *Good Try Investments Ltd v. Easily Development Ltd* [2013] HKEC 7 (unreported, DCCJ 3346/2011, 3 January 2013) (DC) and *Kwan Wing Leung v. Fung Chi Leung* [2014] HKEC 1523 (unreported, DCPI 2489/2013, 15 September 2014) (DC).

[137]   Lord Justice Jackson, *Review of Civil LItigation Costs: Final Report* (London: The Stationary Office, 2009), 53.

[138]   [2014] HKEC 1523 (unreported, DCPI 2489/2013, 15 September 2014) (DC).

[139]   Ibid. at para. 61.

[140]   Ibid. at para. 62.

[141]   See, for example, *Golden Eagle International (Group) Ltd v. GR Investment Holdings* HKLRD 3 [2010] at 273 and *Pacific Long Distance Telephone v. New World Telecommunications Ltd* [2012] HKEC 732 (unreported, HCA 1688/2006, 10 February 2012) (CFI).

fact that the parties were encouraged by the court to mediate at the pre-trial review.[142] The court held that it was inappropriate for the court to deprive some or all of the defendants' costs for their unreasonable refusal to mediate, as any mediation in the context of Section 168A petitions was voluntary per se.[143] Similarly, the judgement in *Good Try Investments Ltd v. Easily Development Ltd* illustrates that the court declined to impose a costs sanction against a party that refused to mediate although there had not been a valid reason for his unreasonable refusal to mediate.[144] A positive explanation may be that the refusing party had accepted the sanction payment in good time, and this act was not considered unreasonable.[145]

However, the court has recently displayed a greater willingness to make any adverse costs order against a party who had failed or refused to engage in ADR processes under the Practice Direction on Mediation. For instance, in *Kwan Wing Leung v. Fung Chi Leung*, the learned Deputy Judge Anthony Chow said that it would be entirely appropriate for the court to deprive the whole or some of the refusing party's costs.[146] First, the court would take non-compliance with the rules and practice direction on mediation seriously. It is entirely appropriate for the court to make an adverse costs order against a party that had failed to comply with the practice direction on mediation, as there was no minimum level of participation agreed to by the parties.[147] Second, given that the CJR has been implemented for a number of years, the costs consequence of refusing to mediate is well known to the local community as well as the legal profession.[148] Thus, it is unlikely to put the refusing party at risk of having the entire costs be deprived for his unreasonable refusal to mediate.

Clearly, the decision in *Kwan Wing Leung* has sent a very clear message to the public that the parties should seriously consider the possibility of using non-litigation modes of dispute resolution to resolve their disputes, as the mediation regime had been implemented for a number of years.[149] This brings greater certainty as to the circumstances in which the court may exercise its powers to penalize a party for refusing to engage in

---

[142] [2010] HKEC 1635 (unreported, HCCW 528/2008, 27 October 2010) 1636 (CFI) at para. 24.
[143] Ibid.
[144] [2013] HKEC 7 (unreported, DCCJ 3346/2011, 3 January 2013) (DC).
[145] Ibid.
[146] [2014] HKEC 1523 (unreported, DCPI 2489/2013, 15 September 2014) (DC).
[147] Ibid. at para. 73.
[148] Ibid. at para. 79.
[149] Ibid.

ADR.[150] Thus, it would be more likely for the courts to impose costs sanction on the party who had failed to exhaust other non-litigation modes of dispute resolution, such as mediation and arbitration in resolving their disputes.[151] As a whole, a court-connected ADR programme in Hong Kong has struck a proper balance in punishing a party in costs for failing to engage in mediation, while at the same time without sacrificing the voluntary nature of informal out-of-court processes.

b. Offering Greater Opportunities to Access Dispute Resolution Forums

A court-based ADR programme can be seen as a way to offer greater opportunities for ordinary citizens to access various types of dispute resolution forums, such as mediation, to resolve shareholder disputes that meet their needs. The application of mediation extended to include shareholders' claims covered by the legal aided schemes embraces the qualitative value of the Basic Law, as it recognizes the freedom to choose various types of dispute resolution processes.[152]

In general, parties with limited financial resources should have the opportunity to adopt a wide variety of dispute resolution processes to resolve shareholder disputes. If policymakers fail to connect the underlying goal of access to various dispute resolution forums with the availability of legal aid funding under a court-connected ADR programme, this may curtail the minority shareholder's right in accessing more affordable means to resolve disputes.[153]

---

[150] It is interesting to contrast the case of *Kwan Wing Leung v. Fung Chi Leung* with the case of *Ansar Mohammad v. Global Legend Transportation Limited* [2010], where Master Levy concluded that 'Had the mediation regime been fully implemented, the defendant may likely be at risk of having its entire costs be deprived. Given the fact that the regime is relatively new, and has only recently become an obligatory part of the CJR, it would not be fair to deprive the defendant's entire costs...'

[151] *Kwan Wing Leung v. Fung Chi Leung* [2014] HKEC 1523 (unreported, DCPI 2489/2013, 15 September 2014) (DC).

[152] Article 38 of the Hong Kong Basic Law stipulates that Hong Kong residents shall enjoy the other rights and freedoms safeguarded by the laws of the Hong Kong Special Administrative Region. Expanding this position would suggest that the Hong Kong Basic Law recognizes the shareholders' freedom to adopt contractual dispute resolution processes for the resolution of intra-close corporate disputes.

[153] Carrie Menkel-Meadow, 'Will Managed Care Give us Access to Justice?', in Roger Smith (ed.), *Achieving Civil Justice: Appropriate Dispute Resolution for the 1990s* (London: Legal Action Group, 1996), 92.

An increasing number of litigants who are unable to resolve their cases through the assistance of a lawyer, that is, represent themselves in court, is a clear signal that the civil justice system is 'in crisis'.[154] Such a crisis generally indicates that there are major barriers for certain litigants to fund their litigation in accessing adequate forums to resolve disputes in a manner which best meets the needs of the parties. Recently, the Hong Kong government increased the types of cases covered under the legal aid scheme.[155] A petitioner who passed a means test under the ordinary legal aid scheme will be entitled to legal aid.[156] Sadly, petitioners of the so-called 'sandwich class' might not be able to get supplementary legal aid to fund unfair prejudice proceedings.[157] This means that our civil justice system is failing to promote equal access to justice, particularly for the middle-income group.

Nevertheless, it is to be welcomed that the Hong Kong government has expanded the operation of the Supplementary Legal Aid Scheme to assist middle-class litigants in resolving shareholder disputes.[158] From this perspective, it seems plausible that the court-institutionalized ADR programme could operate in parallel with the Legal Aid Department in encouraging the aided litigants to consider mediation as a viable option at any time before or during court proceedings. Given that it is not necessary for aided litigants to have tried mediation before being granted legal aid, this preserves the standard orthodoxy of voluntary mediation, as litigants are not forced into mediation either by the court or the Legal Aid Department. This policy objective can improve the opportunity of middle-class litigants to have more affordable means of resolving shareholder disputes.[159] In sum, the policy that seeks to promote greater

---

[154] The Law Reform Commission of Hong Kong, *Report on Conditional Fees*, (2007), paras. 6.55–6.60. In Camille Cameron and Elsa Kelly, 'Litigants in Person in Civil Proceedings: Part I', *Hong Kong Law Journal*, 32 (2002), 313–342 at 316–317. Cameron and Kelly point out that litigants in person is a sign of system breakdown.

[155] Schedule 2 of the Legal Aid Ordinance (Cap. 91).

[156] Section 5 of the Legal Aid Ordinance (Cap. 91) sets out that an applicant who has financial resources (i.e., the aggregate of annual disposal income and disposal capital) below $260,000 will qualify for legal aid for civil proceedings under the Ordinary Legal Aid Scheme.

[157] Section 5A of the Legal Aid Ordinance (Cap. 91) stipulates that legal aid funds would be limited to certain categories of cases mentioned in Part I of Schedule 3 instead of proceedings mentioned in Part II of that Schedule.

[158] The Law Society of Hong Kong, *Working Party on Conditional Fees: Response for the Law Reform Commission's Report on Conditional Fees* (2007), paras. 4.1, 4.11–4.16.

[159] Final Report of the Working Party on Civil Justice Reform, para. 838. The report recommended that the DLA should have power in suitable cases to limit its initial funding of

opportunities for access to various dispute resolution forums is consistent with the constitutional values under the Hong Kong Basic Law.[160]

4.5 Conclusion

The chapter has argued that the court rules and practice directions on mediation issued by the Hong Kong Judiciary help to improve the legitimacy of the court in exercising its case management power to promote the greater use of out-of-court processes to resolve shareholder disputes among the local business and legal professional community. This argument rests on the assumption that these objectives are not only consistent with constitutional values inherent in the Basic Law, but are also in line with social norms underpinning the cultural rules of Hong Kong which emphasize the importance of safeguarding the free operation of business and access to the courts. As such, a court-connected ADR programme for shareholder disputes can secure its legitimacy not purely from the substantive provisions of the Basic Law, but also from social beliefs (such as the primacy of contractual freedom and the emphasis on the maintenance of law that guarantees a citizen's right of access to courts), which are endorsed by the local business and legal professional community. Eventually, judges may be more willing to apply rules in a manner which is consistent with ADR goals. The next chapter considers how recent Civil Justice Reform in Hong Kong provides fresh impetus for the development of extrajudicial processes within the new statutory unfair prejudice regime.

persons who qualify for legal aid to the funding of mediation, alongside its power to fund court proceedings where mediation is inappropriate and where it has failed.

[160] Article 38 of the Hong Kong Basic Law.

5

Reforms of Company Law

Legitimizing the Use of Informal Processes in Conjunction with Court-Based Shareholder Proceedings

5.1 Introduction

Among members of the local business community and legal profession, both the civil procedure rules and the relevant court directives on mediation enhance the legitimacy of the courts to promote greater use of ADR in resolving shareholder disputes. The recent reform of Hong Kong's civil justice system has given further impetus by introducing a specific set of procedure rules, which covers a set of informal private dispute resolution mechanisms under the Companies (Unfair Prejudice Petitions) Proceedings Rules (Cap. 622L). A new set of unfair prejudice petitions rules has been made pursuant to Section 727 of the new Companies Ordinance (CO), which empowers Hong Kong's Chief Justice (CJ) to make rules in regulating the conduct of unfair prejudice proceedings.[1]

The reception of the UK procedural rules for unfair prejudice applications is nonetheless extremely effective in Hong Kong.[2] This is due to the fact that the Hong Kong government is subject to mimetic pressure to introduce a similar UK provision that enhances the court's discretion in granting an order for a stay with a view to mediation or other alternative processes at the petition stage.[3] Such institutional pressure stems primarily from the need of the Hong Kong government to cope with uncertainty about the application of extrajudicial processes to resolve shareholder disputes in Hong

---

[1] The Hong Kong SAR Government, *Press Releases: Companies (Unfair Prejudice Petitions) Proceedings Rules Submitted to Leg Co* (15 May 2013).
[2] Colin J. Bennett, 'How States Utilize Foreign Evidence', *Journal of Public Policy*, 11:1 (1991), 31–54 at 37–38.
[3] Hong Kong Financial Services and the Treasury Bureau, *New Companies Ordinance: Subsidiary Legislation for Implementation of the New Companies Ordinance (Phase Two Consultation Document)* (Hong Kong Financial Services and the Treasury Bureau, 2012), para. 12.6. Rules 4, 5, 6 and 9 of the Companies (Unfair Prejudice Petitions) Proceedings Rules (Cap. 622L) (C(UPP)PR) are formulated with reference to the Companies (Unfair Prejudice Applications) Proceedings Rules 2009 of the United Kingdom.

Kong.[4] A brief introduction of a new set of unfair prejudice proceeding rules relating to the court's discretionary power to make an order for ADR raises deeper questions about whether the application of non-litigious modes of dispute resolution, such as mediation and arbitration, could fit precisely into the new statutory unfair prejudice regime of the CO.

The focus of this chapter is to examine how extrajudicial processes and court-based shareholder proceedings can coexist and be applied simultaneously within the CO's new statutory unfair prejudice regime. It is argued that the new statutory unfair prejudice regime is flexible in accommodating the existence of ADR for the resolution of shareholder disputes. On that basis, extrajudicial processes are perceived as supplementing the operation of court-based unfair prejudice proceedings, rather than merely being substitutive to it in Part 14 of the new CO.[5]

Like in discussions of the fusion of law and equity, there has been a continuing debate in ADR circles regarding the extent to which ADR has become entrenched in the litigation process by law.[6] A brief analysis of the combination of law and equity offers insight into the analysis of the relationship between court-based unfair prejudice proceedings and private dispute resolution methods. The characteristics of equity are inherent in both the ADR process and unfair prejudice proceedings. The concept of unfair prejudice places great emphasis on equitable considerations that is derived from *Ebrahimi* and had subsequently been incorporated into the statutory unfair prejudice provisions. Similarly, the characteristics of traditional equity are echoed in the system of ADR (such as mediation),[7] and ADR becomes an accepted mode of the dispute resolution process within the civil justice system to resolve shareholder disputes. In this regard, the analysis helps to determine how ADR and shareholder litigation can coexist and be applied simultaneously within the new statutory unfair prejudice regime.

---

[4] Paul J. DiMaggio and Walter W. Powell, 'The Iron Cage Revisited: Institutional Isomorphism and Collective Rationality in Organizational Fields', *American Sociological Review*, 48:2 (1983), 147–160 at 151.

[5] See Section 5.2.2.

[6] Jacqueline M. Nolan-Haley, 'The Merger of Law and Mediation: Lessons from Equity Jurisprudence and Roscoe Pound', *Cardozo Journal of Conflict Resolution*, 6 (2005), 57–71 at 53.

[7] Thomas O. Main, 'ADR: The New Equity', *University of Cincinnati Law Review*, 74 (2005), 329–404 at 354–374. Main depicts that there are five main aspects of ADR that echo a theme that is characteristic of equity: (1) saving time and money, (2) procedural flexibility, (3) substantive flexibility, (4) the reflection and reinforcement of community norms and (5) access to justice.

First, the new corporate law in Hong Kong contains a provision that empowers the court to make subsidiary legislation (i.e., the unfair prejudice petition rules) for regulating the conduct of unfair prejudice proceedings.[8] Under this rule, judges may give a direction in requiring each party to consider the possibility of extrajudicial processes to resolve shareholder disputes at the stage of commencing an unfair prejudice action.[9] Recent reform of the statutory unfair prejudice provisions takes a step further to convince both local businessmen and their legal representatives to consider the application of extrajudicial processes for shareholder disputes as statutory backing given to the court to make an order for ADR.[10] Clearly, an individual who refuses to comply with an order to stay an unfair prejudice proceeding to mediate may be open to charge of contempt of court.[11]

In contrast with the current judicial approach towards ADR, the court may impose costs sanctions on the party for either failure to engage in out-of-court processes to the minimum level of participation or without reasonable explanation for attempting extrajudicial processes.[12] This raises a serious concern with respect to an extension of the court's powers under the new statutory unfair prejudice jurisdiction, as out-of-court processes are institutionalized through the legislative mandate instead of through a directive issued by the Hong Kong's Chief Justice.[13]

There would be no lasting solution to the potentate for 'Bleak House problems'[14] highlighted by Dickens within shareholder litigation if reform-minded corporate lawmakers failed to consider local circumstances by

---

[8] Section 727 of the new Companies Ordinance (Cap. 622).

[9] Rule 6(f) of the C(UPP)PR.

[10] Interpretation and General Clauses Ordinance (Cap. 1) defines 'subsidiary legislation' as 'any proclamation, rule, regulation, order, resolution, notice, rule of court, bylaw, or other instrument made under or by virtue of any Ordinance and having legislative effect'. Section 35 of this Ordinance provides that an item of subsidiary legislation is subject to the Legislative Council's scrutiny under the positive vetting procedures or the negative vetting procedures.

[11] *Halsbury's Law of Hong Kong*, (2nd ed. 2011), Vol. 37, para. 110.051. According to Halsbury's Law of Hong Kong, it is a civil contempt of court to refuse or neglect to do an act required by a judgement or order of the court within the time specified in the judgement or order, or to disobey a judgement or order requiring a person to abstain from doing a specified act, or to act in breach of an undertaking given to the court by a person, on the faith of which the court sanctions a particular course of action or inaction.

[12] Order 62 of the Rules of the High Court (RHC), paras. 4 and 5 of Practice Direction 31.

[13] This issue raises the serious concern of whether the proposed inclusion of ADR into the subsidiary legislation of the new company law would seriously undermine Article 35 of the Hong Kong Basic Law.

[14] Hazel Genn, 'Civil Justice Reform and ADR', Conference on *Civil Justice Reform: What Has It Achieved?* (Hong Kong, 15 April 2010). The term '*Bleak House* problems' was coined

incorporating a similar provision taken from the UK legislation.[15] This chapter employs theories of economics and law to analyse the relationship between out-of-court processes and formal court-based proceeding for shareholder disputes. Previous scholars such as Fiss noted that there is a distinction between public court adjudication and out-of-court processes.[16] The former promotes public values as it is designed for articulating constitutional values and rights which are enshrined in the country's constitution, whereas the latter serves 'individual preferences through consensual and democratic processes'.[17] Under this private/public dichotomy, it is uncertain whether the inclusion of out-of-court processes within the new statutory unfair prejudice regime could either weaken or strengthen the public function of the court for protecting minority shareholders' rights and interests under the corporate law.

Second, the question remains of what, exactly, is meant by 'integration' if extrajudicial processes are incorporated into the statutory unfair prejudice regime. In other words, does this mean that ADR is perceived as complementing an effective operation of shareholder proceedings in Part 14 of the new CO? Logically, if ADR and a court-based approach to the resolution of shareholder disputes are compatible, the two processes can sit happily alongside one another. In this regard, it is essentially important to conceptualize the relationship between ADR and unfair prejudice proceedings. This conceptualization helps to determine how the two processes are compatible. In general, there are two possible ways to determine what, exactly, is meant by 'compatibility'. One way of answering this is to give a short description of the essence of first, the claim of substitution, and second, the claim of complementary.[18]

As a whole, this chapter argues that the new statutory unfair prejudice regime (which took effect on 3 March 2014) is flexible in accommodating the existence of extrajudicial processes for the resolution of shareholder disputes. Both extrajudicial processes and unfair prejudice proceedings are compatible on the basis that the two processes, while similar, have their own unique functions. Although the private/public dichotomy is the

---

by Professor Genn and she notes that the 'Bleak House problems' include 'delay, cost and complexity'.

[15] See supra note 3.

[16] Owen M. Fiss, 'Against Settlement', The Yale Law Journal, 93:6 (1984), 1073–1090 at 1156.

[17] Amy J. Cohen, 'Revisiting Against Settlement: Some Reflections on Dispute Resolution and Public Values', Fordham Law Review, 78 (2009), 1143–1170 at 1156.

[18] Judith Resnik, 'Many Doors? Closing Doors? Alternative Dispute Resolution and Adjudication', The Ohio State Journal on Dispute Resolution 10:2 (1995), 211–265 at 254.

dominant view among legal practitioners and legal scholars,[19] the integration of private dispute resolution mechanism into the new statutory unfair prejudice regime recognizes that the informal dispute resolution process is an important supplement to court-based shareholder proceedings in Hong Kong. The corporate policy approach towards ADR has struck a proper balance between the importance of maintaining the flexibility of ADR processes and the needs to secure the public values of the court to improve the ability of shareholders to seek judicial enforcement of their rights. As such, the minority protection provisions in the new Hong Kong company law are formulated in line with the current objectives of the court-connected ADR programme, which recognize the important role of the Judiciary in promoting the voluntary use of informal out-of-court dispute resolution processes, while at the same time placing certain limits on the scope of judicial discretion in referring cases to ADR at various stage of unfair prejudice proceedings. Section 5.2 reviews law and economics theories in order to determine how informal out-of-court processes can coexist harmoniously within the statutory unfair prejudice regime. This analysis reveals that the incorporation of ADR process into the statutory unfair prejudice regime may improve the enforcement regime in Hong Kong. Apart from that, it examines approaches to institutionalizing ADR process within the formal legal system. Section 5.3 determines whether the corporate policy approach towards ADR is broadly in line with the voluntary court-connected ADR scheme. Section 5.4 suggests that ADR is often ancillary to public court adjudication of shareholder disputes from two main aspects. Section 5.5 concludes that the reform of provisions concerning the protection of minority shareholders facilitates the coexistence of both informal out-of-court processes and unfair prejudice proceedings.

5.2 The Coexistence of Informal Dispute Resolution Methods and Court-Based Shareholder Proceedings

In order to determine how informal out-of-court processes can coexist coherently within the statutory unfair prejudice regime, it is necessary to examine the nature and function of the two dispute resolution methods by reviewing law and economic theories. A number of theorists suggested that companies are merely voluntary associations of individuals

---

[19] Richard C. Reuben, 'Constitutional Gravity: A Unitary Theory of Alternative Dispute Resoltuion and Public Civil Justice', *UCLA Law Review*, 47 (2000), 949–1104 at 953.

joined by contract and their goal is to maximize wealth for shareholders.[20] Corporate law, in particular, establishes a private ordering regime that shareholders are free to dictate the terms for governing their behaviour and resolving disputes. However, the use of contractual mechanisms such as accounting-based debt convents or bonus plan may not be effective in minimizing the various contracting costs (or agency costs) associated with the contract between shareholders and managers.[21] The effective use of contractual mechanisms may actually be quite limited in a concentrated ownership system. In particular, controlling shareholders are typically able to extract money out of the firm 'by entering into non-arms' length deals with the firms or by exploring corporate opportunities'.[22] Thus, most legal and economics scholars, such as La Porta, Lopez-de-Silanes, Shleifer and Vishny, contend that law can be viewed as an effective corporate governance mechanism that aligns the interests of managers/controlling shareholders with those of minority shareholders.[23]

However, recent findings show that private formal enforcement or governance mechanism (such as minority shareholder actions) is not critical for strong enforcement, as it plays a more limited role in constraining corporate directors.[24] This line of thought reveals that extralegal substitutes have their role to play in creating an optimal corporate governance regime in aligning the interests of controlling minority shareholders under concentrated ownership. This is particularly so, as Confucian

---

[20] J. E. Parkinson, *Corporate Power and Responsibility* (Oxford: Clarendon Press, 1993), 27.

[21] William R. Scott, *Financial Accounting Theory*, 3rd ed. (Toronto: Prentice Hall, 2003), 273–279. Scott depicts that firm managers may choose accounting policies in their own best interest, which may not necessarily also be in the firm's best interest. However, firm managers are more likely to select accounting procedures that shift earnings from future periods to the current period so as to avoid the breach of debt agreement. This form of contractual mechanism, namely, debt covenant, may to some degree align the interests between the managers and shareholders such that if these covenants are violated, the debt agreement may impose penalties, such as constraints on dividends or additional borrowings.

[22] Martin Gelter, 'The Dark Side of Shareholder Influence: Managerial Autonomy and Stakeholder Orientation in Comparative Corporate Governance', *Harvard International Law Journal*, 50 (2009), 129–194 at 155.

[23] See, for example, Tray A. Paredes, 'A System Approach to Corporate Governance Reform: Why Importing US Corporate Law Isn't the Answer', *William and Mary Law Review*, 45 (2003), 1005–1157 and Rafael La Porta, et al., 'Investor Protection and Corporate Governance', *Journal of Financial Economics*, 58 (2000), 3–27.

[24] John Armour et al., 'Private Enforcement of Corporate Law: An Empirical Comparison of the United Kingdom and the United States', *Journal of Empirical Legal Studies*, 6:4 (2009), 687–722 at 711.

tradition prevails in Hong Kong's business society.[25] Company owners often shy away from the law by employing private resolution in settling their disputes.[26] This helps to keep their private squabbles out of the public eye. The following discussion analyses the policy reasons for incorporating ADR processes into the statutory unfair prejudice regime. It then examines the institutional approaches to legitimization of ADR with the formal legal system.

5.2.1 The Use of ADR to Enhance Effective Enforcement of Shareholders' Rights

This subsection raises the issue of how to improve the ability of shareholders to enforce their rights to obtain appropriate relief through mediation and other out-of-court processes. La Porta, Lopez-de-Silanes, Shleifer and Vishny demonstrate that a strong institutional and legal framework is the prerequisite for a good corporate governance system. A strong legal framework shields shareholders, especially minority shareholders, from being expropriated by controlling shareholders.[27] Their findings are consistent with Weber's analysis of the relationship between law and the development of capitalism. Like Weber, they believe a strong legal institution that embodies 'rational legal orders' nevertheless provides 'sufficient predictability, calculability, and stability' for capitalism to thrive.[28]

Arnour and his colleagues analyse the relationship between corporate law and corporate governance from a different perspective. They argue that in order to determine the degree to which law could facilitate the development of a well-functioning corporate governance system, it is necessary to distinguish between substantive legal doctrine ('law in books') and enforcement ('law in action').[29] According to their analysis, the former focuses mainly on the association between the 'roles of substantive laws' in protecting minority shareholders and corporate ownership

[25] Alex Lau et al., 'In Search of Good Governance for Asian Family Listed Companies: A Case Study on Hong Kong', *The Company Lawyer*, 28:10 (2007), 306–311 at 309.
[26] Ibid.
[27] Rafael La Porta et al., 'Investor Protection and Corporate Governance', 4.
[28] David Trubek, 'Max Weber on Law and the Rise of Capitalism', *Wisconsin Law Review*, (1972), 720–753 at 740. In Paredes, 'A System Approach to Corporate Governance Reform', 1064. Paredes depicts that LLSV endorses strong and enforceable legal protections for shareholders, as this can form a basis for promoting securities markets and economic growth.
[29] Armour et al., 'Private Enforcement of Corporate Law', 687.

patterns around the world.[30] La Porta and his colleagues are the leading authorities in claiming that common law countries such as the United Kingdom, United States and Hong Kong have the relatively strongest corporate governance systems than civil law countries, as the legal systems in common law countries provide strong legal protection for minority shareholders.[31] 'Enforcement', by contrast, places great emphasis on the way in which rules are enforced by a particular actor, or group of actors, and what remedies are potentially available.[32] This highlights that a strong system of rules is almost always paired with a well-functioning court system in order to provide successful civil enforcement for corporate governance disputes. Thus, a well-functioning court system is the prerequisite of an effective enforcement regime.[33]

In Hong Kong, the level of ownership concentration (i.e., family-owned business dominated by controlling shareholders) is prevalent not just in public companies, but also in small business enterprises.[34] Nonetheless, Hong Kong provides a favourable corporate environment, as it offers the strongest legal protection for minority shareholders. Though over the past decades, corporate governance reforms have specifically addressed public corporations in Hong Kong, particular attention has also been given recently to the corporate governance reforms by the amendments of the CO which are tailored to the needs of small privately held companies.[35] The World Bank Doing Business 2016 Report illustrates that Hong Kong's performance in protecting minority shareholders through its legal

---

[30] Ibid.

[31] Rafael La Porta et al., 'Law and Finance', *Journal of Political Economy*, 106:6 (1998), 1113–1155 at 1126–1130.

[32] John Armour, 'Enforcement Strategies in UK Corporate Governance: A Roadmap and Empirical Assessment', in John Armour and Jennifer Payne (eds.), *Rationality in Company Law: Essays in Honour of D. D. Prentice* (Oxford: Hart Publishing, 2009), 77. Armour notes that there are two approaches to analyse the effectiveness of enforcement. One approach is to focus on the corporate legislation by examining the extensiveness of its enforcement powers of a particular actor, or group of actors, at a point in time, and what remedies are potentially available. However, he argues that this approach might not be comprehensive. He suggests another approach is to consider the rate of enforcement by considering the operation of the procedural rules in the legal environment.

[33] See Rafael La Porta et al., 'Law and Finance', 1140.

[34] Rafael La Porta et al., 'Corporate Ownership Around the World', *Journal of Finance*, 54:2 (1999), 471–517; Eelke de Jong, 'Cultural Determinants of Ownership Concentration across Countries', *International Business Governance and Ethics*, 2 (2006), 145–164 at 148.

[35] Hong Kong Financial Services and the Treasury Bureau, *Consultation Paper on the Draft Companies Bill: First Phase Consultation* (Hong Kong Financial Services and the Treasury Bureau, 2009).

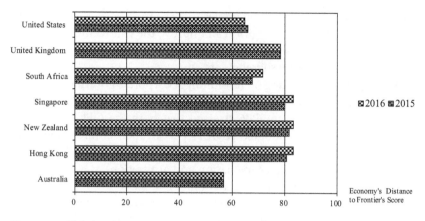

Figure 5.1 Global ranking on investor protection in 2015/2016.

mandates is extremely good, as it is the top ranked country in the world in this respect (see Figure 5.1).[36]

However, a country that offers strong legal protection for minority shareholders could be viewed as only one of the major factors that contribute to a strong enforcement regime.[37] Armour and his colleagues reveal that there are some extralegal factors which could influence the quality of enforcement. Recently, legal academics such as Bouchez and Karpf argue that a crucial prerequisite for successful civil enforcement is the availability of efficient mechanisms of dispute resolution, which include a range of both litigation and non-litigation out-of-court forms of dispute resolution processes, such as mediation and arbitration.[38] Building upon

[36] World Bank Group, *Doing Business 2016: Measuring Regulatory Quality and Efficiency* at www.doingbusiness.org (Accessed 10 September 2016).

[37] Craig G. Doidge et al., 'Has New York Become Less Competitive in Global Markets? Evaluating Foreign Listing Choices Over Time', *Journal of Financial Economics*, 91:3 (2009), 253–277 at 254 and Armour et al., 'Private Enforcement of Corporate Law', 711. Armour finds out that private enforcement of corporate law is not critical for strong securities markets. He further suggests that there might be some extralegal substitutes that might influence the quality of enforcement.

[38] Louis Bouchez and Alexander Karpf, 'The OECD's Work on Corporate Governance and Dispute Resolution Mechanisms', in Louis Bouchez et al. (eds.), *Topics in Corporate Finance: The Quality of Corporate Law and the Role of Corporate Law Judges* (Amsterdam: Amsterdam Center for Corporate Finance, 2006), 3. In addition, the Global Corporate Governance Forum (GCGF), cofounded by the World Bank Group and the Organization for Economic Cooperation and Development, is promoting mediation to resolve corporate governance disputes through a publication entitled *Mediating Corporate Governance Conflicts and Disputes*. For details, see Eric M. Runesson and Marie-Laurence Guy, Mediating Corporate Governance Conflict and Disputes: Global Corporate Governance Forum Focus 4 (2007) at www.gcgf.org/ifcext/cgf.nsf/AttachmentsByTitle/ Focus+Mediation/$FILE/Focus4_Mediation_12.pdf (Accessed 18 August 2009).

their findings, this dissertation argues that the inclusion of ADR into the statutory unfair prejudice regime can improve the enforcement regime of Hong Kong.[39] This approach may widen the spectrum of remedies which are available to minority shareholders.

The exploratory meeting on resolution of corporate governance-related disputes organized by the Organization for Economic Co-operation and Development (OECD) in 2006 stressed that both the OECD and non-OECD countries have adopted ADR as part of their enforcement strategies.[40] This meeting reflects that there is an international significance for the use of ADR (such as mediation and arbitration) as a specific civil enforcement option in settling shareholder disputes.

First, judicial enforcements in some countries are less advanced or reliable and minority shareholders often face difficulties in enforcing their rights.[41] Second, the growth of globalized economies provides a fresh impetus for companies to carry out their business activities across borders. However, minority shareholders find it difficult to obtain redress for grievances if the registered seat of a company is located in a country that offers weak legal protection for minority shareholders.[42] The use of arbitration in this scenario would become a sensible choice, as parties are free to choose different laws and rules to resolve their disputes. Theses include the law in governing the substantive contractual issues (such as substantive rights and obligations of the parties); the law applicable to the arbitration agreement; the law governing the arbitral procedure (institutional or *ad hoc* arbitration rules) and the law of the seat of the arbitration (i.e., the legal place of arbitration which the parties or arbitral tribunal agree).

On top of that, enforcement of arbitration awards can be viewed as a simpler route in the context of cross-border shareholder disputes.[43]

---

[39] Section 727 of the Companies Ordinance.
[40] OECD, *Exploratory Meeting on Resolution of Corporate Governance Related Disputes* at www.oecd.org/dataoecd/48/22/37188704.pdf (Accessed 12 December 2011).
[41] Ibid.
[42] See, for example, *Re Estate of Kam Kwan Sing* [2015] HKEC 2370 (unreported, FACV 4/ 2015, 11 November 2015) (CFA) at para. 17. In this case, the Hong Kong Court of Final Appeal reaffirmed the lower court's decision that the Hong Kong court did not have jurisdiction to determine the petitioner's application for relief under Section 168A of the former Companies Ordinance (Cap. 32) (now Section 724 of the Companies Ordinance (Cap. 622)), as the company had not established a place of business in Hong Kong. However, the court allowed the appeal on jurisdiction under Section 327(3)(c) of the Companies (Winding-Up and Miscellaneous Provisions) Ordinance (Cap. 32) to wind up foreign companies on just and equitable grounds.
[43] Bouchez and Karpf, 'The OECD's Work on Corporate Governance and Dispute Resolution Mechanism', 18.

One plausible explanation may be that cross-broader arbitral awards can be enforced by the Hong Kong courts subject to only limited judicial review, or in the case of an international arbitration, without review of substantive matters.[44] In contrast to the mediation process, there is no equivalent to Section 66 of the Arbitration Ordinance (Cap. 609) for the parties to enforce their mediated settlement agreements as an arbitral award under the Mediation Ordinance.[45] Thus, cross-border enforcement of mediated settlement agreements is subject to private international law.[46]

Domestically, ADR could be used as an enforcement strategy to improve Hong Kong's corporate governance regime. Former Hong Kong Bar Association Chairman Rimsky Yuen Kwok-keung suggests that Hong Kong should develop an effective dispute resolution system which embodies a diverse range of dispute resolution mechanisms that are effective and accessible to the general public in resolving their disputes.[47] Extending this position would suggest that Hong Kong policymakers should promote various approaches that embrace differences between processes, rather than promoting court-based adjudicative processes, which is a generally superior method.[48] However, it would be premature to go down the route of incorporating ADR into the statutory unfair prejudice regime without examining the relationship between court-based unfair prejudice proceedings and private dispute resolution methods (such as mediation). The next section identifies institutional approaches to legitimizing the use of ADR within the formal legal system to resolve shareholder disputes.

---

[44] Section 85 of the Arbitration Ordinance (Cap. 609) stipulates that an arbitral award, whether made in or outside Hong Kong, in arbitration proceedings by an arbitral tribunal is enforceable in the same manner as a judgment of the court that has the same effect, but only with the leave of the court. Enforceability of an arbitral award is subject to exceptions, and they are provided in Section 86 of the Arbitration Ordinance.

[45] Section 66(2) of the Arbitration Ordinance (Cap. 609) sets out that if the parties to an arbitration agreement settle their dispute and enter into an agreement in writing containing the terms of settlement ('settlement agreement'), the settlement agreement will then be treated as an arbitration award for the purpose of enforcement.

[46] Claire Wilson, *Hong Kong Mediation Ordinance: Commentary and Annotations* (Hong Kong: Sweet & Maxwell/Thomas Reuters, 2013), 73.

[47] Albert Wong, 'Bar Chief Backs Reforms on Financial Checks', *The Standard*, 13 January 2009, A3.

[48] John Lande, 'A Guide for Policymaking that Emphasizes Principles, and Public Needs', *Alternatives to High Cost Litigation*, 26:11 (2008), 197–205 at 198.

5.2.2 Strategies for Legitimizing the Use of ADR within the Formal Legal System

This subsection considers the issue of under what circumstances can ADR and court-based shareholder litigation coexist coherently within a statutory unfair prejudice regime. In other words, on what basis is ADR perceived as being compatible with the unfair prejudice proceeding in that each of these methods, while similar, have distinctive functions?

Many who advocate the effectiveness of private dispute resolution as a substitution for the adjudication process base their view on the underlying assumption that 'the image of adjudication has been distorted'.[49] For example, Professor Galanter argues that a sudden and precipitous 'vanishing' of trials from civil court is not an isolated incident, but is closely connected to the pathological adversarial system causing US citizens to lose faith in the government's ability to promote and supply accessible justice.[50] Eventually, there has been a trend towards informal dispute resolution processes and a shrinking from investment in the civil justice system is seen as a public good.[51] The rapid decline in the number of cases that go to trial reveals that the vast majority are settled in the 'shadow' of the adjudicated cases.[52] On such a basis, ADR is sufficiently close to the adjudication process so that ADR is perceived as being compatible with it.

In stark contrast to the school of thought that claims ADR is supplementary to adjudication, ADR and adjudication processes are compatible because the two processes, while similar, have their own unique characteristics. For example, Professor Menkel-Meadow contends that the judicial role at settlement conferences is 'to maximize the usefulness without seriously threatening the appropriate role of judges in formal adjudication'.[53] Lambros, in the same vein, admits that 'settlement and adjudication are complementary; they are not mutually exclusive, nor are they incompatible'.[54] Unsurprisingly, Duncan Kennedy, who is an ADR

---

[49] Ibid. and Marc Galanter, 'A World Without Trial', *Journal of Dispute Resoltuion*, 7 (2006), 7–34.

[50] Galanter, 'A World Without Trial', 19.

[51] Ibid., 20.

[52] Ibid., 28–29.

[53] Carrie Menkel-Meadow, 'For and Against Settlement: Uses and Abuses of the Mandatory Settlement Conference', *UCLA Law Review*, 33 (1985), 485–514 at 486.

[54] Thomas D. Lambros, 'The Federal Rules of Civil Procedure: A New Adversarial Model for a New Era', *University of Pittsburgh Law Review*, 50 (1989), 789–807 at 796.

proponent, claims that 'right-based neo-formalism' (i.e., adjudication) and 'conflicting considerations consciousness' (i.e., private ADR process) can coexist together.[55]

The latter view is to be strongly preferred, as recent case law in Hong Kong echoes the opinion that adjudication is intrinsically superior to ADR. The effectiveness of the ADR process is distinguishable from the court litigation process. In *Eastman Chemical Ltd v. Heyro Chemical Co Ltd*,[56] the plaintiff sought to stay the injunction proceedings and arbitration pending the hearing of the Petition on the ground that Section 16(3) of the High Court Ordinance empowers the courts 'to stay any proceedings [i.e., arbitration tribunal] before it, where the court thinks fit to do so. The court dismissed the plaintiff's application on the grounds that Section 16(3) of the High Court Ordinance is applicable only to proceedings before the court and hence case management powers contained in Order 1B, Rule 1 of the RHC cannot be exercised with respect to arbitral trial.[57]

Previously, academics such as Cappelletti have argued that informal justice (such as court-institutionalized ADR programmes) could be used to complement the formal legal system.[58] Based on his view, it is plausible for Hong Kong to further institutionalize the use of ADR by empowering the Hong Kong's CJ to make subsidiary legislation for regulating conduct of unfair prejudice proceedings.[59] In general, both the Judiciary and lawmakers establish rules to govern referral to ADR processes. Sander identifies the possible ways that the law can be viewed as an institutional approach to legitimizing the use of ADR within the formal legal system. He distinguishes 'categorical' from 'discretionary' in referring to ADR.[60]

---

[55] Amy J. Cohen, 'ADR and Some Thoughts on the Social in Duncan Kennedy's Third Globalization of Legal Thought', *Comparative Law Review*, 3:1 (2012), 1–11, at 5 (citing Duncan Kennedy, 'Three Globalizations of Law and Legal Thought: 1850–2000', in David M. Trubek and Alvaro Santos (eds.), *The New Law and Economic Development: A Critical Appraisal* (Cambridge: Cambridge University Press, 2006), 36 and 63. Kennedy observes that in the third globalization (it began during the second half of the twentieth century), both an informal dispute resolution process and a right-based adjudication process can coexist.

[56] [2012] 2 HKLRD 135 at 141–142.

[57] Ibid., 146–147.

[58] Mauro Cappelletti, 'Alternative Dispute Resolution Processes within the Framework of the World-Wide Access-to-Justice Movement', *The Modern Law Review*, 56 (1989), 282–296 at 289.

[59] Section 727 of the Companies Ordinance.

[60] Frank E. A. Sander, 'Another View of Mandatory Mediation', *Dispute Resolution Journal*, 16 (2007), 16.

The former approach applies when a legislative mandate provides that certain categories of cases must undergo ADR.[61] He argues that despite a presumption that certain cases would particularly benefit from an interest-based resolution, the statute should have an opt-out provision that allows a party to petition the court for good cause in refusing to attempt ADR.[62] The latter approach refers to judges who are given the authority to refer any case they deemed appropriate to ADR.[63]

However, there has been continuing debate in ADR circles regarding the precise meaning of 'coercion' if rules or regulations are provided to the court in administering a mediation programme. Disputing parties may feel that they are being coerced to attempt ADR even though court referral to mediation 'is a procedural step along the way to a court hearing if the case does not settle at mediation'.[64] This can be explained by the fact that 'coercive isomorphism' is a form of institutionalization based on legal rules.[65] Citizens should generally honour their legal commitments, as the legitimacy of the rules stems from the legal officials, who have the capacity to establish rules.[66] Notably, the risk is heightened when rules are developed by lawmakers based on their own thoughts instead of the norms or social beliefs that they presume are accepted by most others.

Goldberg, Green and Sander attempt to define the term 'coercion' precisely by making a clear distinction between 'coercion within' the mediation process and 'coercion into' mediation.[67] However, they did

---

[61] An example includes Section 3170(a) of the California Family Code and it provides that 'if it appears on the face of a petition, application, or other pleading to obtain or modify a temporary or permanent custody or visitation order that custody, visitation, or both are contested, the court shall set the contested issues for mediation' (quoting the footnote from Dorcas Quek, 'Mandatory Mediation: An Oxymoron? Examining the Feasibility of Implementing A Court-Mandated Mediation Program', *Cardozo Journal of Conflict Resolution*, 11 (2010), 479–509 at 481).

[62] See, for example, Section 214 of the Australian Corporations Act 2001 stipulates that the court *may* make any orders, and give any directions that it considers appropriate in relation to statutory derivative proceedings, including requiring mediation.

[63] Sander, 'Another View of Mandatory Mediation', 16.

[64] Hazel Genn et al., *Twisting Arms: Court Referred and Court Linked Mediation Under Judicial Pressure* (Ministry of Justice Research Series, Series 1/07, 2007) at 15.

[65] DiMaggio and Powell, 'The Iron Cage Revisited', 150–151.

[66] Ibid. and Richard W. Scott, *Institutions and Organizations*, 2nd ed. (Thousand Oaks, CA: SAGE, 2001), 51–58.

[67] Stephen B. Goldberg, et al., 'ADR Problems and Prospects: Looking to the Future', *Judicature*, 69 (1985), 291–299 at 293. Goldberg and his colleagues distinguish between coercion 'into' the mediation process and coercion 'within' mediation. The former approach is justifiable as it allows ignorant, inexperienced or innocent disputants to appreciate the beauty of the

not provide a satisfactory result to demarcate the difference between correction 'into' and 'within' mediation precisely.[68] Although empirical researchers attempt to adopt settlement rate as an indicator (or proxy) to determine whether coercion exists, their results are tentative and somewhat speculative.[69] The vast majority of empirical researchers fail to investigate whether other factors/variables, such as the role of the mediator, or the strengths and weaknesses of the cases are likely to be proxies for determining the interrelationship among other causal factors.[70] In addition, there would be no difference in settlement rates between compulsory and voluntary mediation programmes if both parties showed their willingness to engage in ADR at an early stage.[71] Obviously, an evaluation of how other jurisdictions administer a mandatory mediation programme also fails to tell the reader what is the real and exact meaning of 'coercion'.[72]

However, this chapter is not interested in debating whether ADR is either voluntary or mandatory based on the criteria of 'coercion in mediation' and 'coercions within mediation'. A different approach is taken by analysing the relationship between ADR and unfair prejudice proceedings. An analysis of the coexistence of ADR and the court-based approach to the resolution of shareholder disputes in the new statutory unfair prejudice provisions is, potentially, very significant. It raises a line of argument that both ADR and shareholder litigation processes are compatible on the basis that each process, while similar, has different functions. Both processes can be applied contemporaneously within the new statutory unfair prejudice regime. The following discussion examines the relationship between private informal dispute resolution processes and unfair prejudice proceedings.

---

mediation process. By contrast with coercion 'within' mediation, this approach may run counter to the core notion of self-determination.

[68] Timothy Hedeen, 'Coercion and Self-Determination in Court-Connected Mediation: All Mediations Are Voluntary, but Some Are More Voluntary Than Others', *The Justice System Journal*, 26:3 (2005), 273–291 at 64.

[69] Roselle L. Wissler, 'Court-connected Mediation in General Civil Cases: What We Know from Empirical Research', *Ohio State Journal on Dispute Resolution*, 17 (2002), 641–704 at 697.

[70] For an excellent discussion on the ways to conduct an empirical research on court-connected mediation programme see John Lande, 'Commentary: Focusing on Program Design Issues in Future Research on Court Connected Mediation', *Conflict Resolution Quarterly*, 22:1–2 (2004), 89–100 at 90–91.

[71] Quek, 'Mandatory Mediation', 487.

[72] Ibid., 488–490.

5.3 Taking 'Integration' Seriously: Exploring a Link between ADR and the Unfair Prejudice Proceeding

This section contends that ADR and court-based shareholder litigation can coexist coherently within the statutory unfair prejudice regime.[73] First, both ADR and unfair prejudice proceedings can coexist, as both dispute resolution methods support the consensual nature of contractual agreements.[74] Second, an analysis of contemporary theories of law (systems theory) regarding the nature of unfair prejudice proceedings in the Hong Kong context points out that the new statutory unfair prejudice regime is sufficiently flexible to accommodate the existence of ADR for the resolution of shareholder disputes.[75] A flexible procedural regime is one that is subordinated to the CO, the latter retaining the discretionary powers of the court to refer matters to ADR for shareholder disputes after the court proceedings are issued.

5.3.1 Relating ADR and the Statutory Unfair Prejudice Proceedings to the Principle of Freedom of Contract

This section contends that both ADR and unfair prejudice proceedings can coexist, as each of these methods recognizes the effect of contractual agreements made by the parties.[76]

Section 724 (and its predecessor Section 168A) of the Hong Kong CO developed from the principles of contract law that the relationship between the members is governed not solely by the company's constitution or any collateral shareholders' agreements.[77] This provision in addition imported the doctrine of good faith from the law of partnership which recognizes some personal relationship or personal dealings between the members in a small quasi-partnership type of private limited company.[78] In a small family business, it is justified for the court to grant relief under the statutory remedies where there is a breach of some promise or arrangement between the members in which equity would be regarded as contrary to good faith. The flexibility of the unfair

---

[73] Section 727 of the Companies Ordinance.
[74] See Section 5.3.1.
[75] See Section 5.3.2.
[76] See Section 5.3.1.
[77] *Re Yung Kee Holdings Ltd* 3 [2014] 2 HKLRD 313 at 344–45 (citing Robin Hollington, *Hollington on Shareholders' Rights*, 7th ed. (London: Sweet & Maxwell, 2013), 195–196).
[78] Ibid.

prejudice provision permits the Hong Kong courts to choose either a robust (assessing the shareholder's reasonable expectations based on the traditional equitable principles) or a restrictive approach (reviewing whether that there is a breach of terms in the company's constitution or any collateral agreements between shareholders) to reviewing the actions of majority shareholders.[79] This is consonant with Lord Hoffman's reasoning in *O'Neill v. Philips* that the sanctity of the contract should be considered and reflected as the guiding principle for the court to determine relief under the statutory remedies.[80]

By comparison, participation in private informal out-of-court processes is premised on the mutual contractual ADR agreement made by the parties in advance or after the dispute between them had arisen.[81] The approach that recognizes the effect of contractual agreements made by the parties is in line with the 'market-based' ADR model.[82] Although a court-connected ADR programme is now embedded in the normal operations of many Hong Kong courts, neither the court nor the amended court rules state explicitly that the court is the best 'forum' for allocating various types of disputes to different dispute processes.[83] This illustrates that the approach that has been adopted by the Hong Kong Judiciary in promoting ADR is entirely different from those in Singapore and the United States.[84] For example, ADR services are considered to be an integral part of the justice system in Singapore. Singapore has a multi-door courthouse (i.e., the Court Dispute Resolution at the Primary Dispute

---

[79] Paul Davies, *Introduction to Company Law* (Oxford: Oxford University Press, 2010), 234–236.

[80] [1999] BCC at 606–607.

[81] Main, 'ADR', 353.

[82] Nadjia Alexander, 'Visualising the ADR Landscape', *ADR Bulletin*, 7:3 (2004), 1–3.

[83] At present, the court-connected initiatives include not only the establishment of the Mediation Information Offices that provide litigants with relevant information on mediation. In addition, the Hong Kong Judiciary worked together in 2001 with the private sector such as the Hong Kong Mediation Council, the Hong Kong Bar Association, the Law Society of Hong Kong, the Chartered Institute of Arbitrators (East Asia Branch), the Hong Kong Institute of Arbitrators, the Hong Kong Institute of Architects, the Hong Kong Institute of Surveyors and the Hong Kong Mediation Centre to set up The Joint Mediation Helpline Office in offering one-stop mediation referral services.

[84] Henry J. Brown and Arthur Marriott, *ADR Principles and Practice*, 2nd ed. (London: Sweet & Maxwell, 2011), 92. The concept of 'Multi-Door Courthouse' was originated from Professor Frank E. A. Sander at the Pound Conference, which was sponsored by the American Bar Association in the year of 1976. In this conference, Professor Sander notes that ADR processes might be used in conjunction with, or as alternatives to, formal litigation processes, as this might improve the efficacy of the court system in view of the bourgeoning dockets and congestion in the courts.

Resolution Centre) for its subordinate courts.[85] A typical feature of this model is that the court usually provides adequate infrastructure for either assisting or directing parties to choose the most appropriate dispute resolution mechanism, either a formal court litigation process or an extrajudicial procedure.[86]

The Hong Kong Judiciary, by contrast, places emphasis on voluntariness as an essential feature of a court-connected ADR programme.[87] It is fair to say that the judge-led ADR model in Hong Kong has maintained a clear distinction between the role of an adjudicator, who is responsible for exercising its case management powers to expedite the trial preparation process leading to conclusion of proceedings,[88] and the role of a 'dispute resolver' or 'dispute manager', who offers a range of formal and informal dispute resolution processes to assist the parties in resolving their disputes.[89] This is particularly true because the court outsources ADR services instead of treating ADR services as an integral part of the justice system.[90] This means that a trained mediator is contracted to offer mediation services not only at the stage of case management conferences, but also at different stages in the litigation proceedings.

Nonetheless, the involvement of the Hong Kong court in assisting in the effective use of ADR seems necessary. Courts are generally involved in the areas of enforcing contractual arrangements made by the parties for the resolution of shareholder disputes, making various forms of judicial practices on mediation (such as Practice Directions 3.3 and 31) to assist the parties in engaging a mediation process sincerely.[91] On such a basis,

---

[85]   The Subordinate Courts of Singapore include the District Courts, the Magistrates' Courts, the Specialized Courts and the Small Claims Tribunals. With effect from 7 March 2004, the Subordinate Courts of Singapore will be renamed 'State Courts'. For an excellent discussion about the development of ADR in Singapore, see Marvin Bay et al., 'Note: The Integration of Alternative Dispute Resolution within the Subordinate Courts' Adjudication Process', *Singapore Academic of Law Journal*, 16 (2004), 501–515 at 509 and Michael Hwang et al., 'ADR in East Asia' in J. C. Goldsmith et al. (eds.), *ADR in Business: Practice and Issues across Countries and Cultures*, Vol. I (The Hague: Kluwer Law International, 2006), 154–155.

[86]   Alexander, 'Visualising the ADR Landscape', 2.

[87]   Hong Kong Judiciary, *Reform of the Civil Justice System in Hong Kong*, Final Report of the Working Party on Civil Justice Reform (Hong Kong Judiciary, 2004), paras. 826–827.

[88]   Order 1A, Rule 4(2)(2)(b) to (d) and (f) to (l) of the RHC provides that judge must exercise his or her case management powers to expedite the trial preparation process, which includes identifying the key issues in the case, summarily disposing of some irrelevant issues, making the order and fixing timetables for the procedural steps in preparing cases for trial.

[89]   Order 1A, Rule 4(2)(b) of the RHC provides that the judge must exercise his or her case management powers to encourage the parties to use ADR procedures where appropriate.

[90]   Alexander, 'Visualising the ADR Landscape', 2.

[91]   Practice Direction 31, para. 13 provides that parties may make a joint application to the court when they were unable to reach agreement on certain proposals in the Mediation

court-connected ADR initiatives for shareholder disputes in Hong Kong are orientated towards the voluntary-based ADR model. This model puts undue emphasis on the clear division of labour between the supporting roles of the court to enforce the contracts made by the parties and the privately funded ADR organizations that offer various ADR devices and experienced neutral third parties for litigants to choose in resolving their disputes.

In sum, both the Hong Kong government and Judiciary recognize the notion of voluntariness as the key factor that constitutes the market-based ADR model.[92] Unsurprisingly, the voluntary-based ADR model in Hong Kong fits well with unfair prejudice proceedings, in which the Hong Kong courts endorsed the sanctity of contract for determining relief under the statutory remedies.[93] If the parties have included ADR clauses in their articles or shareholder agreements in advance for contracting out of the statutory minority remedies of unfair prejudice, the courts might be willing to facilitate rather than displace this form of contractual mechanism.[94] On such a basis, both ADR and unfair prejudice proceedings can coexist.

This analysis highlights the policy implications with regard to the future development of ADR for the resolution of shareholder disputes in Hong Kong. It is probably desirable to incorporate ADR into the statutory unfair prejudice provisions, as both ADR and unfair prejudice proceedings support the consensual nature of contractual arrangements. However, this analysis raises another issue of how the new statutory unfair prejudice regime in Hong Kong can accommodate the existence of private dispute resolution mechanisms for shareholder disputes.

5.3.2 Including ADR in Developing New Procedural Rules

This section suggests that the new statutory unfair prejudice regime is sufficiently flexible to accommodate the existence of ADR for the resolution of shareholder disputes. This premise is based on the assumption that the statutory unfair prejudice provisions are ideologically committed to the

---

Notice and Mediation Response in relation to the mediation. This means that the court may assist the parties to explore an appropriate ADR process. Recent case law illustrates that parties are generally unable to reach agreement on the following matters: (1) choice of mediators (2) minimum level of participation and (3) stay of proceedings until the result of mediation.

[92] See Civil Justice Reform: Final Report, supra note 83, paras. 826–827.
[93] *O'Neill v. Phillips* [1999] BCC at 607 and *Re Kam Fai Electroplanting Factory Ltd* [2004] HKEC 556 (unreported, HCCW 534/2000, 8 December 2003) (CFI) at paras. 39–40.
[94] *Quiksilver Greater China Ltd v. Quiksilver Glorious Sun JV Ltd* [2014] HKEC 1241 (unreported, HCCW 364 and 365/2013, 25 July 2014) (CFI).

constitutional values in the Hong Kong Basic Law. This analysis can be understood from two aspects.

First, the relative autonomy of the statutory unfair prejudice provisions with respect to the political sphere captures the interest of private enterprises by safeguarding the free operation of business affairs through contractual mechanisms.[95] Second, the statutory unfair prejudice regime remains relatively autonomous from the judicial sphere as ethical considerations are generally taken by the court in articulating public values in the constitution. On such a basis, the court will not make any order to compel the parties resort to ADR in lieu of the traditional court litigation process for shareholder disputes.[96] Subsystem theories become relevant here as law is being viewed as a 'relatively self-contained social subsystem' that can accommodate itself to social change.[97]

The most influential systems theorist in the legal discipline is Luhmann. He views society as a functionally differentiated social system that comprises a number of functional subsystems.[98] The legal system is, therefore, regarded as one of the functional subsystems within a society, and it can be viewed as an 'autopoietic system'. Even though law is a normatively closed system, it is a cognitively open one by transforming various external factors for responding to external social, economic and political changes.[99] However, this model may not fit nicely into the analysis of the main function of the unfair prejudice provisions. This is due to the fact that Luhmann's vision of 'autopoietic legal system' is rooted in the European Continental perspective of law.[100]

However, it is impossible to treat law as a unique set of binary codes of lawful/unlawful, legal/illegal in analysing the common law legal system.[101]

---

[95] Article 110 of the Hong Kong Basic Law.
[96] Article 35 of the Hong Kong Basic Law.
[97] Lawrence M. Friedman, 'Legal Culture and Social Development', *Law & Society Review*, 4 (1969), 29–44 at 37.
[98] Sharyn L. Roach Anleu, *Law and Social Change* (London: SAGE, 2010), 44–45.
[99] Ibid., p. 46 and Richard Lempert and Ann Arbor, 'The Autonomy of Law: Two Visions Compared' in Gunther Teubner (ed.), *Autopoietic Law: A New Approach to Law and Society* (Berlin: Walter de Gruyter, 1988), 178–179. Law is a normatively close system means that law follows its internal legal logics (an abstract legal proposition) instead of norms derived from any social or political groups. This means that law reproduces itself but does not insulate itself from social and economic forces. However, law can change to the extent that external factors are filtered selectively into legal structures according to their own legal logic of development.
[100] Roach Anleu, 'Law and Social Change', 45.
[101] Lempert and Arbor, 'The Autonomy of Law', 184. According to Lempert and Arbor, Luhmann's 'vision of autopoiesis appears quite close to the ordinary Anglo-American perspective on how common law courts produce and reproduce the law'.

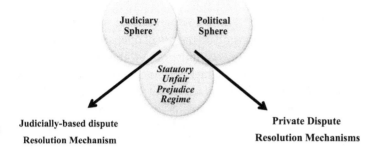

Figure 5.2 An analysis of the statutory unfair prejudice provisions.

This is partly due to the fact that the law has its own distinctively legal meaning entailing specific consequences.[102] On the contrary, an understanding of the idea of relative legal autonomy illuminates that a statutory unfair prejudice regime sits at the intersection of the political and judicial domains (see Figure 5.2).[103] On that basis, it is more appropriate to view the new statutory unfair prejudice provisions as being relatively autonomous from the Judiciary and the political system. My justification is based on the following two grounds.

First, the new statutory unfair prejudice regime remains relatively autonomous from the political sphere. This means that the law is cognitively open to the influence of political issues. This argument rests on the assumption that the function of the law-making process is assigned to the legislative branch of the polity.[104] In particular, the corporatist style

---

[102] Ibid., 158–159 and 169 and Gunther Teubner, 'Introduction to Autopoietic Law', in Gunther Teubner (ed.), *Autopoietic Law: A New Approach to Law and Society* (Berlin: Walter de Gruyter, 1988), 7. Lempert and Arbor contend that the autonomy of legal system 'is, at best, a relative matter; that is, it can be at most partial.' This means that the legal system can look to itself, as it has its set of forms to which it can fit actors and actions. Thus, the Anglo-American approach is able 'to distinguish varying degrees of autonomy by defining empirically testable criteria of relative autonomy'. In contrast with the European Continental approach, its legal system distinguishes norms from facts, and thus norms can be developed only by applying an abstract legal proposition (unique binary code) to a concrete fact situation.

[103] This argument was based on the assumption that 'the idea of legal autonomy can be more closely achieved in the law application or judicial process than in the law creation or legislative process. The legislature sits at the intersection of the political and legal spheres'. For details, see Lempert and Arbor, 'The Autonomy of Law', 159–161.

[104] Talcott Parsons, 'Law as an Intellectual Stepchild', in Harry M. Johnson (ed.), *Social System and Legal Process: Theory, Comparative Perspectives and Special Studies* (San Francisco: Jossey-Bass, 1978), 23–32 and Lempert and Arbor, 'The Autonomy of Law', 161.

of law-making processes in Hong Kong invariably privileges big business and elite professional groups to vest their substantial political interests into the law-making process.[105] From this perspective, corporatist tendencies may lead to a rapid expansion of 'the use of open-ended standards and general clauses in legislation, administration, and adjudication'.[106] However, it is fair to say that the maintenance of Hong Kong's status as an international financial hub had a place in the government's drive for corporate law reform.[107] By contrast, corporate scandals were the key impetus of the British government to enact the statutory unfair prejudice provisions to regulate the abuse of powers by majority shareholders.[108] On that basis, the substantive provisions of the corporate law in Hong Kong are orientated towards the free market-approach.

Undoubtedly, statutory unfair prejudice provisions can also be characterized as the 'voluntaristic model of law' that facilitates contractual arrangements made by shareholders.[109] This view can be reflected in the current law reform in Hong Kong as lawmakers opted for statutory reinstatement of the arrangements in Section 168A of the CO with slight modifications.[110] Although the new 2014 legislation does not provide any authoritative guidance on the definition of 'unfairly prejudicial' conduct, the shareholders' contractual agreement and the conduct of the company's affairs provides benchmarks for analysing whether the defendant's conduct amounts to being 'unfairly prejudicial.'

The unfair prejudice provisions remain relatively autonomous from the political sphere as they place emphasis on open-ended legal principles in regulating the unfair prejudicial conducts.[111] Nonetheless, the unfair prejudice provisions are ideologically committed to the constitutional

---

[105] Angus Young, 'Reforming Directors' Duties in Hong Kong: The Journey, Stakeholders and Oversights', *International Company and Commercial Law Review*, 23:4 (2012), 142–154 at 144.

[106] Roberto Magabeira Unger, *Law in Modern Society: Toward A Criticism of Social Theory* (New York: Free Press, 1976), 193–194.

[107] The HKSAR Chief Executive Donald Tsang, *The 2006–07 Policy Address: Proactive Pragmatic Always People First* (2006), para. 21.

[108] David Sugarman, 'Reconceptualising Company Law: Reflections on the Law Commission's Consultation Paper on Shareholder Remedies: Part 1', *The Company Lawyer*, 18:8 (1997), 226–247 at 231.

[109] See supra note 89.

[110] Hong Kong Financial Services and the Treasury Bureau, *New Companies Ordinance: Subsidiary Legislation for Implementation of the New Companies Ordinance (Phase Two Consultation Document)* (Hong Kong Financial Services and the Treasury Bureau, 2012), para. 12.3.

[111] Lempert and Arbor, 'The Autonomy of Law', 160.

value under the Hong Kong Basic Law as it facilitates the free operation of business through private contracting mechanisms.[112] In sum, this analysis reveals that big business enterprises and professional groups in Hong Kong have exerted their political influences in formulating and implementing the corporate law for safeguarding the free operation of businesses.

Second, the statutory unfair prejudice provisions which place emphasis on both open-ended standards and discretionary approaches have led to the expansion of judicial discretion in resolving shareholder disputes. This illustrates that the relative autonomy of the unfair prejudice provisions is justifiable by the fact that the statutory interpretation and sanctioning of legal norms are generally handled by the Judiciary.[113] In any case, the use of 'purposive' statutory construction of the statute will often produce the same result as a 'literal' interpretation.[114] This argument rests on the assumption that the function of the Judiciary is to apply legal provisions in accordance with general principles. Thus, an argument in favour of expanding the court's power in the unfair prejudice jurisdiction to promote alternative forms of private dispute resolution methods is to be welcomed.[115]

Nevertheless, the discretion and powers bestowed upon the court by Section 727(1)(a) of the new CO for regulating the conduct of unfair prejudice proceedings should not be undermined. This legislation recognizes the two benefits of judicial discretion to make a relevant court order to adjourn the unfair prejudice proceeding by requiring both parties to attempt ADR processes. First, the new provisions of the minority protection are couched in a high level of generality through open-ended statutory languages and principles. The 2014 statutory unfair prejudice regime allows judges to make discretionary and flexible rules in managing unfair prejudice proceedings. Under the rules, the court may give a direction in requiring each party to stay unfair prejudice proceedings until the parties have attempted ADR. This procedural regime strikes the right balance between allowing judges' discretion to make an order to refer a matter to

---

[112] See Article 110 of the Hong Kong Basic Law.
[113] The 'literal' rule of statutory interpretation states that words used in the statute must be given their plain, ordinary or literal meaning. Thus, the judges interpreted legislation in a cautious and conservative manner. Cheffins illustrates a good example of how judges interpreted the term 'oppression' under Section 210 of the Companies Act 1948 in a cautious manner. For details see Brian R. Cheffins, *Company Law: Theory, Structure, and Operation* (Oxford: Clarendon Press, 1997), 353.
[114] Ibid., 350–351.
[115] See Section 5.3.3(a).

ADR and at the same time creating certainty as ADR referral is made in accordance with Practice Direction 3.3.

Although the new companies legislation permits the Judiciary to make procedural rules in regulating the conduct of unfair prejudice proceedings, this does not mean that the rule provides an extensive set of detailed codes/guidelines for the court to refer cases to any form of informal dispute resolution processes. This procedural rule may create hardship and mischief if it does not contain any specific circumstances that referral cases to any form of out-of-court processes could be considered inappropriate and problematic.[116] It is to be welcomed that the rule would provide broad discretionary rights for the judges to exclude certain cases if an out-of-court process is considered inappropriate in some special circumstances. This suggested framework may prevent judges from exercising their discretionary power to refer cases to any form of informal dispute resolution processes in an arbitrary manner. This framework also provides a hierarchy of principles to ameliorate the difficulties that could be created by strict and technical applications of subordinate rules to refer cases to ADR.[117]

Second, the Judiciary interprets the rules in a fashion which fulfils the original ADR policy goals.[118] This rests on the assumption that judges prefer to strive for the true meaning of the constitutional value by applying the law in accordance to legal principles.[119] In this regard, judges are obliged to comply with constitutional value under the Basic Law for safeguarding the right of access to the court.[120] If the judges observe the legal rights of disputants to access the court expressed in the Constitution, the inclusion of a set of informal out-of-court processes into the companies unfair prejudice petitions rules would not hamper the fundamental rights of a shareholder to obtain redress from the court. On such a basis, the incorporation of an ADR scheme into the statutory unfair prejudice regime would not of itself amount to a compulsory ADR programme, particularly in the Hong Kong corporate context.

In sum, the new statutory unfair prejudice provisions are flexible in accommodating the existence of extrajudicial processes for shareholder disputes. The statutory unfair prejudice provisions can be conceptualized

---

[116] Thomas O. Main, 'Traditional Equity and Contemporary Procedure', *Washington Law Review Association*, 78 (2003), 429–515 at 513.

[117] Ibid.

[118] See Chapter 4.

[119] Owen M. Fiss, 'The Supreme Court 1978 Term Forward: The Forms of Justice', *Harvard Law Review*, 93 (1979), 1–58 at 12–14.

[120] Article 35 of the Hong Kong Basic Law.

as the dichotomy between court adjudication of shareholder disputes, applying publicly created rules and principles, and a private (extralegal) contractual regime, applying privately developed rules in resolving shareholder disputes.[121] The distinctive nature of the statutory unfair prejudice provisions renders both ADR and court-based shareholder litigation processes compatible. Nevertheless, the new statutory unfair prejudice regime empowers judges to understand the differences between ADR and unfair prejudice proceedings with concern for the 'underlying objectives' outlined in Order 1A of the civil procedure rules.

5.4 Improving the Effective Use of ADR to Supplement Unfair Prejudice Proceedings

This part suggests that ADR should be included in the statutory unfair prejudice regime to complement the court-based shareholder litigation process. This argument rests on the assumption that ADR is perceived as being compatible with the unfair prejudice proceedings, as each of these methods, while similar, has unique functions.

Many have come to the view that there is a tension between ADR and the court adjudication process.[122] This tension is partly due to the fact that ADR is incapable of promoting public values, whereas the court can articulate public values expressed in the Constitution through the adjudication process.[123] This analysis illustrates that both ADR and the court adjudication process should be separated and operated in two distinctive systems (i.e., private/public dispute resolution systems).[124] Under this bipolar system, each dispute resolution process should be treated as an autonomous entity.[125]

But even assuming that both extrajudicial process and public court adjudication processes are performing different functions, the two dispute resolution processes can coexist and be applied within the legal system in a complementary manner. The advent of a court-connected ADR programme exemplifies that ADR takes place under the auspices of the

---

[121] Rule 6(f) of the C(UPP)R.

[122] Owen M. Fiss, 'Out of Eden', *The Yale Law Journal*, 94:7 (1985), 1669–1673 at 953 and Jean R. Sternlight, 'Is Alternative Dispute Resolution Consistent with the Rule of Law? Lessons from Abroad', *DePaul Law Review*, 56 (2006), 569–592 at 582.

[123] Amy J. Cohen, 'Revisiting Against Settlement: Some Reflections on Dispute Resolution and Public Values', *Fordham Law Review*, 78 (2009), 1143–1170 at 1148–1157.

[124] Reuben, 'Constitutional Gravity', 953.

[125] Ibid.

legal system. Informal dispute resolution devices can be used to deal with the problems associated with lengthy and costly shareholder litigation. Nonetheless, rule makers may encounter teething problems to sustain this virtue by preserving both the public and private dispute resolution within a single unified legislative framework. For example, courts might not be able to exercise their quality control by scrutinizing mediated settlement agreements if the legislation provides express provisions in relation to the duty of confidentiality.[126] This is due to the fact that lawmakers fail to recognize the fact that both ADR and unfair prejudice proceedings can coexist on the ground that each of these processes originates from different functions despite being similar.

Indeed, both extrajudicial process and unfair prejudice proceedings provide alternatives to the traditional legal rule-bound approach to dispute resolution. Like the ADR process, the statutory unfair prejudice regime moderates the rigidity of the *Foss v. Harbottle* Rules by empowering the court to exercise its discretionary power in regulating the conduct of a company's affairs.[127] Apart from that, the doctrine of good faith, which is well established in partnership contract, is imported into company law in cases where a special relationship existed between shareholders, justifying the court to apply equitable principles of good faith to restrain on the conduct of the majority shareholders.[128] Thus, the statutory unfair prejudice regime offers a wider range of remedies, albeit it usually limits remedies to monetary damages, injunctive relief or court-ordered buyout relief.[129]

Each process, however, varies greatly in the following aspects. First, an ADR process such as mediation is not a self-sufficient system in generating public norms that public judicial institutions could really support.[130] The division of two separate regimes that governs the procedural aspects of the presentation of an unfair prejudice petition (such as a court-ordered referral to ADR) and substantive requirements of unfair prejudice remedies should be maintained under the company law. This prevents the court from interpreting the company law arbitrarily by identifying the relevant procedural solutions (such as ADR) that may be applicable to an analysis of the substantive unfair prejudice provisions.

---

[126] Section 8(2) of the Mediation Ordinance (Cap. 620) relates to the issue of confidentiality of mediation communications. This section provides that in general, a person must not disclose mediation communication except as provided by subsection (2) or (3).

[127] D. D. Prentice, 'The Theory of the Firm: Minority Shareholder Oppression: Sections 459–461 of the Companies Act 1985', *Oxford Journal of Legal Studies*, 8:1 (1988), 55–91.

[128] Hollington, 'Shareholders' Rights', 251–254.

[129] Section 725 of the Companies Ordinance.

[130] Reuben, 'Constitutional Gravity', 953.

At present, the new Companies Ordinance maintains the boundary separating a regime to deal with the substantive matters of shareholders' rights[131] and the procedural regime where the court may offer effective solutions to redress shareholder grievances.[132] The statutory change with respect to the subordinate procedural rules that empowers the court to make an order to refer cases to ADR is to be welcomed. The law neither abridges nor modifies substantive rights in an unfair prejudice proceeding as ADR is merged into the procedural regime of the primary mandate, while leaving the substantive matters related to shareholders' rights to litigate intact.

In particular, clarity and accessibility of ADR can be achieved as the Companies (Unfair Prejudice Petitions) Proceedings Rules which applied to petitions made under Section 724 confer on the court a wide discretion to make an order that the proceeding or any part of it could be referred to mediation or other alternative processes.[133] In this sense, the new procedural rules relating to proceedings under Section 724 provide clarity on what is expected of the court in exercising its case management power to facilitate parties to engage in ADR.[134] This prevents the Hong Kong courts from misusing their case management powers to compel parties to postpone the court proceeding until parties have attempted ADR.

Moreover, neither the court nor the lawmakers in Hong Kong state explicitly that an individual who refuses to comply with an order to attempt ADR may be open to a charge of contempt of court.[135] Instead, it would seem probable that an individual's refusal to comply with an order to attempt ADR may amount to contempt by disobedience to a judgement, order or process (i.e., civil contempt).[136] Thus, it is likely that the contemnor will be punished by a fine.[137] Such a procedural device that empowers the court to make an order for ADR at the stage of petition is much in line with the policy of the Civil Justice Reform (CJR) in Hong Kong that mediation and other alternative processes should remain voluntary.[138] On that basis, the inclusion of ADR in the statutory unfair prejudice regime is only ancillary and intended to assist the courts to operate the provisions

---

[131] Sections 723–725 of the Companies Ordinance.
[132] Section 727 of the Companies Ordinance.
[133] Rule 6(f) of the Companies (Unfair Prejudice Petitions) Proceeding Rules (Cap. 622L).
[134] Order 1A, Rule 1(e) of the Rules of the High Court.
[135] Shirley Shipman, 'Compulsory Mediation: The Elephant in the Room', Civil Justice Quarterly, 30:2 (2011), 163–191 at 163. It has been suggested that an individual's refusal to comply with a compulsory order to mediate may trigger either imprisonment for contempt of court or discontinuance of the action.
[136] Halsbury's Law of Hong Kong, para. 110.082.
[137] Ibid., paras. 110.073–110.074.
[138] Final Report of the Working Party on Civil Justice Reform, para. 827.

of the minority protection in the principal legislation in a more effective manner.

Second, private dispute resolution mechanisms (particularly mediation) should be treated as a necessary complement to unfair prejudice proceedings so that shareholders can apply a multitude of non-legal principles to enforce their contractual relationships. Contemporary legal theorists generally assume that a corporation is best understood as a 'nexus of contract' that individuals voluntarily joined together to form an association by contract.[139] In private companies, the contractual terms in governing the affairs of the company are highly flexible and incomplete. The flexibility of this contractual arrangement allows shareholders to adjust their ongoing relationship in accommodating the fast-changing commercial world. This means that a 'relational contract'[140] is likely to have a role to play, in particular for sustaining long-term relationships and avoiding adversarial tendencies among shareholders in a private company.

The relational extent of such a contract may be measured by a variety of factors such as cooperation, organizational culture, trust, good faith or duration of contract.[141] In this regard, contractual factors in governing the relational extent of a contract between shareholders in a private company are not limited to legal factors, such as the contractual duties of good faith which are owned in equity in the case of quasi-partnerships.[142] The centrality of non-legal factors should not be overlooked in analysing the

---

[139] Melvin A. Eisenberg, 'The Conception that the Corporation Is a Nexus of Contracts, and the Dual Nature of the Firm', *The Journal of Corporation Law*, 24 (1998), 819–836 at 819. Eisenberg said: '[T]he conception that the corporation is a nexus of contacts ... has dominated the law and economics literature in corporate law.' See also John Parkinson, 'Inclusive Company Law', in John de Lacy (ed.), *The Reform of United Kingdom Company Law* (London: Cavendish, 2002), 27.

[140] Ian R. Macneil, 'Contracts: Adjustment of Long-Term Economic Relations under Classical Neoclassical, and Relational Contract Law', *Northwestern University Law Review*, 72:6 (1978), 854–905 at 886–887. According to Macneil, 'relational contract' is generally used to govern a long-term relationship in which all contingencies and performance standards cannot be specified in advance. See also Oliver E. Williamson, 'Transaction-Cost Economics: The Governance of Contractual Relations', in Peter J. Buckley and Jonathan Michie (eds.), *Firms, Organizations and Contract: A Reader in Industrial Organization* (Oxford: Oxford University Press, 1996), 172.

[141] Ibid.

[142] Hollington, 'Shareholders' Rights', 251. The contractual duties of good faith can be divided into two broad categories. The first type is 'express contractual duties of good faith' which are not originated from a purely commercial, arm's length, relationships between 'competing businessmen'. Such provisions used to be relatively unusual in dealing with personal relationships or personal dealings between members in a closely held corporation. The second type is 'implied duty of good faith' which is established in partnership contracts.

underlying causes which contribute to the breakdown of personal relationships between shareholders in a private company.

Rights-based, determinative dispute resolution processes such as unfair prejudice proceedings are oriented towards formal justice system.[143] Proceedings for relief from unfair prejudice often entail complex factual investigation, as a finding of unfair prejudice conduct is often based on the cumulative nature of the supporting allegations of facts instead of focusing on the parties' real motivations or underlying interests in the dispute.[144] In particular, the open-ended language of the statutory unfair prejudice provision frees the court from a technical consideration of legal rights, which allow judges to construe the scope of shareholders' interests as broadly as intended by the law to give the court wide discretion to grant relief. Therefore, the types of shareholders' interests that fall within Section 724 are not limited to conduct affecting the strict legal rights of members under the articles of association, but extend to wider interests of members, with the court entitled to take into account equitable considerations.[145] In other words, the types of shareholders' interests that fall within the provision can only be determined objectively by the court, in which case, the contractual duties of good faith owed in a quasi-partnership type company could be implied or inferred from an agreement or understanding between shareholders enforceable in equity.

Apparently, the courts rely heavily on an elusive legal concept, the partnership concept of good faith (such as fiduciary duty), as the criterion governing the contractual relationship between members in a private company.[146] Moreover, the courts are acting in a manner which is consistent

In a case of the relationship between shareholders as a 'quasi-partnership', it is justified for the court to apply the principles of good faith derived from the law of partnership.

[143] Mary Rowe and Corinne Bendersky, 'Workplace Justice, Zero Tolerance, and Zero Barriers', in Thomas A. Kochan and David B. Lipsky (eds.), *Negotiaions and Change: From the Workplace to Society* (Ithaca, NY: Cornell University Press, 2003), 119.

[144] English Law Commission, *Shareholder Remedies Consultation* (Law Commission Consultation Paper No. 142, 1996), para. 1.7.

[145] Prentice, 'The Theory of the Firm', 61. Prentice points out that the types of interests of a member in a quasi-partnership type of company are as follows: (1) the right to participate in the affair of the company so as to guarantee some return on his investment; (2) the right to protect his investment in the company which will often take the form of the investment of skills and labour; and (3) the ability to monitor the conduct of his co-venturers. See also Stefan H. C. Lo and Charles Z. Qu, *Law of Companies in Hong Kong* (Hong Kong: Sweet & Maxwell/Thomas Reuters, 2013), 439.

[146] Jonathan R. Macey, *Corporate Governance: Promise Kept, Promise Broken* (Princeton, NJ: Princeton University Press, 2008), 22. According to Macey, fiduciary duties are part of the contractual nature of the corporation and exist to fill in the blanks and inevitable oversights in the actual contracts used by business organizations. The purpose of fiduciary

with the 'hypothetical bargaining model' by focusing on the contractual foundation that the parties themselves have established.[147] Consequently, the 'types of shareholders' interests' that may be protected under the statutory unfair prejudice provision are artificially constructed by the judge instead of through the natural language of interests that derives from the parties' real motivations or underlying interests in the disputes.

In general, the underlying interests in shareholder disputes include 'people's feelings about what is basically desirable' and these form a part of the parties' motivations and aspirations, including needs and values.[148] There are several dimensions that can be used to describe 'the underlying interests' of the parties, as some are tangible such as material goods, some are intangible such as power and others are specific to certain parties.[149] This stands in sharp contrast against the types of shareholders' interests which are covered under Section 724 of the Ordinance.

In a private company limited by shares, personal and business affairs of shareholders are closely intertwined, and it is inevitable that from time to time the overlapping relationship between family and business ownership and management could lead to personality clashes and family quarrels.[150] It is not surprising that personal interests of the party (such as power or wealth) are primary causes of shareholder disputes. Without exploring the underlying interests of the parties, it would hardly be possible for the parties to generate an effective solution that meet their needs. Interest-based dispute resolution processes such as facilitative mediation seem to be the most appropriate methods of identifying the parties' underlying interests, as these are oriented towards the community justice system.[151] Mediation opens channels of communication between the shareholders, and seeks to assist them to focus and prioritize their personal interests instead of their respective legal rights of the disputes. Shareholders are

---

duties is to provide people with the results that they would have bargained for if they had been able to anticipate the problem at hand and had contracted for its resolution in advance. Thus the law of business organizations in general and corporations in particular is highly contractual in nature.

[147] Cheffins, 'Company Law', 329.

[148] Dean G. Pruitt and Sung Hee Kim, *Social Conflict: Escalation, Stalemate, and Settlement*, 3rd ed. (New York: McGraw-Hill Higher Education, 2004), 15.

[149] Ibid., 16.

[150] Benjamin Means, 'NonMarket Values in Family Business', *William & Mary Law Review*, 54 (2013), 1185–1250, at 1214–1216. Typically, the fundamental understanding of minority shareholders in a quasi-partnership type of company is that they expect to actively participate in the management of the family business.

[151] Rowe and Bendersky, 'Workplace Justice', 119.

encouraged by the third party neutral (the mediator) to generate a mutually acceptable compromise or a creative solution that meets their real needs or underlying interests. The focus of parties' personal interests makes it possible to go to the roots of shareholder disputes, while avoiding harm to the business reputation and even preserving the relationship between the parties.[152] On that basis, the inclusion of mediation and other alternative processes into the procedural rules relating to unfair prejudice proceedings is entirely appropriate, as shareholders can apply a range of non-legal principles to enforce their contractual relationships.

In sum, different modes of dispute resolution methods (especially interest-based dispute resolution processes such as mediation) are important supplements to unfair prejudice proceedings. This can be explained by the fact that the court has construed the notions of 'unfairness' narrowly. The concept of unfairness under Section 724 is grounded on the contractual agreements and understandings made between the members.[153] The promissory nature of the concept of unfair prejudice often gives rise to evidentiary problems for the petitioners to prove that the alleged complaints could amount to unfairly prejudicial conduct as the concept of unfair prejudice is narrowly construed by the court.[154]

Courts, on the other hand, have reinforced the notions of early settlement following the House of Lords decision in *O'Neill v Phillips*.[155] This reflects that there could be no presumption in favour of court proceedings as the default procedure for the resolution of shareholder disputes. This judicial approach is particularly welcomed, as needs-based negotiation may not be suitable in some instances. For example, if there is uncertainty about the strengths and weaknesses of each party's claim, disputing parties may find it difficult to establish a range of possible solutions for them to reach an early settlement. On such a basis, rights-based procedures (such as early evaluation) might be the preferred first choice of

---

[152] Christian Bühring-Uhle, *Arbitration and Mediation in International Business* (The Hague: Kluwer Law International, 2006), 175.

[153] See, for example, *Re Ching Hing Construction Co Ltd* [2001] HKEC 1402 (unreported, HCCW 889/1999, 23 November 2001) (CFI) at para. 34; *Wong Man Yin v. Ricacorp Properties Ltd & Others* [2003] 3 HKLRD 75 PP. 88–89; *Re Kam Fai Electroplating Factory Ltd* [2004] HKEC 556 (unreported, HCCW 534/2000, 8 December 2003) at para. 82 and *Re Yung Kee Holdings Ltd* 3 [2014] 2 HKLRD 313 at 346.

[154] Jennifer Payne, 'Sections 459–461 Companies Act 1985 in Flux: The Future of Shareholder Protection', *Cambridge Law Journal*, 64:3 (2005), 647–677 at 660, citing *O' Neill v Phillips* [1999] BCC 600.

[155] [1999] BCC at 607.

the parties.[156] Early evaluation could possibly be more effective than the court-adjudicative process. The main objective of the early evaluation process is to help the disputing parties to develop a case plan that is narrowly tailored to manage the case efficiently.[157]

The policy objective behind the incorporation of an ADR provision into the statutory unfair prejudice regime is consistent with the recent judicial approach towards early settlement of shareholder disputes.[158] The new corporate regime gives the judicial substantial discretion to moderate the rigidity of both the legal and equitable remedies by directing the parties to attempt extrajudicial methods to resolve their disputes. If one effect of the reform of civil procedure rules in Hong Kong is to urge the court to consider the possibility of using ADR to resolve shareholder disputes at an early stage, then those cases that go to the trial are likely to be the most contentious, and therefore the use of court order to direct parties to attempt ADR is particularly justified at an early stage, either pre-action or after proceedings have been issued but before trial.

5.5 Conclusion

This chapter has analysed the relationship between private out-of-court processes and court based shareholder proceedings in Hong Kong. It has argued that both private out-of-court processes and public adjudicative unfair prejudice proceedings can coexist harmoniously within the new statutory unfair prejudice regime. This argument rests on the assumption that the new statutory unfair prejudice regime is flexible in accommodating the existence of informal dispute resolution methods for the resolution of shareholder disputes. As a whole, both ADR and unfair prejudice proceedings are compatible on the basis that the two processes, while similar, have their own unique functions.

The integration of ADR into the new statutory unfair prejudice regime recognizes that ADR is an important supplement to public court adjudication of shareholder disputes in Hong Kong. The corporate policy approach towards ADR is broadly in line with the voluntary court-connected ADR scheme. This can be explained by the fact that the new statutory unfair

---

[156] William L. Ury et al., *Getting Disputes Resolved: Designing Systems to Cut the Costs of Conflict*, 1st ed. (San Francisco: Jossey-Bass, 1988), 16.

[157] John Lande, 'The Movement Toward Early Case Handling in Courts and Private Dispute Resolution', *Ohio State Journal on Dispute Resolution*, 24:1 (2008), 81–130 at 99.

[158] Order 1A, Rule 1(d) of the RHC.

prejudice provision recognizes the role of the Judiciary in promoting the voluntary use of ADR while at the same time placing certain limits on the scope of judicial discretion in referring cases to ADR at the stage of commencing an unfair prejudice action.

Although ADR procedures such as mediation are generally accepted as an appropriate mode to resolve shareholder disputes through the enactment of the new corporate law, it is uncertain whether ADR have widely been used within the local legal professional community. The next chapter examines the diffusion of ADR practices among Hong Kong lawyers for the resolution of shareholder disputes in light of the recent reform of the civil justice system in Hong Kong that began in 2009.

Diffusion of Procedural Innovations

An Empirical Analysis of Hong Kong Lawyers' Attitudes about the Use of ADR for Shareholder Disputes

6.1 Introduction

Traditionally, most legal practitioners in Hong Kong employ the dominant model of 'adversarial lawyering philosophical map' for lawyering practice that assumes the dichotomous win–lose solution is largely determined by the application of authoritative legal principles.[1] The traditional assumption of the lawyer–client relationship is that the parties play more passive roles to participate in the process themselves whereas lawyers actively control the decision-making process.[2] The landscape of legal dispute in Hong Kong has changed dramatically since the Civil Justice Reform (CJR) began in 2009. The central aim of introducing a new set of court rules and case management directives relating to out-of-court processes is to bring about changes in lawyers' attitudes towards dispute resolution.[3] It seeks to shift their focus away from a traditional, litigation-centred approach to dispute resolution which relies solely on the court to apply legal rules and principles, and towards the use of pragmatic and cost-effective approaches to resolving shareholder disputes.

In particular, the dictum of Lam JA in *Lam Chi Tat Anthony v. Kam Ye Wai Andrew (No. 2)* is, potentially, very significant, as a failure by the legal practitioners to comply with a provision (i.e., Order 1A, rule 3 of the Rules of the High Court (RHC)) relating to their duty to assist the court's case management power to explore the possibility of using ADR to help their clients resolve disputes can be triggered by an adverse costs

---

[1] Hong Kong Judiciary, *Reform of the Civil Justice System in Hong Kong*, Interim Report and Consultative Paper on Civil Justice Reform (Hong Kong Judiciary, 2000), paras. 26–35.6. See also Leonard L. Riskin, 'Mediation and Lawyers', *Ohio State Law Journal*, 43 (1992), 29–60 at 43–48.

[2] Ibid.

[3] Johnson Lam Man-Hon, 'Mediation in the Context of CJR: The Role of the Judiciary', Conference on *CJR: What Has It Achieved?* (Hong Kong, 15 April 2010).

order, including wasted costs orders.[4] It is thus expected that Hong Kong lawyers are more responsive to significant changes in the disputing environment by encouraging their clients to participate voluntarily in ADR processes pursuant to the production of a mutually acceptable solution on their own terms.

Recent reforms of both the civil process and corporate law in Hong Kong have made mediation and other alternative processes integral parts of the unfair prejudice proceedings. The new disputing landscape creates an opportunity for Hong Kong lawyers to develop innovative models of disputing (such as mediation) for assisting their clients to resolve shareholder disputes. Hong Kong lawyers are more prepared to be involved in institutionalizing a new paradigm of dispute resolution practice into their normal disputing practice as a result of normative pressures which generally stem from professionalization.[5] Professionalization occurs when a group of powerful lawyers endeavour to monopolize the field of mediation, arbitration and other alternative processes from other professional experts through the development of a set of codes and training standards.[6]

Indeed, a group of powerful lawyers such as the Judiciary and the leaders of the two branches of the Hong Kong's legal profession, namely the Law Society of Hong Kong (the Law Society) and the Hong Kong Bar Association (the Bar Association) can accelerate the pace of institutionalization of private dispute resolution policy for shareholder disputes within the legal community. This is attributable to the fact that there is a linkage between normative legitimacy which is derived from a group of powerful lawyers and the diffusion of procedural innovations among members of the local legal professions.[7] Thus, it is not surprising that lawyers could exercise their influence over their clients to support the greater use of ADR for shareholder disputes and to institutionalize innovative dispute resolution models into their everyday practices through accreditation and training.[8]

---

[4] [2013] HKLRD 1085 at.1086. Order 62, rule 8 of the RHC empowers the court to make a wasted costs order against a legal representative.

[5] Paul J. DiMaggio and Walter W. Powell, 'The Iron Cage Revisited: Institutional Isomorphism and Collective Rationality in Organizational Fields', *American Sociological Review*, 48:2 (1983), 147–160 at 152–153.

[6] Eliot Freidson, *Professionalism: The Third Logic* (Cambridge, UK: Polity, 2001), 17 and Penny Brooker, *Mediation Law: Journey through Institutionalism to Juridification* (London: Routledge, 2013), 251.

[7] DiMaggio and Powell, 'The Iron Cage Revisited', 156.

[8] See Section 6.3.2.

The primary purpose of this chapter is to evaluate Hong Kong lawyers' attitudes towards the use of ADR for shareholder dispute since the CJR began in 2009. This focus is particularly relevant to the following discussion on how Hong Kong lawyers' approaches to resolving shareholder disputes are in conformity with ADR policy goals. At present, no prior empirical research has completely examined the relationship between legitimacy of ADR practices within the legal environment and the spread of ADR practice among lawyers in the Hong Kong context. Arguably, if mediation and other alternative processes are deemed to be legitimate and acceptable methods of settling shareholder disputes within the legal professions themselves, Hong Kong lawyers are more willing to adopt such practices in assisting their clients to resolve shareholder disputes. This argument rests on the following assumptions.

First, the legal professional organizations and law faculties in various universities are developing ADR courses and actively promoting mediation through the organization of workshops and conferences. The robustness of ADR training programmes offered by the legal professional organizations and the universities constitute a common cognitive basis and a shared legitimization among the legal professions in the Hong Kong community.[9] This provides justification for lawyers to act as 'dispute resolvers' or 'dispute managers' in offering a broad range of methods to assist their clients to resolve shareholder disputes, as they believe that they are competent and knowledgeable in ADR practices.[10]

Second, the Judiciary and the legal professional organizations could exert their tremendous influences either directly or indirectly on lawyers regarding the essential characteristics of mediation and other informal out-of-court processes for the resolution of shareholder disputes in Hong Kong.[11] This provides justification for lawyers to believe that ADR processes could be used as cost-effective alternatives to court-based shareholder proceedings.[12]

---

[9] Ibid.

[10] See Section 6.4. The statistical analysis illustrates that there was a significant result that supports the hypothesis that Hong Kong lawyers who are familiar with the ADR processes are more likely to adopt ADR in assisting their clients to settle shareholder disputes.

[11] See Section 6.3.2.

[12] See Section 6.4. The statistical analysis illustrated that there was a significant result that supports the hypothesis that when the ADR process is perceived as being compatible with Hong Kong lawyers' existing legal approaches to resolving shareholder disputes, those lawyers will tend to adopt ADR in assisting their clients to resolve shareholder disputes.

Third, Hong Kong lawyers often occupy powerful position within the legal field to promote the greater use of ADR for shareholder disputes, as they are bound to give advice to their clients about the risks of costs of refusing to attempt mediation or other methods of ADR.[13] Lawyers might in some cases simply avoid costs penalties and possibly encourage their clients to attend mediation sessions with no intention to attempt settlement.[14] Based on the aforementioned arguments, this research study seeks to gain further insight into the policy challenges involved in institutionalization of ADR within the court system.

Section 6.2 begins analysing the spread of ADR adoption among Hong Kong lawyers by reviewing theories on institutional entrepreneurs and the diffusion of innovations generally. Section 6.3 identifies the key factors affecting Hong Kong lawyers' decisions about the use of private dispute resolution methods for shareholder disputes. Section 6.4 presents the results of statistical analysis relating to the propensity of Hong Kong lawyers to adopt mediation and other informal out-of-court processes in assisting their clients to resolve shareholder disputes. Finally, it discusses the theoretical implications with regard to the limitations of this current study and other related issues, which are clearly worth investigating in future studies.

6.2 Diffusion of ADR Practices among Hong Kong Lawyers

This section contends that the degree to which mediation and other alternative processes have been generally accepted among Hong Kong lawyers depends on the types of influences exerted by the key agents (such as the Judiciary, the two branches of the Hong Kong's Legal profession, ADR service providers, sociolegal scholars and the law schools in Hong Kong). The following discussion begins to identify those parties who could play very important roles in the promotion of mediation and other out-of-court processes for the resolution of shareholder disputes. It then considers how the diffusion model fits into the present empirical analysis of Hong Kong lawyers' acceptance of the use of informal dispute resolution processes for the resolution of shareholder disputes.

---

[13] Order 1A, Rule 3 of the RHC and para. 4, Practice Direction 31.

[14] See Section 6.4. The statistical analysis runs contrary to the author expectations, as there was a negative association between the perceived advantage of ADR and the likelihood of Hong Kong lawyers to choose extrajudicial processes for shareholder disputes. One plausible line of reasoning of this is that ADR has its weaknesses (such as the possibility of using ADR as a fishing exercise to evaluate an opponent's case with no intention to settle through the mediation process).

6.2.1 The Critical Role of Key Agents in Articulating the Characteristics of ADR

Theorists in sociological institutionalism assert that there is an inextricable link between the key institutional entrepreneurs and institutional change.[15] The term 'institutional entrepreneur' refers to the change agents that 'have an interest in a particular institutional arrangement and who leverage resources to create new institutions or to transform existing one.'[16] Although they are viewed as being embedded in the existing institutional field, they hold a powerful and dominant position in facilitating the adoption of new practices.[17]

Recently, the introduction of court-connected ADR programmes, judicial case management techniques and judicial support for determining the fair value of the party's shares[18] have revealed that some influential members of the legal profession have expressed their dissatisfaction with the limits of traditional litigation approached to shareholder dispute resolution.[19] Influential actors who are dissatisfied with the traditional adversarial advocate approaches to resolving shareholder disputes are the Judiciary, legal practitioners, ADR service providers (such as the Hong Kong International Arbitration Centre, the Hong Kong Mediation Council and the Hong Kong Mediation Centre) and the law faculties of the three universities (University of Hong Kong, Chinese University of Hong Kong and City University of Hong Kong).[20] They act as the key agents in facilitating the adoption of new dispute resolution models that

---

[15] DiMaggio and Powell, 'The Iron Cage', 152–156 and Michael Lounsbury, 'Institutional Rationality and Practice Variation: New Directions in the Institutional Analysis of Practice', *Accounting, Organizations and Society*, 33 (2008), 348–361 at 353–355.

[16] Paul DiMaggio, 'Interest and Agency in Institutional Theory' in Lynne G. Zucker (ed.), *Institutional Patterns and Organizations: Culture and Environment* (Cambridge: MA:: Ball inger, 1988).

[17] Cynthia Hardy and Steve Maguire, 'Institutional Entrepreneurship' in Royston Greenwood, et al. (eds.), *The SAGE Handbook of Organizational Institutionalism* (Thousand Oaks, CA: SAGE, 2008), 198–199.

[18] *O' Neill v. Phillips* [1999] BCC at 613–615. This decision provides considerable judicial support for early fair buyout offers as a means of settling shareholder disputes. This decision was applied in the Hong Kong court case of *Re Prudential Enterprises Ltd* [2002] 3 HKLRD 388 (HK) and *Re Ranson Motor Manufacturing Company Limited* [2007] 1 HKLRD 751.

[19] Wong Yan-Lung, 'The Use and Development of Mediation in Hong Kong', *Asian Dispute Reivew* (2008), 54–56.

[20] Hong Kong Department of Justice, *Report of the Working Group on Mediation* (Hong Kong Department of Justice, 2010), para. 5.8.

focus on 'practical problem solving rather than on expensive legal argument and arcane procedures'.[21] They use their professional status and intellectual capacities to challenge the incumbent rights-based strategic approach to resolving disputes and to construct the meanings of ADR for securing its legitimacy. In this way, key agents created a new landscape of dispute in which belief about positive effects (such as cost-effectiveness) of using ADR become 'taken-for-granted' among Hong Kong lawyers.

Basically, there are two explanatory streams in supporting that key agents can initiate significant changes in altering lawyers' traditional, litigation-centred values and practices to resolve shareholder disputes. The first reason relates to the special positions of the key actors.[22] In the new disputing landscape of Hong Kong, judges occupy subject positions, with legitimacy with respect to their supportive role to enforce contractual ADR agreements made by the parties and to assist the parties to explore an appropriate ADR under the Practice Direction on Mediation.[23] Similarly, lawyers are expected to perform their positive pre-litigation duties to assist the court in furthering the 'underlying objectives' by advising their clients to consider the possibility of ADR to resolve their disputes seriously.[24]

Apart from the Judiciary, both the Bar Association and the Law Society issued the Codes Conduct and Professional Practices requiring their members to give proper advice to their clients in relation to the use of ADR processes for resolving disputes.[25] In addition, the Judiciary, the Law Society and the Bar Association try to facilitate such changes by raising awareness and providing facilities to educate the lawyers about the use of mediation (such as training courses offered by the Bar Association and the Law Society, 'Mediation' page on the Hong Kong Judiciary website).[26] In this regard, judges and legal professional bodies have occupied subject

---

[21] Julie MacFarlane, 'The Evolution of New Lawyer: How Lawyers Are Reshaping the Practice of Law', *Journal of Dispute Resolution* (2008), 61–81 at 62.

[22] Hardy and Maguire, 'Institutional Entrepreneurship', 200–201.

[23] Part C of Practice Direction 31 provides that where one or more of the parties is not legally represented, the court, may either on application of a party or on its own motion to give directions about whether mediation is appropriate.

[24] Order 1A, Rule 3 of the RHC and para. 5 of Practice Direction 31.

[25] According to para. 116A of the Code of Conduct issued by the Hong Kong Bar Association, it stipulates that where appropriate, a barrister should consider with his or her clients the possibility of attempting to resolve a dispute or any particular issue thereof by way of mediation. Similarly, Chapter 10, para. 10.17(3) of the Hong Kong Solicitors' Guide to Professional Conduct provides that a litigation solicitor should consider and if appropriate advise his client on ADR such as mediation, conciliation and the like.

[26] The Report of the Working Group on Mediation, para. 6.65.

positions that allow them to exert their powers in facilitating a change in lawyers' core practices and attitudes to the conduct of dispute resolution that emphasizes on the needs to 'shift from the traditional litigious mode to a broadened horizon of weighing the options in resolving a disputes satisfactorily and effectively'.[27]

The second reason relates to the special characteristics and intellectual capacity of the key actors.[28] Neo-institutionalists place great emphasis on the cognitive-cultural dimension of institutions, which represents a significant shift away from 'a-rational mimicry and stability' towards a new focus that places great emphasis on 'institutional rationality and on-going struggle and change'.[29] This strand of institutional argument rests on the assumption that actors are rational-centred (i.e., they have material interests in the field) and they have sufficient cognitive capacities to conceive new visions and social reasons for change.[30] Key actors employ 'institutional meaning-making' strategies that link new practices (such as mediation) to attributes of pre-existing practice (e.g., public court adjudication) that are fundamentally embedded in the legal cultural systems.[31]

For example, sociolegal academics assert that ADR processes (such as mediation and arbitration) do not exist in isolation from the public court adjudication process. Instead, these informal dispute resolution devices are institutionally located in the family of dispute processing, frequently contested with formal dispute resolution mechanisms and sometimes reordered.[32] Shapiro depicts that the prototypical adjudicative processes inherently possess the general attributes of mediation processes. Like in mediation processes, the Judiciary offers feasible remedies such as monetary or equitable remedies instead of a dichotomous decision in which one of the parties was assigned the legal rights and the other was found wrong.[33] Unlike the orthodox view of mediation, judicial outcomes are

---

[27] Lam, 'Mediation in the Context of CJR', 9–10.

[28] Hardy and Maguire, 'Institutional Entrepreneurship', 201–202.

[29] Lounsbury, 'Institutional Rationality and Practice Variation', 349.

[30] Roger Friedland and Robert R. Alford, *Powers of Theory: Capitalism, the State, and Democracy* (Cambridge: Cambridge University Press, 1985), 244–246 and Lounsbury, 'Institutional Rationality and Practice Variation', 351–353.

[31] DiMaggio, 'Interest and Agency in Institutional Theory', 14–15, the creation of institutions depends on whether the institutional entrepreneurs have successfully articulated the legitimating accounts of a new practice.

[32] Friedland and Alford, 'Bringing Society Back', 245; Martin Shapiro, *Courts: A Comparative and Political Analysis* (Chicago: University of Chicago Press, 1986), 10 and Marc Galanter, 'Adjudication, Litigation, and Related Phenomena', in Leon Lipson and Stanton Wheeler (eds.), *Law and the Social Sciences* (New York: Russell Sage Foundation, 1986), 160–164.

[33] Shapiro, 'Courts', 10.

not freely bargaining based solely on the wills of the parties, but conducting legalized bargaining under the shadow supervision of the court.[34] On
such a basis, it may be justifiable for the key agents to employ 'institutional meaning-making' strategies that connect ADR practices to local
legal cultures in advancing the legitimacy of ADR practices.

Clearly, the Hong Kong Judiciary, the legal professional organizations,
ADR service providers, sociolegal scholars and universities serve as agents
of legitimacy or institutional entrepreneurs supporting the development
of ADR policy within the legal professional community in Hong Kong.[35]
They use their intellectual and cognitive capacities to convince lawyers to
help their clients to resolve shareholder disputes through informal dispute resolution methods.[36] The legitimacy of ADR derives from a cognitive process through which ADR promoters employ symbolic (such as the
use of law) or rhetorical (the use of language) devices that connect ADR
practice to the existing legal culture.[37]

It will not be surprising that legitimization of extrajudicial practices
for the resolution of shareholder disputes among legal practitioners can
be achieved through the use of rhetorical strategies by institutional entrepreneurs, such as legal professional bodies, sociolegal scholars and the
Judiciary. In general, ADR proponents try to connect the benefits of informal dispute resolution processes to a system of rules, beliefs and norms
which can be considered as legitimate and acceptable to the public.[38] For
example, sociolegal scholars such as Marc Galanter and John Lande claim
that informal dispute resolution methods are inexpensive, speedy, flexible,
consensual in nature, constructive rather than destructive, among others.[39]
Similarly, most judges in Hong Kong will employ their professional

---

[34] Ibid. and Robert H. Mnookin, and Lewis Kornhauser, 'Bargaining in the Shadow of the Law: The Case of Divorce', The Yale Law Journal, 88:5 (1979), 950–997.

[35] John Lande, 'The Diffusion of a Process Pluralist Ideology of Disputing: Factors Affecting Opinions of Business Lawyers and Executives', PhD thesis, University of Wisconsin-Madison (1995), 35 and The Report of the Working Group on Mediation, para. 5.8.

[36] Roy Suddaby and Royston Greenwood, 'Rhetorical Strategies of Legitimacy', Administrative Science Quartely, 50 (2005), 35–67 at 37.

[37] Ibid.

[38] Lynne G. Zucker, 'The Role of Institutionalization Cultural Persistence' in Walter W. Powell and Paul J. DiMaggio (eds.), The New Institutionalism in Organizational Analysis (Chicago: University of Chicago Press, 1991), 85.

[39] Marc Galanter and John Lande, 'Private Courts and Public Authority', Studies in Law, Politics, and Society, 12 (1992), 393–415 at 395–397; Leonard L. Riskin et al., Dispute Resolution and Lawyers, 3rd ed. (Eagan, MN: West, 2006), 10 and Hailary Astor and Christine M. Chinkin, Dispute Resolution in Australia (Sydney: Butterworths, 1992), 12–13.

discourses to articulate a number of appealing characteristics of ADR. For instance, Justice Lam Man-Hon identified four positive features of mediation: consensuality, voluntariness, satisfaction and cost-effectiveness.[40] In this way, mediation and other out-of-court processes can be considered as a legitimate or acceptable means of dispute resolution.

ADR has a clear advantage in both cost-effectiveness and high levels of satisfaction. However, the claimed advantage of ADR is not the only factor in measuring the characteristics of informal out-of-court processes.[41] Indeed, private dispute resolution methods can be viewed as important supplements to the court, as the use of informal out-of-court processes can indeed be compatible with shareholder litigation processes.[42] In addition, critics highlight that there are some negative effects or potential pitfalls in using private dispute resolution methods to resolve shareholder disputes. The most frequently cited barriers to the facilitative, interest-based dispute resolution processes, such as mediation were the informality of the procedure; the enforceability of mediated settlement; the lack of reviewability of settlement decisions; and a dispute resolution system that involves a stratified, multiple layers of directions for mediation.[43]

As a whole, this section suggests that factors included in the following statistical analysis are (1) the compatibility of ADR processes with court-based shareholder proceedings; (2) the relative advantage of out-of-court processes; and (3) potential barriers to out-of-court settlements. This provides a better understanding of how the Hong Kong Judiciary, the professional organizations of both branches of Hong Kong's legal profession, ADR service providers, sociolegal scholars and the three law schools in Hong Kong exert their influence over Hong Kong lawyers' decision towards the use of ADR for the resolution of shareholder disputes.

6.2.2 Integrating Diffusion Models into the Empirical Analysis of ADR Adoption

This section aims to apply the theory of 'diffusion of innovation' to generate a model in explaining the variations of lawyers' attitudes towards

---

[40] Lam, 'Mediation in the Context of CJR', 1–4.
[41] See supra note 39.
[42] See Chapter 5.
[43] Galanter and Lande, 'Private Courts and Public Authority' at 397; Simon Roberts and Michael Palmer, *Dispute Processes: ADR and the Primary Forms of Decision-Making*, 2nd ed. (Cambridge: Cambridge University Press, 2005), 53–65; Hailary and Chinkin, 'Dispute Resolution in Australia', 12–15; and Ettie Ward, 'Mandatory Court-annexed Alternative Dispute Resolution in the United States Federal Courts: Panacea or Pandemic?', *St. John's Law Review*, 81 (2007), 77–98 at 89.

the use of informal out-of-court processes for shareholder disputes in the post-CJR era, and, where necessary, to guide future reform. This empirical analysis seeks to explore the key factors contributing the adoption of ADR among Hong Kong lawyers for shareholder disputes since the CJR began in 2009. This would provide judicial policymakers with the kind of rich and detailed understanding of the key factors that drive Hong Kong lawyers to adopt ADR in helping their clients to resolve shareholder disputes.

To begin with, it briefly reviews the literature on diffusion of innovations. Innovation diffusion is concerned with the spread of abstract ideas and concepts and actual practices through a population of potential adopters within a social system over time and/or space.[44] Everett Rogers first developed the concept of diffusion of innovations. He defined the term 'innovations' as 'ideas or practices perceived as new by practitioners'.[45] This theory has been widely applied in the areas of public management, social policy, health service organizations, marketing and the housing association sector.[46]

Unlike the research studies which have been done in the field of organization and management, there is paucity of ADR studies on innovation diffusion. Among the ADR studies on that topic, Lande is the first socio-legal scholar to examine the spread of 'legal pluralist ideology' among business lawyers and executives in the United States.[47] However, he applied the theory of early institutional diffusion in determining the spread among business lawyers and executives since numerous ADR programmes were established around the United States in the 1960s. According to his analysis, Lande argues that professionalization is the key mechanism of diffusion that contributes to institutional change.[48] Based on this assumption, he identifies a range of factors affecting the spread of ADR beliefs among corporate lawyers

---

[44] Richard A. Wolfe, 'Organizational Innovation: Review, Critique and Suggested Research Directions', *Journal of Management Studies*, 31:3 (1994), 405–431 at 407; Everett M. Rogers, *Diffusion of Innovations*, 5th ed. (New York: Free Press, 2003), 5–6 and Barbara Wejnert, 'Integration Models of Diffusion of Innovations: A Conceptual Framework', *Annual Review of Sociology*, 28 (2002), 297–326 at 297.

[45] Rogers, 'Diffusion of Innovations', 12.

[46] Richard M. Walker et al., *Managing Public Services Innovation: The Experience of English Housing Associations* (Bristol: Policy Press, 2001), 14 and Trisha Greenhalgh et al., 'Diffusion of Innovations in Service Organizations: Systematic Review and Recommendations', *The Milbank Quarterly*, 82:4 (2004), 581–629 at 589.

[47] Lande, 'The Diffusion of a Process Pluralist Ideology of Disputing', 31–33.

[48] Ibid.

and executives in the United States. These factors are classified into four main groups: [49]

- Demographic, organizational and professional factors
- Disputing experience of each individual
- Opinions about courts
- Opinions about the use of out-of-court processes, such as mediation and arbitration for the resolution of commercial disputes

Lande's empirical analysis suffers a number of weaknesses in the following aspects. First, he fails to take into account the important fact that legal contextual factors (i.e., origins of legal system) may influence the spread of ADR among individuals.[50] Second, he fails to identify the similarities and differences between ADR and innovation. In the absence of any sound evidence in supporting that ADR is characterized as innovation, it is dangerous to generalize that 'ADR is more than an incremental technical innovation.'[51]

Last but most importantly, he fails to construct a list of attributes that could accurately measure the characteristics of ADR.[52] The lack of a broadly accepted list of sophisticated attributes in measuring the characteristics of ADR may result in the lack of significance among these variables.[53] Consequently, the research results may not be consistent with the existing literature on ADR. Nonetheless, Lande provides further insights into the empirical analysis of the diffusion of informal dispute resolution ideologies among US lawyers and executives in the US-listed companies.

This section suggests that Rogers's influential model of innovation diffusion should be applied in analysing the spread of ADR practices for the resolution of shareholder disputes among Hong Kong lawyers.[54] The premises underlying this argument are as follows.

---

[49] Ibid.
[50] Barbara Wejnert, 'Integration Models of Diffusion of Innovations: A Conceptual Framework', *Annual Review of Sociology*, 28 (2002), 297–326 at 310–318. Wejnert notes that environmental factors are associated with the diffusion of innovations.
[51] Lande, 'The Diffusion of a Process Pluralist Ideology of Disputing', 10.
[52] In the field of public management, academics have developed sophisticated attributes in measuring the characteristics of innovation. For details, see Wolfe, 'Organizational Innovation', 417–420 and Walker et al., 'Managing Public Services Innovation', 23–27.
[53] George A Boyne et al., 'Explaining the Adoption of Innovation: An Empirical Analysis of Public Management Reform', *Environment and Planning C: Government and Policy*, 23:4 (2005), 419–435 at 432.
[54] Roger, 'Diffusion of Innovations', at 5–6.

First, ADR has the inherent characteristics of innovation. Like for innovation, it is difficult to offer a precise definition in defining the term 'ADR' properly.[55] ADR is broadly similar to innovation, as it is commonly associated with procedures that are intended to supplement – not replace or limit – existing court adjudicative process.[56] In Hong Kong, the introduction of innovative disputing procedures into the court system embraces some types of change. The policy reasons underlying the procedural change is to improve the accessibility of the civil courts and to bring about a change in lawyers' attitudes towards the conduct of resolving disputes on behalf of their clients.[57] In addition, out-of-court informal dispute resolution procedures are characterized as innovation, as these extrajudicial dispute resolution methods may be discontinued over time. This is particularly true if policymakers fail to create a sustainable ADR programme that maintains the essential values of ADR and is sufficiently flexible to satisfy the needs of key stakeholders in using the court system.[58]

Second, Rogers's model of innovation diffusions helps to examine the behaviour of individuals, as it focuses on the potential impact of an innovation's adoption by an individual actor.[59] The potential impact may include the improvement of living standards, enhancement of a person's reputation or increase in a company's productivity.[60] Along similar lines, the introduction of innovative disputing procedures into the courthouse may lead to private consequences affecting the livelihood of individual lawyers in Hong Kong. These private consequences may at least either improve lawyers' reputations or increase their productivity. This is particularly true as the change in lawyers' core practices and attitudes to the conduct of dispute resolution may produce the desired policy goal of curtailing lawyers' discretion to employ the fullest possible range of

---

[55] See Chapter 1.

[56] See Chapter 5 and Judith Resnik, 'Many Doors? Closing Doors? Alternative Dispute Resolution and Adjudication', *The Ohio State Journal on Dispute Resolution*, 10:2 (1995), 211–265 at 254.

[57] Hong Kong Judiciary, *Reform of the Civil Justice System in Hong Kong*, Interim Report and Consultative Paper on Civil Justice Reform (Hong Kong Judiciary, 2000).

[58] Lande, 'Principles for Policymaking about Collaborative Law and Other ADR Processes', 662–663.

[59] Ibid., 118–119; Greenhalgh et al., 'Diffusion of Innovations in Service Organizations', 589–590 and Richard M. Walker, 'Innovation Type and Diffusion: An Emprical Analysis of Local Government', *Public Administration*, 84:2 (2006), 311–335 at 312.

[60] Wejnert, 'Integration Models of Diffusion of Innovations', 299–300.

adversarial tactics.[61] Moreover, recent procedural changes in the disputing environment have created opportunities for innovative lawyers to deliver legal services that meet the clients' needs to resolve disputes at reasonable cost. For example, legal work can be decomposed into tasks, each of which would be sourced in a variety of ways[62] or alternatively, a market can be developed for all types of cost-effective dispute resolution process, including mediation.[63]

Third, Rogers develops an innovation adoption model with five variables that determine the rate of adoption (i.e., the relative speed with which members of a social system adopt an innovation).[64] He defines the term 'adoption' as 'a decision to make full use of an innovation as the best course of action available'.[65] Current legal practitioners in Hong Kong may argue that they have adopted ADR in order to legitimize new practices and ideas for the resolution of shareholder disputes on their clients' behalf.

The objective of applying the model of innovation diffusion in this study is to explain or predict rates and patterns of ADR adoption over time and/or space. This analysis helps to explain how lawyers can account for the adoption of ADR, particularly in today's climate in which lawyers are urged to advise their clients to adopt a more pragmatic, time-efficient approach to resolving shareholder disputes. In addition, factors that have been found to influence diffusion can be used in analysing the rate of ADR adoption among Hong Kong lawyers. These factors include:[66]

- The characteristics of innovations. Relative advantage, compatibility and complexity are the perceived attributes of innovations.
- The type of innovation decision. This refers to the fact that the social system within which the innovation is to be adopted can influence the likelihood of adoption through the types of decisions that can be taken.
- The process by which an innovation is communicated.
- The social network to which the adopters belong.

---

[61] A. A. S. Zuckerman, 'Reform in the Shadow of Lawyers' Interests', in A. A. S. Zuckerman and Ross Cranston (eds.), *Reform of Civil Procedure: Essay on "Access to Justice"* (Oxford: Clarendon Press, 1995), 62.

[62] Richard Susskind, *The End of Lawyer: Rethinking the Nature of Legal Services*, rev. ed. (Oxford: Oxford University Press, 2010), 42–50.

[63] Julie MacFarlane, 'ADR and the Courts: Renewing our Commitment to Innovation', *Marquette Law Review*, 95 (2012), 927–940 at 930.

[64] Roger, 'Diffusion of Innovations', 222.

[65] Ibid., 221.

[66] Ibid., 15–31.

- The role of change agents' promotional efforts. Their efforts can be seen as 'critical masses' in influencing innovation decisions towards the adoption of innovations.

In sum, Rogers's conceptual model does offer insights into the development of an innovation adoption model with relevant variables for determining the spread of ADR among legal practitioners in Hong Kong. The following sections will apply the conceptual and theoretical models of innovation diffusion proposed by both Rogers for hypothesis formulation.

6.3 Factors Affecting Hong Kong Lawyers' Attitudes towards the Use of Out-of-Court Processes

This section begins to review the current literature on innovation adoption, theories of the legal professional, and law and economics theories. It then constructs effective measures about the attributes that influence Hong Kong lawyers' decisions in adopting extrajudicial processes for the resolution of shareholder disputes.

6.3.1 Extraction of Key Factors Affecting Hong Kong Lawyers' Attitudes towards the Use of ADR

The purpose of this section is to build up a group of inter-related variables or factors that might be used to measure some common underlying dimension.[67] Given that the primary purpose is to examine the rate of ADR adoption among Hong Kong lawyers for shareholder disputes since the CJR came into effect in 2009, it is necessary to explore factors affecting the use of mediation and other out-of-court processes. To date, no prior empirical research work has been done in exploring the key factors contributing to ADR adoption among Hong Kong lawyers in a programme of the CJR that involves the influence of the court rules, practice directions or court orders. Exploratory factor analysis is a powerful analytical tool in elucidating the important determinants and associated predictor variables that drive Hong Kong lawyers to adopt ADR in helping their clients to resolve shareholder disputes. First, this analytical tool helps to reduce a large number of items from a questionnaire to a smaller number of components for the measures of predictor variables.[68] Second, this analysis is

---

[67] Rebecca M. Warner, *Applied Statistics: From Bivariate Through Multivariate Techniques* (Thosand Oaks, CA: SAGE, 2008), 753–760.
[68] Ibid.

particularly useful in measuring the attitudes, beliefs or experiences of the respondents in this study, as it creates a new multiple-item scale that is convenient for analysis.[69] On such a basis, factor analysis helps to extract key factors affecting Hong Kong lawyers' decisions about the use of ADR.

Factor analysis in the form of Principle Component Analysis with Varimax rotation with Kaiser Normalization was used to obtain the grouping results. The results presented in Table 6.1 show that twenty-three survey items were reduced to six dimensions based on the pattern of associations corresponding to the characteristics of ADR, personal experiences with ADR processes and the impact of the legal environment for resolving shareholder disputes in Hong Kong as mentioned in Section 6.2.2.

6.3.2 Developing a Series of Testable Arguments for Analysing the Behavioural Changes of Hong Kong Lawyers towards the Use of ADR

As previously discussed, the propensity of Hong Kong lawyers to adopt mediation and other out-of-court processes in assisting their clients to resolve shareholder disputes is believed to be dependent on various factors.[70] These factors can be classified into the following three groups:

1. The characteristics of innovative disputing procedures
2. Lawyers' personal experiences with informal out-of-court processes for shareholder disputes
3. The impact of legal environment for resolving shareholder disputes

Based on these three groups, six hypotheses were developed as follows.

The Characteristics of Innovative Disputing Resolution Procedures

The first set of hypotheses is concerned with factors in relation to the characteristics of informal dispute resolution processes. Rogers indicates that innovation displays the following features: (1) relative advantage, (2) compatibility and (3) complexity that help to explain the rate of adoption.[71] Three hypotheses were developed in order to analyse three distinctive features of out-of-court processes that may, to a greater or lesser extent, affect the rate of ADR adoption for the resolution of shareholder

---

[69] Ibid., 851.
[70] See Section 6.2.
[71] Rogers, 'Diffusion of Innovations', 15–16.

Table 6.1 *Factors Affecting the Use of ADR among Hong Kong Lawyers*

Factors	A Total of 23 Survey Items	Factor Loadings Coefficient[a]	Cumulative Variance Explained (%)
Compatibility	Practice Direction 3.3 creates no tension between the lawyers' traditional adversarial role and their settlement role within a voluntary court-connected ADR programme.	0.619	43.04
	ADR can complement litigation process by increasing access to various dispute resolution processes for minority shareholders.	0.80	
Advantage	Speedy	0.85	43.64
	Preserves business relationships	0.85	
	Helps the parties to focus on their interests and needs	0.82	
	Consensual participation is a crucial element for a successful mediation.	0.75	
	The issuance of Practice Direction 3.3 has led to a shift in lawyers' practical orientation towards consensus-building as an alternative to a rights-based adjudication.	0.53	
Barrier	Enforcement	0.80	62.33
	Delay	0.77	
Familiarity	Knowledge and skills of ADR	0.90	65.50
	Experience in using ADR	0.90	
	Prior experience as a neutral third party in ADR processes	0.70	
	Prior experience in representing the parties in ADR processes	0.60	
	Acquiring sufficient ADR training in law schools at the postgraduate levels (e.g., LLM) or ADR service providers (such as Hong Kong International Arbitration Centre [HKIAC])	0.73	

(continued)

Table 6.1 (*continued*)

Factors	A Total of 23 Survey Items	Factor Loadings Coefficient[a]	Cumulative Variance Explained (%)
Network	Judicial pressure to settle through mediation or other alternative processes	0.66	30.54
	The effectiveness of the court's case management powers	0.66	
	Court's encouragement to settle shareholder disputes	0.76	
	Judicial competence to give direction in relation to mediation or other ADR processes	0.76	
	The Judiciary's Mediation Information Office provides lawyers with relevant information on mediation.	0.69	
	The legal professional bodies offer various training activities, including seminars and conferences.	0.54	
Legal Culture	Legal certainty as to the application of statutory minority protection remedy	0.58	49.37
	Judicial competence to determine whether the alleged conduct is unfairly prejudicial to the interests of the minority.	0.76	
	The statutory relief can be viewed as the most effective legal means to protect the interests of the minority shareholders.	0.791	
Sample size = 67			

[a] Factor loadings are the correlations of the variables with the factor, the weighted combination of variables which best explains the variance. Each factor is sorted by the size of the loading coefficient. Variable groups with factor loading below ± 0.4 are not listed.

disputes among Hong Kong lawyers since the CJR was implemented in 2009. Three distinctive features of informal dispute resolution processes are (1) relative advantage of out-of-court processes, (2) potential barriers to out-of-court settlements and (3) the compatibility of ADR process with court-based shareholder proceedings.

The Compatibility of ADR Process with Court-Based Shareholder Proceedings   According to Rogers, compatibility is the degree to which innovation is perceived as being consistent with the existing values, past experiences and needs of potential adopters.[72] Similarly, Boyne and his colleagues contend that the term 'compatibility' has been used normatively in referring to the 'values of the adopters (what they think about or feel about an innovation) and practically or operationally to what people do in response to an innovation.'[73] On such a basis, there may be a positive correlation between the rate of ADR adoption and the perceived relative advantage of innovation.

Consistent with prior studies, the findings of the factor analysis reveal that ADR is being perceived as compatible with lawyers' existing legal approaches to resolving shareholder disputes. Professor MacFarlane identifies that conflict resolution skills (such as mediation skills) are rooted in the skills and knowledge of traditional legal practice, notably information assimilation, legal research, effective oral communication, strategic planning and insider knowledge.[74] She argues that lawyers who are experienced in mediation advocacy are able to apply trial advocacy skills effectively by assisting their clients to achieve durable settlements that meet their interests and needs.[75]

Chapter 5 indicates that ADR and the unfair prejudice proceedings are indeed compatible on the basis that informal dispute resolution processes can complement shareholder litigation.[76] This analysis reveals that out-of-court processes can complement the unfair prejudice proceeding as the two compatible dispute resolution processes, while similar, have their own unique characteristics. Both dispute resolution processes are similar, as both processes support the contractual relationship. The House of Lords decision in *O'Neill v. Phillips* supported the contractual relationship

---

[72] Ibid., 15.
[73] Boyne et al., 'Explaining the Adoption of Innovation', 424.
[74] Julie MacFarlane, *The New Lawyer: How Settlement Is Transforming the Practice of Law* (Vancouver, B.C.: UBC Press, 2008), 68.
[75] Ibid.
[76] See Chapter 5.

of the parties by holding that to prove unfair prejudice conduct, minority shareholders must show that there is some breach of their formal (legally binding) or informal (binding under equity) rights.[77] Along similar lines, the ultimate basis of extrajudicial processes such as mediation and arbitration is contractual. However, the two compatible dispute resolution processes display some differences in terms of their natures and functions.[78] In this regard, informal out-of-court process can serve as a complement to shareholder litigation by making access to dispute resolution for minority shareholders less costly and less adversarial.

Another possible reason is that there might be an increasing tendency in favour of early settlement following the court decisions in *O'Neill v. Phillips*.[79] Out-of-court settlement, such as early fair offers to buyout in shareholder disputes, became legitimized and ultimately 'taken-for-granted' as a social fact before the CJR began in 2009. In general, corporate lawyers can play an advisory and supportive role in assisting their clients to make a reasonable offer to buyout of the interest of the petitioner. This approach could negate any unfairness conducts of the respondent if he or she makes a reasonable offer at the earliest possible stage.[80] This indicates that courts provide effective alternatives to adjudication for parties to settle their differences to avoid lengthy and costly shareholder litigation through the mechanism of shareholder buyout. This approach is consistent with the underlying objectives of the CJR.[81] These arguments lead to the following hypothesis (stated in the alternative form).

Hypothesis 1: When the ADR process is perceived as being compatible with Hong Kong lawyers' existing legal approach to resolving shareholder disputes, those lawyers will tend to adopt ADR in helping their clients to resolve shareholder disputes.

The Relative Advantage of ADR   Rogers asserts that the relative advantage is the degree to which an innovation is perceived as better than the idea it replaces.[82] By the same token, ADR processes such as mediation

---

[77] The Hong Kong Courts placed considerable reliance on a line of the *O'Neill v. Phillips* authority; see *Re Kam Fai Electroplating Factory Ltd* [2004] HKEC 556 (unreported, HCCW 534/2000, 8 December 2003).

[78] See Chapter 5.

[79] [1999] BCC.

[80] Ibid., 613.

[81] Order 1A, Rule 1(e) of the RHC provides that one of the 'underlying objectives' of the CJR is to facilitate the settlement of disputes.

[82] Rogers, 'Diffusion of Innovations', 15.

have their own relative advantage in terms of both cost-effectiveness and high level of satisfaction. The findings of the factor analysis are consistent with the previous literature. With respect to the quantitative argument that ADR (such as mediation) is regarded as a cost-efficient dispute resolution process, ADR displays several appealing characteristics in reducing cost and time associated with shareholder litigation. This is particularly true, as the extrajudicial process is a voluntary and non-legalistic process.[83] Given that ADR is characterized as an informal process of dispute resolution, its procedures are relatively simple and short in duration as compared with the court rules. Unsurprisingly, corporate lawyers often value mediation, as it helps the parties to reach speedy settlements within an appropriate time frame.[84]

In stark contrast with the qualitative argument that emphasizes the impact of the parties' level of satisfaction with the mediation process, this process focuses on the parties' underlying needs and interests.[85] Undoubtedly, the informality of the extrajudicial process by comparison with a trial offers parties the opportunity to play a greater role in the management of their disputes.[86] This empowers the parties to work towards a mutually acceptable outcome that reflects each of their interests and needs.[87] This process is particularly useful in preserving the ongoing relationship between the disputants.[88]

In addition, ADR will increase the likelihood of successful mediation, as our judicial policymakers reinforce the notion of the voluntary nature of a court-connected ADR programme.[89] If parties show their willingness to cooperate, this increases the likelihood of the parties to compromise.[90] These arguments lead to my second hypothesis (stated in the alternative form).

[83] Nadja Alexander, 'Global Trends in Mediation: Riding the Third Wave' in Nadja Alexander (ed.), Global Trends in Mediation (The Hague: Kluwer Law International, 2006), 206–209.
[84] John Lande, 'Using Dispute System Design Methods to Promote Good-Faith Participation in Court-Connected Mediation Programs', UCLA Law Review, 50 (2002), 70–141 at 120–122.
[85] Carita Wallgren, 'ADR and Business', in J.C. Goldsmith et al. (eds.), ADR in Business: Practice and Issues across Countries and Cultures, Vol. I (The Hague: Kluwer Law International, 2006), 9 and Christian Bühring-Uhle, Arbitration and Mediation in International Business (The Hague: Kluwer Law International, 2006), 206.
[86] Alexander, 'Global Trends in Mediation', 10 and Hazel Genn, Judging Civil Justice, The Hamlyn Lectures 59th Series (Cambridge: Cambridge University Press, 2010), 86–89.
[87] Ibid.
[88] Bühring-Uhle, 'Arbitration and Mediation in International Business', 206.
[89] See Chapter 4.
[90] Bühring-Uhle, 'Arbitration and Mediation in International Business', 229.

Hypothesis 2: When ADR has its own relative advantage in terms of both cost-effectiveness and high level of satisfaction by the parties, those lawyers tend to adopt extrajudicial processes in helping their clients to resolve shareholder disputes.

Potential Barriers to the Use of ADR for Settlement   Rogers defines the term 'complexity' as the extent to which an innovation is difficult to understand and use, as perceived by potential adopters.[91] This implies that innovations may have some inherited barriers or constraints, which make them difficult to operate in reality. Likewise, enforceability of a mediation agreement is generally regarded as the major barrier to ADR as the parameters of enforceability of mediation agreements are still unclear.[92] The fundamental legal issues in relation to the enforceability of mediation settlements arise generally at the post-mediation stage.

Given that one central feature of mediation is its consensual nature, the deficiencies of the legal framework that provides effective legislative provisions for enforcing mediation agreements makes its implementation difficult. This is particularly true as a mediated outcome can take different forms, including non-binding agreements such as memoranda of understanding, standard legal contracts, various categories of settlement deed and court orders.[93] In general, the common law courts maintain their position by stipulating that enforceability of mediation agreements largely depends on the good faith requirement to mediate, clarity in specifying the mediation process and that mediated settlement must take the form of standard contracts.[94] For instance, the English courts decided that for a mediated settlement to be considered effective and enforceable would nonetheless depend not only on formal writing requirements, but most importantly, on the consent of all parties.[95]

Indeed, it is unlikely that parties who do consent to participate in mediation will later challenge any agreement to mediate.[96] However, the

---

[91] Rogers, 'Diffusion of Innovations', 16.

[92] At present, the Mediation Ordinance does not include a provision for the enforcement of an agreement to mediate. See also David B. Lipsky and Ronald L. Seeber, 'Patterns of ADR used in Corporate Disputes', *Dispute Resolution Journal*, 54:1 (1999), 68–71 at 24–29.

[93] Nadja Alexander, *International and Comparative Mediation: Legal Perspectives* (The Hague: Kluwer Law International, 2009), 303.

[94] The Report of the Working Group on Mediation, para. 7.63.

[95] *Brown v. Rice & Patel & ADR Group* [2007] EWHC (Ch.) 625.

[96] In general, the UK courts set aside mediated settlement on the grounds of fraud, see *Brown v. Rice & Patel & ADR Group* [2007] EWHC (Ch.) 625 and *Crystal Decisions (UH) Ltd v. Vedatech Corp* EWHC (Ch.) 1062.

position in the Hong Kong courts is unclear in dealing with enforcing mediation agreements. In particular, the Hong Kong Judiciary displayed considerable scepticism and hostility towards mediated agreements before the implementation of the CJR. This line of argument is consistent with a landmark case decided before the Hong Kong courts. In *Hyundai Engineering and Construction Co. Ltd v. Vigour Ltd*,[97] the Hong Kong Court of Appeal distinguished the reasoning in *Cable and Wireless Plc*[98] and held that a dispute resolution clause that contains the words 'submit to third party mediation procedure' was unenforceable for lack of uncertainty.

In addition, ADR (such as mediation) has its inherent weakness, as this process depends on the cooperation of all parties.[99] If parties or their lawyers are pursuing mediation purely for tactical benefits (such as fishing expeditions) or are reluctant to engage mediation sincerely, a consensual procedure may simply be exploited for delay.[100] These arguments lead to the third hypothesis (expressed in alternative form).

Hypothesis 3: Potential barriers to the use of ADR for settlement are negatively associated with Hong Kong lawyers' decisions about the use of ADR for shareholder disputes.

Lawyers' Personal Experiences with ADR Processes

The second set of hypotheses is concerned with factors in relation to Hong Kong lawyers' personal experiences with out-of-court processes. MacFarlane notes that lawyers' personal experiences with ADR processes derive not only from their membership in particular cultural groups and communities of practice, but also their familiarity with ADR processes.[101] Hence, two hypotheses were developed to analyse how lawyers' personal experiences with ADR processes, may, to a greater or lesser extent, affect the rate of ADR adoption for the resolution of shareholder disputes among Hong Kong lawyers since the CJR was implemented in 2009. Lawyers' personal experiences with ADR include (1) lawyers' familiarity with using ADR and (2) the influence of both the Judiciary and legal professional bodies, including the Law Society and the Bar Association.

---

[97] [2005] HKLRD 723 at 734–735.
[98] *Cable & Wireless Plc v. IBM United Kingdom Ltd* [2002] EWHC 2059.
[99] Bühring-Uhle, 'Arbitration and Mediation in International Business,' 209.
[100] Ibid., 209–210.
[101] MacFarlane, 'The New Lawyer', 37–42.

Lawyers' Familiarity with ADR   Sociolegal theorists such as Abel argue that the rationale underlying the desire of lawyers to seek control over their markets (i.e., the production *of* producers) through their professional knowledge is to limit the number of producers. The mechanism of closure (i.e., market control) through a monopolization of esoteric knowledge and associated skills enables the profession to maintain its high social status and to gain public status from their clients.[102] Clearly, the legal profession's successful control of their market in this manner may impact the perception of an individual lawyer to develop effective negotiation and settlement skills in three generally aspects. First, Individual lawyers begin to market themselves as mediation or alternative dispute resolution 'specialists' by virtue of learning from practical experience and formal legal education. Lawyers who are specialized in effective negotiation and settlement skills then become experts, as they are able to construct a valuable commodity.[103] This is particularly true as Professor MacFarlane notes that[104]

> Once the skills associated with effective settlement advocacy become recognized as a commodity that has economic and reputational consequences the profession will buy into what they regard as a significant means of ensuring their professional status.

Second, lawyers place considerable effort into acquiring effective negotiation and settlement skills through formal legal education and practical experience. The profession traditionally restricted entry to maintain members' social status, prestige and financial reward by means of academic education, professional examinations and apprenticeship.[105] In Hong Kong, there are certain conditions governing eligibility for admission either as a qualified barrister or solicitor. In general, a person who seeks to qualify as a solicitor in Hong Kong has to comply with examination and course requirements offered by the universities or other bodies which are recognized by the Law Society.[106] In addition, he or she has to

---

[102] Richard L. Abel, *American Lawyers* (Oxford: Blackwell, 1991), 25–27. According to Abel, the status of a professional is affected by two principle factors: membership and clientele. Limitations on entry influence the profession's compositions as well as its members.

[103] MacFarlane, 'The New Lawyer', 18.

[104] Ibid., 18–19.

[105] Richard L. Abel, 'Lawyers and Legal Services' in Peter Cane and Mark Tushnet (eds.), *The Oxford Handbook of Legal Studies* (Oxford: Oxford University Press, 2003), 97.

[106] Section 4(1)(a) of the Legal Practitioners Ordinance (Cap. 159). See also Michael Wilkinson and Michael Sandor, *The Professional Conduct of Lawyers in Hong Kong* (Hong Kong: Butterworths, Asia, 2008), 15–19.

comply with the obligation prescribed by the Law Society with respect to employment as a trainee solicitor for a two-years period.[107] Likewise, a person who seeks to qualify as a barrister has to comply with similar admission requirements as well. A major difference between the two branches for admission to practice is the period of time for apprenticeships. In Hong Kong, a potential barrister is required to undertake a qualifying period of active practice commonly known as 'pupillage' for a period of not less than one year in the chamber before being qualified as a practicing barrister.[108]

However, lawyers tend to employ a large proportion of practical knowledge and a moderate proportion of formal knowledge which is learnt from the law schools in handling disputes on behalf of their clients. This argument rests on the assumption that the legal profession is classified as a 'discretionary manual specialization' involving tasks that require discretionary judgement and action.[109] Given that the tasks are highly technical rather than routine clerical work, special knowledge is required in order to perform them successfully. Along similar lines, Abel argues that formal legal education serves purposes other than market control, and thus lawyers place great emphasis on practical knowledge instead of their formal legal education in dealing with issues relating to legal disputes.[110] The preceding discussion suggests that lawyers seek to acquire reputations for specializing ADR practices through practical training instead of formal legal education. They attempt to become familiar with ADR practices so as to accommodate a new disputing landscape, especially the demands of consumers.

An analysis of the theoretical approaches to the legal profession reveals that there is an association between the intellectual capacities of individual lawyers and the familiarity with the operation of extrajudicial process for conflict resolution.[111] This means that if individual lawyers are able to demonstrate their dexterity in resolving disputes through extrajudicial processes, this increases familiarity with the use of ADR to deal with

---

[107] Ibid.

[108] Section 31(2) of the Legal Practitioner Ordinance and Rule 4(3) of the Barristers (Qualification for Admission and Pupillage) Rules.

[109] Freidson, 'Professionalism', 23–24, 34.

[110] Abel, 'American Lawyers', 22.

[111] Freidson, 'Professionalism', 24–27. Intellectual capacity refers to the dexterity of an individual in applying substantive knowledge and skills in order to accomplish a task. This means that people must acquire substantive knowledge and experience (tactical skills) in order to accomplish a task.

disputes. Their capability of accomplishing a certain task in helping their clients to resolve disputes by means of ADR largely depends on the relative proportion of each type of knowledge and skills they employ. Given that lawyers place considerable efforts in handling disputes through technical knowledge instead of formal legal education, survey items that are all related to the use of practical knowledge in dealing with conflict resolution are associated with familiarity with the use of ADR for conflict resolution.[112]

Of the two measures of academic study in relation to ADR, the empirical results suggest that lawyers' familiarity with ADR processes is associated with ADR training courses offered either by the Law Faculties at the postgraduate level (e.g., LLM) or private ADR organizations (e.g., HKIAC).[113] Two plausible lines of reasoning for the relationship are as follows. First, Hong Kong lawyers may acquire practical, real-world experience in the fields of negotiation, mediation and conflict management either through the university law school curriculum at the postgraduate level or ADR service organizations.[114] For example, a lawyer who has successfully completed both mediator accreditation courses and assessments offered by various institutions which provide mediator training in Hong Kong is eligible to be considered for inclusion on the panel of accredited mediators.[115]

Following completion of relevant training and accreditation of mediators, a lawyer may gain status from his or her clients by performing an effective mediation advocacy. Second, ADR training courses under the LLB curriculum provide formal legal knowledge relating to the operation of ADR processes. Lawyers cannot apply formal legal knowledge to assist their clients in handling their disputes directly through ADR, as the undergraduate courses put undue emphasis on abstract theories and concepts.[116] This leads to my fourth hypothesis (stated in the alternative form).

Hypothesis 4: Hong Kong lawyers who are familiar with the ADR processes are more likely to adopt ADR in assisting their clients to settle shareholder disputes.

---

[112] See Table 6.1.
[113] See Table 6.1.
[114] The Report of the Working Group on Mediation, para. 6.19 General Accreditation Bodies in Hong Kong are The Hong Kong International Arbitration Centre, The Law Society of Hong Kong; The Hong Kong Mediation Centre, The Hong Kong Institute of Surveyors, Royal Institution of Chartered Surveyors Hong Kong and Hong Kong Institute of Architects.
[115] Ibid., para. 6.21.
[116] Freidson, 'Professionalism', 28–29.

The Influence of the Judiciary and Legal Professional Bodies on ADR Professional associations play important roles in the professional project in knowledge exchange and building capacity of lawyers to adopt a variety of public and public processes in assisting their clients to resolve shareholder disputes.[117] More recently, Mather and her colleagues have developed a conceptual framework in arguing that the legal profession, as a whole, provides the 'collegial communities' of practice.[118] The 'collegial communities' are crucial to defining professional norms and values through the 'mediated influence of collegiality'.[119] This means that the 'collegial communities' of legal practitioners can be viewed as 'interpersonal networks' that comprise a group of members with similar educational backgrounds, beliefs, socioeconomic status, practices and similar within the legal professional organizations.

The networks of both the Bar and the Law Society have a positive effect in persuading their peers or colleagues to accept innovative dispute resolution methods for shareholder disputes. This is due to the fact that the legal professional organizations provide meaningful reference points, such as the common ideology, language and norms of the legal profession, which repeatedly draw lawyers' attention to their general professional identities and their differences from non-professionals.[120] Undoubtedly, the legal professional organizations contribute directly to professional developments by translating the general and often contradictory professional identities and norms into guiding principles for daily application for their members.[121] They will use appropriate interpersonal communication channels (such as organizing numerous seminars and conferences) to give lawyers a better understanding about the operation of ADR. Interpersonal channels are particularly useful in convincing individual lawyers to adopt informal out-of-court processes when the experience of close colleagues shared in courses or seminars which are organized by the legal professional organizations suggest that such processes would be very effective modes of resolving shareholder disputes.[122]

---

[117] Richard Abel, 'England and Wales: A Comparison of the Professional Projects of Barristers and Solicitors', in Richard Abel and Philips C. Lewis (eds.), *Lawyers in Society* (Berkeley: University of California Press, 1995), 72–74.

[118] Lynn Mather et al., *Divorce Lawyers at Work: Varieties of Professionalism in Practice* (Oxford: Oxford University Press, 2001), 41–42 and MacFarlane, 'The New Lawyer', 34–37.

[119] Mather et al., 'Divorce Lawyers at Work', 34–37.

[120] Ibid., 42–43.

[121] Ibid., 61–62.

[122] See Table 6.1.

However, the 'social network' theory suggests that the influence from institutional networks (such as the Hong Kong Judiciary) contributes to the adoption of innovations by individuals.[123] Recently, scholars and legal practitioners in the field of ADR have suggested that judicial institutions play an important role by creating awareness and providing facilities to educate legal practitioners about ADR.[124] Notably, the impact of ADR information, education and training might be enhanced, as the Judiciary has taken account of potential lawyers' needs by giving them a better understanding about the use of ADR.[125] In addition, judicial encouragement of ADR, either by its case management powers or through the use of appropriate communication channels, may have positive impact on the use of ADR by Hong Kong lawyers.[126] Hence, both the Hong Kong Judiciary and legal professional bodies could exert influences on lawyers' attitudes towards the use of extrajudicial processes for shareholder disputes from various sources of promotional channels.[127] These arguments lead to the following hypothesis (stated in the alternative form).

Hypothesis 5: The existence of both the Judiciary and legal professional bodies are likely to facilitate the change in Hong Kong lawyers' attitudes towards the use of ADR for shareholder disputes.

Legal Environment for Resolving Shareholder Disputes

Previous academics noted that the impact of environmental variables such as local cultural environment, political conditions, economic globalization and other kinds of contextual factors on organizational innovativeness in the public sector are rather sparse.[128] They argue that a detailed analysis of the relationship between the influence of environmental factors and the spread of innovations helps to determine whether the implementation of innovations can be sustained over a long period of time.[129]

---

[123] Rogers, 'Diffusion of Innovations', 18–19. Rogers defines the term 'communication channel' as the 'means by which messages get from one individual to another'.

[124] Roselle L. Wissler, 'Barriers to Attorneys' Discussion and Use of ADR', *Ohio State Journal on Dispute Resolution*, 19:2 (2004), 459–508 at 495; Lord Justice Jackson, *Review of Civil Litigation Costs: Final Report* (London: The Stationary Office, 2009), paras. 3.9–3.10; and Hazel Genn, 'What Is Civil Justice For? Reform, ADR, and Access to Justice', *Yale Journal of Law and the Humanities*, 24:1 (2012), 397–417 at 416.

[125] Ibid.

[126] See Table 6.1.

[127] See Table 6.1.

[128] Boyne, et al., 'Explaining the Adoption of Innovation', 421. In general, the most effective way to promote the awareness of out-of-court processes for shareholder disputes includes conferences, press releases, TV drama, radio broadcasts and newspapers.

[129] Ibid.

This is particularly true because the best way to ensure sustainability of ADR programme in a country hinges on the capacities and belief systems of local stakeholders (such as lawyers and judges) to affect procedural changes involving the development of a set of private dispute resolution methods.[130] This is due to the fact that the local legal culture not only defines the appropriate styles of playing legal roles for local stakeholders, but also prescribes the use of different modes of dispute resolution processes for the resolution of disputes.[131] In addition, local legal culture may be important to the understanding of the interaction between the court-connected ADR initiatives for shareholder disputes and lawyers' beliefs about the use of ADR.[132] This empirical analysis helps to determine whether the current policy initiatives can successfully change lawyers' attitudes towards the use of informal out-of-court processes for shareholder disputes in the Hong Kong corporate context. On such a basis, the local legal culture is likely to influence the belief systems of individual lawyers to behave in a manner which is consistent with the objectives of the reform of the civil process in Hong Kong.

Promoting a Culture of Early Settlement in Resolving Shareholder Disputes   The courts had been promoting a culture of early settlement to cope with lengthy and expensive unfair prejudice proceedings prior to the introduction of the CJR in Hong Kong.[133] The rationale underlying the courts' promotion of a culture of early settlement in unfair prejudice cases under the statutory unfair prejudice provisions is consistent with the 'underlying objectives' underpinning the reform of the civil process in Hong Kong.[134] The impact of procedural developments with respect to the unfair prejudice proceedings is nonetheless far reaching, as it may subsequently influence lawyers' attitudes towards the use of ADR in the post-CJR era. This is due to the fact that the Hong Kong courts have expressly adopted Lord Hoffman's guidelines in motivating litigants to

---

[130] Lukasz Rozdeiczer and Alejandro Alvarez de la Campa, *Alternative Dispute Resolution Manual: Implementing Commercial Mediation - Small and Medium Enterprise Department* at http://rru.worldbank.org/Documents/Toolkits/adr/adr_fulltoolkit.pdf (Accessed 18 August 2009), 7–8.

[131] Galanter, 'Adjudication, Litigation, and Related Phenomena', 181.

[132] MacFarlane, 'The Evolution of New Lawyer', 250.

[133] The House of Lords decisions in *O'Neill v. Phillips* was decided in 1999. Hong Kong cases of *Re Prudential Enterprises Ltd* [2002] 1 HKLRD 267 (HK) and *Re Ranson Motor Manufacturing Company Ltd* [2007] 1 HKLRD 751 were decided before the implementation of the CJR in 2009.

[134] Order 1A, Rule 1(e) of the RHC.

settle disputes out-of-court through negotiation with respect to an early fair-buyout offer.[135] This creates legal certainty in assessing 'reasonableness' of offer which is made by the respondents to buyout the interests of a petitioner at an early stage. Lord Hoffman's guidance in *O'Neill* on what constitutes a reasonable offer was subsequently applied in the Hong Kong courts, and the judicial guidance is listed as follows:[136]

- There exists an offer to purchase the shares at fair value, which would normally involve the price being determined on a pro rata basis.
- The value, if not agreed, should be determined by a competent value.
- The valuer's determination would not need to provide for arbitration. The objective is 'economy and expedition'.
- The offer should provide for equality of arms between the parties.
- The issue of costs should be addressed and often the payment of costs would need to be included in the offer.

Undoubtedly, the general culture of judicial support for early fair buy-out offers has laid down a set of norms and values shared by the community of legal practitioners as well as the litigants. On one hand, corporate lawyers are more willing to encourage their clients to settle their disputes at an early stage, as this can reduce the time and expenses associated with shareholder litigation. On the other hand, this enhances the prospects of the parties in settling disputes through the company's buyout offer at an early stage. This perhaps is attributable mainly to the fact that a petitioner would not obtain everything to which he was entitled if he fails to accept a reasonable offer which was made by the respondents.[137] It concludes that recent procedural developments have enhanced legal certainty regarding judicial remedies available to aggrieved minority shareholders under Section 725 of the new Companies Ordinance. These arguments are in parallel with the factor analysis results.[138]

---

[135] The guidelines given by Lord Hoffman in *O'Neill v. Phillips* [1999] BCC at 614–615 were applied in Hong Kong. See *Re Prudential Enterprises Ltd* [2002] 1 HKLRD 267 and *Re Ranson Motor Manufacturing Company Ltd* [2007] 1 HKLRD 751.

[136] Ibid.

[137] In *O'Neill v. Phillips* [1999] BCC at 613, Lord Hoffman stated that if the petitioner was offered everything to which he has been held entitled, the respondent may, as in the case of a *Calderbank* letter, be entitled to say that the costs after the date of the offer should be made by the successful petitioner, who ought to have accepted the offer and brought the litigation to an end. On the other hand, a petitioner who contested a petition for nearly three years would not obtain everything to which he is entitled unless there is an offer of costs.

[138] See Table 6.1.

Arguably, legal certainty regarding judicial relief to aggrieved minority shareholders under Section 725 may have either a small positive or no impact on lawyers' enthusiasm for ADR processes. In particular, no prior suggestions were made for a way forward in reforming the statutory unfair prejudice provisions that extend the scope of arbitral power in dealing with disputes regarding valuation of shares for a buyout order in Hong Kong.[139] Although buyout relief sought by the minority shareholder under Section 725 is court based, a court ordered buyout order has promoted a culture of early settlement in the unfair prejudice proceedings. The preceding discussion leads to the following hypothesis.

Hypothesis 6: Legal certainty regarding judicial relief to aggrieved minority shareholders under Section 725 of the new Companies Ordinance may have either a small positive impact or no impact on lawyers' enthusiasm for ADR.

Appendix 1 further discusses the operationalization of the dependent and independent variables for this research. It provides a summary of the operational definitions, parameters, expected relationships and the way in which the six hypotheses have been formulated in this chapter.

6.4 Implications of the Research Findings for ADR Policy

In an overall view, the results of statistical analysis indicate that the proposed statistical model fits the analysis of Hong Kong lawyers' attitudes towards the use of ADR for shareholder disputes in the post-CJR era.

First, a review of the Variance Inflation Factor (VIF) of all the tested factors indicates, as shown in Table 6.2, that the highest score in the six equations was 2.304, and so basically there were no problems of multicollinearity.[140] In other words, each of the factors has an independent effect on the likelihood of Hong Kong lawyers' acceptance towards the use of out-of-court processes for shareholder disputes. Based on this result, the sample data collected from this research study can then be used to estimate the propensity of Hong Kong lawyers to adopt mediation and other

---

[139] Hwang Hokyu and Walter W. Powell, 'Institutions and Entrepreneurship', in Sharon A. Alvarez et al. (eds.), *Handbook of Entrepreneurship Research: Disciplinary Perspectives* (New York: Springer, 2005), 208.

[140] Damodar N. Gujarati, *Basic Econometrics*, 4th ed. (New York: McGraw Hill, 2003), 362. Gujarati suggests that multicollinearity is unlikely to be problematic if the VIF scores are below 10.0.

Table 6.2 *Multicollinearity Diagnostics for the Function of ADR Adoption by Hong Kong Lawyers*

Determinants that Drives HK Lawyers to Adopt ADR	Collinearity Statistics
	Variance Inflation Factor (VIF)
Compatibility	2.304
Advantage	1.895
Barrier	1.067
Familiarity	1.257
Network	1.558
Legal Culture	1.082

informal out-of-court processes in assisting their clients to resolve shareholder disputes.

Second, the statistical results depicted in Table 6.3 suggest that the model accounts for a significant amount of the variation in whether or not individual Hong Kong lawyers adopt out-of-court processes for shareholder disputes since the CJR began in 2009. This means that the overall model is highly significant ($p < 0.000$) as the Cox and Snell pseudo-R^2 statistic is 47 per cent (see Table 6.3).[141] In further attempt to assess model fit, the author computed the Hosmer–Lemeshow goodness-of-fit statistics. The Hosmer–Lemeshow goodness-of-fit test put observations into groups based on estimated probabilities and then computes a Pearson Chi-square statistic based on the observed and estimated expected frequencies in each of the groups.[142] A significant Hosmer–Lemeshow statistic suggests differences between the observed and expected frequencies in the groups, and thus a lack of model fit.[143] In this case, the Hosmer–Lemeshow goodness-of-fit statistic is 0.792 and not significant ($p > 0.05$), suggesting that the data fit the model at an acceptable level (see Table 6.3).

Third, Table 6.3 presents the results of the binary logistic regression model used to test the relationship between three groups of predictor variables and lawyers' decisions regarding whether or not to adopt ADR for shareholder disputes since the CJR began in 2009. The results illustrated

[141] The Cox and Snell pseudo-R^2 statistic is based on the log likelihood for the model compared to the log likelihood for a baseline model. See generally David Roxbee Cox and E. Joyce Snell, *The Analysis of Binary Data*, 2nd ed. (London: Chapman & Hall, 1989).

[142] David W. Hosmer and Stanley Lemeshow, *Applied Logistic Regression*, 2nd ed. (Hoboken, NJ: John Wiley & Sons, 2000), 148.

[143] Ibid.

Table 6.3 *Logistic Regression of Hong Kong Lawyers' Attitudes Towards the Use of ADR for Shareholder Disputes*

Logit (ADOP) = $\beta_0 + \beta_1$ COMPATIBILITY + β_2 ADVANTAGE + β_3 BARRIERS + β_4 FAMILIARITY + β_5 NETWORK + β_6 LEGAL CULTURE

Variable	Predicted Relation	β	S.E	Wald	df	Exp(β)
Intercept	?	−23.075	12.103	3.635	1	0.000
COMPATIBILITY	+	2.407	1.059	5.167[a]	1	11.101
ADVANTAGE	+	−1.105	0.449	6.049[a]	1	0.331
BARRIERS	−	1.619	0.846	3.663	1	5.046
FAMILIARITY	+	0.832	0.296	7.912[a]	1	2.298
NETWORK	+	−0.714	0.456	2.450	1	0.490
LEGAL CULTURE	+/none	1.081	0.576	3.526	1	2.947
Number of observations		63[b]				
Chi-square for model		39.56				
p-value		(0.000)				
Pseudo-R^2 (the Cox & Snell R^2)		0.47				
Hosmer–Lemeshow statistic		0.792				
p-value		(0.999)				

[a] Indicates statistically significant at the < 5% level.

[b] Outliers were detected in the analysis and four cases were removed for interpretation.

Note: The residuals were checked for outliers. Prior to the removal of outliers, the accuracy rate of the logistic regression model is 88.1 per cent. After removing outliers, the accuracy rate of the logistic regression model is 95.2 per cent. Given that the logistic regression omitting outliers has a classification accuracy rate that is higher than the logistic regression for all cases, the model excluding outliers is preferred for regression analysis.

Key to Table 6.3

α	=	Constant, or the *y*-intercept of the regression plane
β	=	Coefficient variable. This represents the change in the logit of the dependent variable associated with a one-unit change in the predictor variable.
S.E.	=	Standard error. This represents the standard deviation between sample means.
Wald	=	The Wald Chi-square statistic is used to determine whether the predictor variable is statistically significantly different from zero. If the Wald test is significant, then the predictor variable is making a significant contribution to the outcome and this variable should be included in the model.
d.f.	=	Degrees of freedom
Exp(β)	=	This can be interpreted as a change in odds resulting from a unit change in the predictor. If the value is > 1 then, as the predictor increases, the odds of an outcome occurring increases.

Source: The key to Table 6.3 was adapted from Walker and his colleagues; for details see Walker et al., 'Managing Public Services Innovation', 76.

that there were a few statistically significant results and suggest that the outcome of Hong Kong lawyers' acceptance towards the use of out-of-court processes for shareholder disputes owes more to observable factors used in the present analysis than to the unobservable factors (e.g., a mix of complicated factors).[144] Thus, the explanation for Hong Kong lawyers' acceptance towards the use of informal out-of-court processes for shareholder disputes could mostly be found in the following factors, which are related to the determinants of ADR adoption by Hong Kong lawyers.

6.4.1 *The Compatibility of ADR Process with Court-Based Shareholder Proceedings*

The statistical result indicates that compatibility was the significant determinant of the likelihood of Hong Kong lawyers accepting the use

---

[144] Comparing it with Hazel Genn et al., *Twisting Arms: Court Referred and Court Linked Mediation Under Judicial Pressure* (Ministry of Justice Research Series, Series 1/07, 2007), 64. Genn and her colleagues conducted an empirical research identifying the factors that most likely affect the rate of mediation settlement. The report illustrates that there were few statistically significant results and suggest that 'the outcome at mediation owes more to chance or unobservable factors than to the observable factors used in the analyses.'

of out-of-court processes to assist their clients in resolving shareholder disputes (see Table 6.3).[145] The empirical result is confirmed by arguments made in Chapter 5 that both informal out-of-court and traditional court adjudication processes are compatible on the basis that both dispute resolution processes are complementary.[146]

6.4.2 The Relative Advantages of ADR

The empirical results indicate that there is a negative association between the perceived advantages of ADR and the likelihood of Hong Kong lawyers to choose informal out-of-court processes for the resolution of shareholder disputes (see Table 6.3).[147] One plausible line of reasoning of this is that informal out-of-court processes have their weaknesses. Prior quantitative studies on ADR support this contention, indicating that out-of-court processes (such as mediation, arbitration and negotiation) are neither faster nor cheaper than formal adjudication.[148] The finding indicates that Hong Kong lawyers who believe that out-of-court processes have their own relative advantages in both aspects of cost-effectiveness and high level of satisfaction are 67 per cent less likely to adopt ADR for shareholder disputes.

The reason for the negative association between the probability of ADR adoption for shareholder disputes among Hong Kong lawyers and the relative advantage of ADR lies in the following aspect. The adversarial lawyering model that places particular emphasis on winner-take-all decisions about legal rights and wrongs have deeply influenced Hong Kong lawyers' attitudes towards the use of ADR for shareholder disputes. Hong Kong lawyers may not yet find themselves in combining both the rights-based litigation strategies and practical problem-solving skills in meeting the demand of a less adversarial, earlier settlement culture.[149]

The finding seems to support MacFarlane's pathway that lawyers may take an adversarial approach to ADR despite her research findings were mainly based on face-to-face interviews with legal counsels in Ottawa

---

[145] The significant beta coefficient for compatibility suggests that the likelihood of ADR adoption is associated positively with the compatibility of ADR (p <0.05).

[146] For details, see Chapter 5.

[147] The results illustrated that the beta coefficient for advantages is in the opposite direction despite the fact it is statistically significant (p < 0.05).

[148] Thomas O. Main, 'ADR: The New Equity', University of Cincinnati Law Review, 74 (2005), 329–404 at 396–397.

[149] MacFarlane, 'The New Lawyer', 20.

and Toronto.[150] Most commonly, lawyers may use the mediation process as a 'fishing expedition' to discover the weaknesses in the other side's case or as a delaying tactic towards disclosure of documents, with no real interest in assisting their clients to work a solution through the mediation process sincerely.[151] The reasons for Hong Kong lawyers to employ a variety of adversarial strategies in the mediation process is partly due to the direction on mediation, which provides that parties are required to first attempt out-of-court procedures before resorting to court proceedings.

The Legislative Council has raised serious concerns regarding the 'sham mediation' after the implementation of Practice Direction 31 on mediation.[152] The term 'sham mediation' means that lawyers may employ a variety of adversarial tactics such as concealment of significant information to gain leverage for later negotiation or to try to psyche out the opponent in the mediation process. These tactics may also be termed as 'Rambo tactics' as 'ADR was just another stop in the "litigation game" which provides an opportunity for the manipulation of rules, time, information, and ultimately, money.'[153] The research finding seems to support the observations made by Justice Poon as well:[154]

> Parties only take mediation as just another interlocutory step in the litigation process which they need to go through. They just pay lip service to the process in order to avoid any possible costs sanction. There is no genuine attempt to mediate at all.... All the efforts will, however, come to naught if there is no material change in the culture in the conduct of dispute resolution.

Apparently, legal protection for the confidentiality of mediation communication is needed, as this prevents the parties and their legal representatives

---

[150] See MacFarlane, 'The Evolution of New Lawyer', 266–268. MacFarlane's study illustrates that Toronto lawyers tend to use court-connected mediation programs as an instrument to gain partisan advantage.

[151] Ibid. and Carrie Menkel-Meadow, 'Pursuing Settlement in an Adversary Culture: A Tale of Innovation Co-opted or 'The Law of ADR'', *Florida State University Law Review*, 19 (1991), 1–46 at 3. Professor Menkel-Meadow contends that 'lawyers may use ADR not for the accomplishment of a better result, but as another weapon in the adversarial arsenal to manipulate time, methods of discovery, and rules of procedure for perceived client advantage.' See also Interim Report and Consultative Paper on Civil Justice Reform, para. 636.

[152] LegCo Panel on Administration of Justice and Legal Services, *Development of Mediation Services and Mediation Services for Building Management Cases* (2011), 4.

[153] Lande, 'Using Dispute System Design Methods to Promote Good-Faith Participation in Court-Connected Mediation Programmes', 122–123 and at 17.

[154] Justice Poon, 'Opening Remarks'.

from using mediation as a strategic way of discovering information about the strengths and weaknesses of the other party's case. This is also in line with Rogers VP's reasoning in *S v. T (Mediation: Privilege)*, which stated that there would be no incentive for parties to engage in open and frank discussion if the court refused to protect the confidentiality of communications made in the mediation process.[155] The new legislation on mediation is particularly welcomed as it offers the protections of the confidentiality of mediation communications.[156] The Ordinance not only provides greater certainty with regard to the confidentiality of mediation communication, but also encourages the parties and their legal representatives to participate in the mediation process in a sincere manner.

6.4.3 Potential Barriers to the Use of ADR for Settlement

The statistical results run contrary to the expectation that barriers to settlement may reduce the likelihood of Hong Kong lawyers to using ADR processes to help their clients resolve shareholder disputes (see Table 6.3). The finding seems to support the recommendations made by the Working Group on Mediation, which indicate that the introduction of legislative provisions in dealing with enforcement of a mediation agreement may hinder the voluntary use of ADR.[157] At present, the new Mediation Ordinance does not contain a statutory mechanism for enforcing mediation agreements. Where necessary, enforcement of mediation settlements can be dealt with by the court in ordinary cases of enforcement of contracts.[158] The main reasons for the judge to determine the enforceability of mediation agreements on a case-by-case basis may be attributable to a number of factors.

The first reason is that the opposite parties are less likely to repudiate or challenge the mediation agreement subsequently as the grounds for setting aside mediation agreement or refusing to attend ADR are generally limited in the Hong Kong context.[159] Another possible reason may be

---

[155] [2011] 1 HKLRD 534 at 535–537.

[156] Section 8 of the Mediation Ordinance (Cap. 620) sets out the general proposition that mediation communication must not be disclosed. However, this rule is not absolute. Exceptions to the disclosure of mediation communications are provided in Sections 8(2) and (3) of the Ordinance.

[157] The Report of the Working Group on Mediation, para. 7.26.

[158] Nadja Alexander, The New Hong Kong Mediation Ordinance: Much Ado About Nothing? (2012) at http://kluwermediationblog.com (Accessed on 16 April 2012).

[159] Recent court decisions made by the Hong Kong courts provided reference regarding any challenges to the validity of mediated agreements. For instance, in *Upplan Co Ltd v. Li Ho*

attributable to the role of the common law judge in exercising its discretionary power in accordance with rules laid down in legislation or leading judicial precedents. Recent legislation on mediation in Hong Kong gives the court more flexibility in exercising its case management power to facilitate early settlement. This fulfils the primary purposes of the mediation law which maintains the flexibility of the mediation process, while at the same time, providing a basic statutory framework for the conduct of mediations.[160]

In addition, with the underlying objectives of the RHC in mind, it may be expected that Hong Kong judges would be willing to exercise their case management powers to facilitate settlement if a mediation agreement is drafted in significant detail that includes all practical issues relating to the operational framework for mediation.[161] This includes the mediation rules of a named dispute resolution organization, an agreed procedure for the appointment of the mediator, the time frame for mediation, costs incurred in the mediation process and so on.[162] On that basis, the flexibility of the court's powers to deal with the issues relating to the enforceability of the mediation agreement is desirable. This enables the Hong Kong court to interpret the words of the Mediation Ordinance and the court rules in light of the policy objectives of promoting mediation within the local business community and legal profession.

6.4.4 Lawyers' Familiarity with ADR

The empirical findings reveal that Hong Kong lawyers who are more familiar with ADR are more likely to use private dispute resolution processes to

---

Ming [2010] HKEC 1257 (CFI) at para. 25, the court held that the parties were still at liberty to determine whether they might have mediation to resolve their disputes. In contrast with the power of the court, the role of the court is to determine any adverse costs order against a party under para. 5 of the Practice Direction 31 if a party fails to provide a reasonable explanation for not engaging in mediation. However, some legal commentators note that the lack of certainty in defining the level of participation may create addition hurdles for the court to encourage the parties to participate in mediation sincerely. This argument rests on the assumption that lack of clarity in defining the level of participation results in 'satellite litigation and greater uncertainty as well as lack of confidence in the confidentiality of the mediation process.' For details, see Dorcas Quek, 'Mandatory Mediation: An Oxymoron? Examining The Feasibility of Implementing A Court-Mandated Mediation Program', *Cardozo Journal of Conflict Resolution*, 11 (2010), 479–509 at 492–494.

[160] Legislative Council, *Bills Committee on Mediation Bill: Background Brief Prepared by the Legislative Council Secretariat* (2011).

[161] Order 1A, Rule 4(2)(e) of the RHC.

[162] Zhao Yun, 'Revisiting the Issue of Enforceability of Mediation Agreements in Hong Kong', *China-EU Law Journal*, 1(2013), 115–133, 124–126.

help their clients resolve shareholder disputes (see Table 6.3).[163] The result also indicates that Hong Kong lawyers who are more familiar with the application of extrajudicial processes are 130 per cent more likely to adopt ADR in assisting their clients to resolve shareholder disputes. The finding is confirmed by Wissler, who notes that there is a positive association between the efforts to increase lawyers' familiarity with ADR processes and the use of ADR.[164] One policy implication derived from the result obtained from the statistical analysis is that where solicitors were familiar with, or understood the mediation process, the presence and active involvement of lawyers in representing the weaker parties in the facilitative mediation process might reduce the effects of inequalities.[165] One possible reason for this is that lawyers have acquired knowledge of both the adjudicative and consensus-building models of disputing.[166] They are professional dispute handlers who are competent to make an assessment on whether a settlement offer is consistent with the expected outcome in court.[167] On that basis, it is justifiable for the Hong Kong Mediation Code to provide measures (such as the representation of both parties) to reduce the effects of power imbalances and inequalities between parties in the mediation process.[168]

6.4.5 The Influence of the Judiciary and Legal Professional Bodies on ADR

The statistical results indicate that a network was not a significant determinant of the likelihood of Hong Kong lawyers to choose extrajudicial processes for the resolution of shareholder disputes (see Table 6.3).[169] The results thus fail to offer evidence to support that the influence of both the Judiciary and legal professional networks can change Hong Kong lawyers' attitudes towards using of informal out-of-court processes for shareholder disputes. Consequently, the author is unable to confirm whether

---

[163] The results illustrated that the beta coefficient for familiarity was significantly positive ($p < 0.05$).

[164] Wissler, 'Barriers to Attorneys' Discussion and Use of ADR', 495.

[165] Genn et al., 'Twisting Arms', 191 and Oren Gazal-Ayal and Ronen Perry, 'Imbalances of Power in ADR: The Impact of Representation and Dispute Resolution Method on Case Outcomes', Law & Social Inquiry, (2014), 1–33 at 19.

[166] Gazal-Ayal and Perry, 'Imbalances of Power in ADR', 8.

[167] Ibid.

[168] Section 7 of the Hong Kong Mediation Code.

[169] The results illustrated that the coefficient of network is not significantly positive.

Hong Kong lawyers are resistant to acting in a manner that is consistent with the less adversarial norms within their legal professional community.

Another possible reason for the insignificant influence from the Judiciary and legal professional bodies on ADR may be attributable to the fact that professional codes of conduct for the legal profession are open-textured criteria which may be interpreted in different ways by different legal practitioners.[170] Although legal practitioners have both a legal and an ethical duty to encourage clients to settle at an early stage, the Codes provide a general set of professional values guiding lawyers in the exercise of their professional judgement regarding the proper way to encourage their clients to settle.[171] However, the Codes offer very little specific guidelines on how lawyers should behave in a manner that is consistent with the original ADR goals.[172] In this regard, owing to the open-ended nature of the Codes, it will not be surprising that individual lawyers might not offer valuable advice to their clients about the benefits of mediation and other informal out-of-court processes for the resolution of shareholder disputes.

6.4.6 Promoting a Culture of Early Settlement in Resolving Shareholder Disputes

The statistical results support the expectation that legal certainty regarding judicial relief to aggrieved minority shareholders under Section 725 of the new Companies Ordinance does not impact lawyers' enthusiasm for ADR (see Table 6.3). There are two possible explanations to support this empirical result.

First, substantive law developments in unfair prejudice proceedings have enhanced the legal certainty as to the effective way of resolving shareholder disputes through out-of-court settlements. Legal certainty regarding the judicial discretion under the corporate law, such as an order

---

[170] MacFarlane, 'The New Lawyer', 42–46.

[171] Principle 1017 of the Hong Kong Solicitors' Guide to Professional conduct provides that solicitors are under a duty not to waste the time of the court by considering whether a settlement would be in the best interests of their clients and to advise them accordingly. Similarly, barristers must in every case use their best endeavours to avoid unnecessary expense and waste of the court time, and this ethical duty is provided under para. 133 of the Bar Code, promulgated by the Hong Kong Bar Council. At common law, a legal practitioner in Hong Kong is also under a common law duty of skill and care to give advice to his or her clients regarding the terms, offer and acceptance of settlement.

[172] Order 1A, Rule 3 of the RHCs.

for the buyout of the petitioners by the majority shareholders, does not have a direct impact on legal practitioners to champion new practices proactively.[173]

Second, both informal dispute resolution processes and unfair prejudice proceedings are not mutually exclusive. The result is further confirmed by Galanter, who notes that adjudication and self-help measures (for example the inclusion of a pre-dispute resolution clause into the company's articles or shareholders' agreement) are not mutually exclusive, as courts may regulate and authorize self-help mechanisms.[174] The same argument may also explain why Hong Kong lawyers believe that ADR practice is compatible with their litigation-centred approach to resolving shareholder disputes. This further confirms that both ADR and unfair prejudice proceedings may not be true competitive rivals. Informal procedures are not substituted for formal adjudication of shareholder disputes, particularly in Hong Kong.[175] As a whole, the key findings arising from the statistical results can be summarized as follows.

First, the compatibility of the ADR process with court-based shareholder proceedings was the most likely factor affecting Hong Kong lawyers' acceptance towards the use of informal out-of-court processes for shareholder disputes. Based on this finding, the inclusion of out-of-court processes into the new unfair prejudice petitions rules is to be welcomed.

Second, the recent establishments of a single non-statutory, industry-led accreditation body (the Hong Kong Mediation Accreditation Association Limited [HKMAAL]) would also be welcomed, in particular where Hong Kong lawyers might find it difficult to appreciate the benefits of informal out-of-court processes for the resolution of shareholder disputes.[176] This argument was based on the empirical results that there was a negative association between the perceived advantages of extrajudicial processes and the likelihood of Hong Kong lawyers using ADR processes to help their clients resolve shareholder disputes. Some lawyers might

---

[173] Hwang and Powell, 'Institutions and Entrepreneurship', 205. Hwang and Powell note that if the enactment of a particular law were ambiguous regarding standards of compliance and lacked effective mechanisms for enforcement, this opens a new space for personnel experts such as lawyers to initiate change. They explain this phenomenon through the passage of the Equal Employment Law in the United States.

[174] Galanter, 'Adjudication, Litigation, and Related Phenomena', 185.

[175] See Chapter 5.

[176] Legislative Council, *Legislative Council Panel on Administration and Legal Services: Mediation* (2013).

behave opportunistically with respect to the inappropriate use of informal out-of-court processes as alternative means to gain personal advantages through the application of traditional, litigation-centred approaches to intimidate the opposite side.[177]

Although the HKMAAL was formed to provide a unified accreditation system, the Mediation Ordinance does not provide for a single accreditation body that prescribes a standardized system for accrediting mediators. One obvious reason leading to the challenge of the establishment of a new regulatory body for the accreditation of mediators is that it is difficult to persuade the existing mediation service providers to surrender their jurisdictional powers to the authoritative institution.[178]

Hopefully, a statutory accreditation body could be set up to replace the HKMAAL in the future. The merit of a statutory accreditation body is that its legitimacy derives from the Mediation Ordinance, and that it has the necessary legal backing required in promoting accreditation of mediators.[179] Given that the institutional setup and objectives of a statutory accreditation body would be prescribed by the Mediation Ordinance, this enhances public confidence in mediation services, and the credibility of mediation could be maintained. In this regard, Hong Kong lawyers who are performing the function of mediators may be more willing to appreciate the benefits of mediation processes.

Last but not least, it is appropriate to argue that training and practical experiences on out-of-court processes play an important role in raising the awareness of Hong Kong lawyers to search for more cost-effective alternative means to resolve shareholder disputes.

6.5 Limitations and Conclusion

The statistical results offer relatively strong support that the model accounts for almost half of the variation in whether or not individual lawyers have adopted ADR processes for shareholder disputes since the CJR began in 2009. However, the author must acknowledge a number of limitations in the present study. The first one includes issues related to the sample size and sample selection and measurement related issues

---

[177] Ibid.
[178] Gavin Denton and Fan Kun, 'Hong Kong' in Carlos Esplugues and Silvia Barona (eds.), *Global Perspectives on ADR* (Cambridge, UK: Intersentia, 2014), 163.
[179] The Report of the Working Group on Mediation, paras. 6.12–6.16.

in analysing lawyers' attitudes towards the use of out-of-court processes for shareholder disputes. The relatively small size of the sample may lead to the result that many other factors not considered in our model may influence their decisions in using extrajudicial processes for shareholder disputes. Further, the study uses only Hong Kong data from the Hong Kong legal profession. These may not be applicable for cross-country comparative analysis of legal professionals. This is in part because there are significant differences in the nature of work that lawyers do in other jurisdictions.[180] It is also noteworthy that more accurate measures of the characteristics of ADR needed to be devised.

The second limitation of this study includes issues that the data are cross-sectional in nature and relate only to Hong Kong lawyers. In addition, the survey data were heavily drawn from individual lawyers' attitudes towards the use of informal dispute resolution processes with forced-choice question type format. Ideally, triangulating this data with secondary data (such as government publications) and actual evidence (such personal interviews or experimental studies with lawyers) would greatly strengthen the results of the study.[181] In addition, the sampling frame may also be enlarged to include judges, court staffs, business executives and accountants for a more comprehensive analysis of the impact of the civil justice reform on the use of informal dispute resolution methods for the resolution of shareholder disputes.

The third limitation of this study relates to the measurement of dependent variables. Given that the dependent variable was operationalized as a dichotomous 'yes–no' answer for ADR adoption, this is not an effective measure in determining the degree of actual utilization of ADR.[182] The development of an index or the implementation of a rating scale to measure ADR adoption is appropriate, as this helps to capture the variation in lawyers' behaviour in accepting the use of ADR for shareholder disputes.[183] Last, but not least, the results of the factor analysis are purely exploratory in nature.

---

[180] Lawrence M. Friedman, 'Lawyers in Cross-Cultural Perspective', in Richard L. Abel and Philips C. Lewis (eds.), *Lawyers in Society: Comparative Theories*, Vol. III, (Berkeley: University of California Press, 1989), 1. For example, civil law countries.

[181] But these were beyond the scope of this research study. See also Walker, 'Innovation Type and Diffusion', 331.

[182] See Boyne et al., 'Explaining the Adoption of Innovation', 426–427.

[183] Ibid.

These limitations lead to the conclusion that the suggested logistic regression model I used here reaches some tentative conclusions about the general use of alternatives to formal court litigation processes for shareholder disputes among individual Hong Kong lawyers. Hopefully, future researchers may tackle these limitations by following the suggested research directions in this book and cooperating closely with scholars in other social sciences.[184]

---

[184] Sir Jack I. H. Jacob, *The Fabric of English Civil Justice* (London: Stevens, 1987), 254.

PART III

The Future Development of ADR in
Hong Kong: Codification of ADR for Shareholder
Disputes in Hong Kong

7

Innovative Approaches to the Future Codification of ADR for Shareholder Disputes in Hong Kong

Borrowing Models from the United Kingdom, New Zealand and South Africa

7.1 Introduction

In Hong Kong, the prohibitive costs of litigation and significant trial delays further encourage the Judiciary to take a pragmatic approach to the development of a court-based ADR programme through the 2009 Civil Justice Reform (CJR).[1] Such a court-appended approach to alternative dispute resolution would be considered as the optimal type of institutionalization. First, the discretionary jurisdiction which the Rules of the High Court (RHC) confers on the court to manage the conduct of civil cases has been considerably expanded.[2] Under the new court rules, the court is prompted to stray from passivity and to take a more proactive approach to encouraging the parties and their lawyers to consider the possibility of ADR to resolve their disputes before a trial begins.[3] Thus, the judicial case management role has evolved from a 'passive case manager' who is responsible for adjudicating questions of facts and question of law in accordance with materials produced by the parties and their lawyers, to an 'active dispute manager' who offers a range of formal and informal dispute resolution processes to assist the disputing parties in resolving their disputes.

Second, there is a great deal of flexibility of the court to give directions as he or she thinks appropriate, including directions regarding the appropriateness of early mediation and other alternative processes in some types of shareholder disputes.[4] Although the CJR was implemented with

---

[1] Hong Kong Judiciary, *Reform of the Civil Justice System in Hong Kong*, Interim Report and Consultative Paper on Civil Justice Reform (Hong Kong Judiciary, 2000), paras. 3–5.
[2] Order 1A, Rule 4(2)(e) of the RHC.
[3] Ibid.
[4] Practice Directions 3.3 and 31.

the objectives to promote a sense of proportionality in relation to the economics of a case, it is unlikely that the court would exercise its case management powers to compel parties to attend ADR in the post-CJR era.[5] This fulfils the underlying policy objectives of maintaining the voluntary nature of ADR processes, including mediation.[6]

In addition, the Hong Kong government has recently taken a positive step to institutionalize the greater use of ADR processes for shareholder disputes through the introduction of the Companies (Unfair Prejudice Petitions) Proceedings Rules.[7] A comprehensive rewrite of corporation statutes relating to the specific procedural rules introduced for unfair prejudice petitions viewed to be innovative. The recent reform of the company law is seen as an important step of the Hong Kong government to embrace 'both novelty and change' to the statutory unfair prejudice provisions relating to new additional powers of the court to make an order for a stay for mediation or other alternative processes for any period as the court thinks fit.[8]

This chapter aims to fill in this research gap by exploring the extent to which foreign law and practices regarding the use of ADR to deal with shareholder disputes could be adopted in Hong Kong with respect to the perspectives of the local legal professional community. This chapter suggests that lessons could be drawn from the United Kingdom, New Zealand and South Africa with respect to the following approaches to the codification of ADR for shareholder disputes:[9]

1. A permissive rule contained in the company law that permits the parties to include an arbitration clause either in the articles of association of the company or in a separate agreement made by all shareholders (i.e., a unanimous shareholder's agreement).
2. The inclusion of mandatory ADR provisions into the company law.
3. The issuance of a voluntary code of governance practice that recommends the company use ADR to deal with minority shareholder disputes. A publically listed company is generally required to disclose how it had complied with the code, and explain in what circumstances

---

[5] Order 1A, Rule 2(2) of the RHC.
[6] Hong Kong Judiciary, *Reform of the Civil Justice System in Hong Kong*, Final Report of the Working Party on Civil Justice Reform (Hong Kong Judiciary, 2004), paras. 826–827.
[7] Rule 6(f) of the Companies (Unfair Prejudice Petitions) Proceedings Rules.
[8] Ibid. and Julia Black, 'What Is Regulatory Innovation?', in Julia Black et al. (eds.), *Regulatory Innovation: A Comparative Analysis* (Cheltenham: Edward Elgar, 2005), 4 and 7.
[9] See Sections 7.2.1–7.2.3.

the company had not applied the code. This is generally referred to as the 'comply or explain' model.

The premises underlying the argument are as follows. First, local legal elites play an important role in channelling the diffusion of foreign materials from the original countries (such as the United Kingdom, New Zealand and South Africa) to the recipient country (i.e., Hong Kong). One plausible line of reasoning of this is that local elite lawyers are not only heavily involved in the lawmaking process, but they also interact closely with government officials, industry groups and international organizations to support the institutionalization of ADR for shareholder disputes through a mix of legal and non-legal policy instruments.[10] For example, the diffusion of arbitral policy from an international organization such as the United Nations Commission on International Trade Law (UNCITRAL) to a domestic regime (such as Hong Kong) occurs through an 'epistemic community', which may consist of professionals from a variety of disciplines and backgrounds (such as lawyers, accountants, business people and similar).[11] On that basis, it is justified to infer that the extent of local lawyers' influence about the adoption of foreign law and practices on ADR for shareholder disputes should not be ignored.[12]

Second, Hong Kong has taken only a small step forward to developing a sophisticated and systematic use of ADR for shareholder disputes under the existing regulatory framework (such as rules and legislations) for shareholder disputes. Future developments of innovative approaches to the codification of shareholder disputes in Hong Kong could be explored further by borrowing the most advanced experience from other common law jurisdictions, such as the United Kingdom, New Zealand and South Africa.[13] The reasons for the adoption of foreign models which are perceived to be more legitimate or more successful in providing a regulatory framework for the use of ADR processes for shareholder disputes are reflected through the following aspects.

First, the similarity of the legal rules and institutions of the recipient country (Hong Kong) to those of the original countries (the United Kingdom, New Zealand and South Africa) increases the likelihood of

---

[10] Katherine L. Lynch, *The Forces of Economic Globalization: Challenges to the Regime of International Commercial Arbitration* (The Hague: Kluwer Law International, 2003), 94–100.

[11] Ibid., 94–95 and 98.

[12] See Sections 7.3.1–7.3.3.

[13] Ibid.

success in adopting foreign ADR policies for shareholder disputes.[14] The adoption of a specific legislation on ADR for shareholder disputes (such as the inclusion of ADR provision into the company law) from the United Kingdom, New Zealand and South Africa could also be driven by the importance of shared language, the common law origin and the formulation of the law and rules based on the global model of corporate law.[15]

Second, the reception of foreign models, notably through a blend of approaches to the codification of ADR for shareholder disputes, is nonetheless extremely effective in generating legitimacy. This is due to the fact that the source of this type of legitimacy stems from the need of the Hong Kong government to cope with uncertainty about the future codification of ADR mechanisms for shareholder disputes, by adopting foreign models which are perceived to be more legitimate or more successful.[16] Thus, experience from other common law jurisdictions could provide future directions for Hong Kong either to incorporate specific ADR provisions into the substantive content of the corporate law or develop corporate governance code or guidelines on the use of ADR contractual clauses to resolve shareholder disputes. Ultimately, the adaption of foreign ADR policies for shareholder disputes could legitimize the greater use of extra-judicial processes in Hong Kong.[17]

The implication of the proposed approaches to the codification of ADR for shareholder disputes will be discussed as follows. Section 7.2 considers how the common law countries, such as the United Kingdom, New Zealand and South Africa have adopted various approaches to the codification of ADR devices for the resolution of shareholder disputes. An analysis is also made on how to incorporate lessons from the United Kingdom, New Zealand and South Africa, which could reduce uncertainty about the future codification of ADR for shareholder disputes in Hong Kong.

---

[14] Mindy Chen-Wishart, 'Legal Transplant and Undue Influence: Lost in Translation or a Working Mis-understanding?', *International and Comparative Law Quarterly*, 62 (2013), 10.

[15] Holger Spamann, 'Contemporary Legal Transplants: Legal Families and the Diffusion of (Corporate) Law', *Brigham Young University Law Review*, 11:6 (2009), 1813–1878.

[16] Paul J. DiMaggio and Walter W. Powell, 'The Iron Cage Revisited: Institutional Isomorphism and Collective Rationality in Organizational Fields', *American Sociological Review*, 48:2 (1983), 147–160 at 151.

[17] Frances Stokes Berry and William D. Berry, 'Innovation and Diffusion Models in Policy Research' in Paul A. Sabatier (ed.), *Theories of the Policy Process* (Boulder, CO: Westview Press, 2007), 223. Berry and Berry depict that the term 'policy innovation' is defined as '… a program that is a new to the government adopting it. This means that a governmental jurisdiction can innovate by adopting a program that numerous other jurisdictions established many years ago'.

Section 7.3 develops three testable series of arguments regarding the conditions under which Hong Kong may learn from the United Kingdom, New Zealand and South Africa experience by examining which foreign law and practices provide the best exemplars for Hong Kong to adapt or follow. Section 7.4 finally concludes with suggestions on the future codification of ADR programme for shareholder disputes in Hong Kong.

7.2 Approaches to the Codification of ADR for Shareholder Disputes: Experience from the United Kingdom, New Zealand and South Africa

This section presents an overview of how the United Kingdom, New Zealand and South Africa rely primarily on the use of company legislation, supported by the judicial institution and the corporate governance codes issued by industry bodies (such as the Institute of Directors) to increase the potential use of arbitration and mediation in facilitating early settlements of shareholder disputes. This section suggests that in order to answer the question of how to formulate a mixture of approaches to the codification of ADR devices for the resolution of shareholder disputes in Hong Kong, it is necessary to analyse the following questions:

1. How to circumvent court-based shareholder proceedings through the inclusion of a pre-dispute arbitration clause into the company's constitutions or a shareholders' agreement?
2. How to include an arbitration provision that operates alongside the framework of mandatory corporate rules?
3. How to increase the public understanding about the use of arbitration and other informal out-of-court processes for the resolution of shareholder disputes through the codes of corporate governance?

7.2.1 The United Kingdom: Practical Considerations for the Inclusion of an Arbitration Clause into the Company's Constitution or a Shareholders' Agreement

This section seeks to consider the practical issues relating to the enforceability of an arbitration clauses contained either in the company's constitutions[18] or a shareholders' agreement. It begins to examine the scope of the concept of arbitrability in relation to disputes between majority and

---

[18] Section 17 of the UKCA 2006 provides that the company's constitution includes the company's articles and any special resolutions, or other resolutions that can effectively bind all members of a class of shareholders without their consent.

minority shareholders in a quasi-partnership type company. This analysis helps to determine whether the UK courts are increasingly willing to recognize the preference of shareholders in relying on a valid arbitration agreement contained in the company's constitution or a shareholder agreement to circumvent the inherent court's jurisdiction to grant relief under Section 996 of the UK Companies Act (UKCA) 2006. Following that, it explores in detail the risk of additional procedural requirements of the shareholders to arbitrate their differences before resorting to litigation under the company's constitution or a shareholders' agreement. Finally, practical constraints on the ability of a minority shareholder to bring court proceedings under an arbitration agreement contained either in the company's constitution or a shareholders' agreement are considered. These issues must be considered in detail in order to determine whether the inclusion of an arbitration clause into the company's constitution or a shareholders' agreement is justifiable.

a. Arbitrability of the Subject Matter of the Disputes

The first issue relates to the question of whether the categories of cases brought under unfair prejudice petitions are capable of being removed by an arbitration agreement (i.e., the issue of arbitrability). The UK courts are generally willing to uphold the validity of an arbitration clause if the subject matter of the dispute falls within the scope of personal membership rights contained in the company's constitution.[19] This can be explained by the following reasons.

First, the courts will not, in general, interfere in the internal affairs of the company, unless the majority shareholders agreed to maintain an action with respect to the alleged wrongs that have been done in the company.[20] On that basis, it is justified to infer that the court would be unlikely to surrender its jurisdictional power over derivative actions to an arbitrator, as there is the possibility that the arbitral tribunal might adopt a more relaxed approach to permit minority shareholders to challenge managerial decisions.[21]

---

[19] *Hickman v. Kent or Romney Marsh Sheep-Breeders' Association* [1915] 1 Ch 881. Section 33 of the UKCA 2006 actually has the effect of creating a contract between the company and its members and each member inter se. There is a similar provision in Hong Kong; see Section 86 of the new Companies Ordinance (Cap. 622).

[20] *Carlen v. Drury* [1812] Vesey and Neames 154; *Shuttleworth v. Cox Bros and Co* [1927] 2 K.B.9; and *Howard Smith Ltd v. Ampol Petroleum Ltd* [1974] A. C. 821.

[21] Andrew Johnston, 'Arbitrability of Company Law Disputes', in Qiao Liu and Wenhua Shan (eds.), *China and International Commercial Dispute Resolution* (Leiden: Koninklijke Brill NV, 2016), 202.

Second, the law has recognized the boundaries in separating personal actions in which members can bring their own rights from other types of rights which would affect third parties or the public at large (including the conduct of company's affairs which may affect the company's rights or the class rights available to all of the company's creditors when a company is insolvent). Hence, it is possible for a party to contract out of his or her statutory right to petition the court for an unfair prejudice remedy if common allegations made in the petition fall purely within the scope of personal membership rights provided in the company's constitution.[22]

Third, the UK courts are more willing to take a pro-arbitration stance by adopting an 'inclusive, permissive approach' to the scope of public policy in the context of enforcement of a company's articles which allowed for arbitration proceedings where there is a dispute between a company and the members and the members inter se.[23] This means that certain types of shareholder disputes which would be considered to be inarbitrable would be limited. This can be explained by the fact that there is no express provision either in the English Arbitration Act or the Companies Act that excludes arbitration as a possible means to resolve disputes between shareholders, nor any implied restriction or rule of public policy applicable to the enforcement of arbitral agreements and awards.[24] Thus, it is expected that the UK courts will continue to display their willingness to enforce the company's articles or a shareholders' agreement which contains a valid arbitration agreement for shareholders to submit their disputes to the arbitral tribunal.

However, it is difficult to separate out general membership rights from personal membership rights, as many breaches of membership rights contained in the articles can be interpreted either as pure internal irregularities, in which case only the company is the proper claimant, or as personal rights which allow the shareholders to sue.[25] In addition, there is much greater willingness of the UK courts to use Section 996 (the so-called unfair prejudice petitions) to secure the redress of corporate wrongs for either breach of directors' fiduciary duties or other misconducts, which

[22] K. W. Wedderburn, 'Shareholders' Rights and the Rule in *Foss v. Harbottle*', *Cambridge Law Journal*, (1957), 194–215 at 209–215.
[23] James Carter and Sophie Payton, 'Arbitration and Company Law in England and Wales', *European Company Law*, 12:3 (2015), 138–143 at 141.
[24] Ibid.
[25] Alan J. Dignam and John Lowry, *Company Law*, 8th ed. (Oxford: Oxford University Press, 2014), 164.

resulted in loss or damages to the company.[26] The judicial recognition of expanding the potential use of Section 996, which enables it to be used as an alternative to the derivative action for minority shareholders, blurs the classical boundary of personal actions which shareholders can bring in their own right, and derivative actions which shareholders can bring on behalf of the company.[27] In this regard, it is questionable whether a member can contract out of his or her statutory right to petition the court for judicial relief if an arbitration clause covered a dispute of corporate wrongs actionable only by the company itself.[28]

b. Using Pre-dispute Arbitration Agreement as a Condition Precedent to the Issue of Unfair Prejudice Proceedings

The use of a pre-dispute arbitration agreement as a condition precedent to the issues of unfair prejudice proceedings poses additional costs and delays of an unsuccessful arbitration. Notably, the Court of Appeal's ruling in *Fulham Football Club (1987) Limited v. Richards* has created a certain degree of ineffectiveness, as it upheld the arbitration provision contained in a shareholders' agreement, and granted a stay of the unfair prejudice proceedings.[29] Under this approach, litigants are required to undergo a two-stage process before they can seek relief from the courts. At the first stage, an arbitrator will adjudicate the issues related to the unfair prejudice claims. At the second stage, if an arbitrator considered that the appropriate remedy is of a type not obtainable in arbitral proceedings (e.g., the conduct of the company's affairs or the supervisory jurisdiction of the court to protect the interests of third party rights such as creditors when the company is insolvent), an arbitrator can revert these matters back to the courts.[30] This implies that the scope of relief sought in the arbitral proceedings is much more limited as compared with the normal relief sought

---

[26] For an excellent discussion about the UK courts to expand the potential use of Section 996 for the redress of corporate wrongs, see generally Rita Cheung, 'Corporate Wrongs Litigated in the Context of Unfair Prejudice Claims: Reforming the Unfair Prejudice Remedy for the Redress of Corporate Wrongs', *Company Lawyer*, 29:4 (2008), 98–104.

[27] David Sugarman, 'Reconceptualising Company Law: Reflections on the Law Commission's Consultation Paper on Shareholder Remedies: Part 2', ibid., 18:9 (1997), 274–282 at 275.

[28] In *Fulham Football Club (1987) Limited v. Richards* [2012] Ch 333, 344, Pattern LJ notes that: 'It is necessary to consider in relation to the matters in dispute in each case whether they engage third party rights or represent an attempt to delegate to the arbitrators what is matter of public interest which cannot be determined within the limitations of a private contractual process.'

[29] *Fulham Football Club (1987) Limited v. Richards* [2012] Ch 333, 360–361.

[30] Ibid., 357.

in the Section 994 petition.[31] Therefore, the requirement for compliance with arbitration as a condition precedent to the issue of the unfair prejudice proceedings may not be justifiable.

First, the condition that the matters fall within the scope of the arbitration clause should first be heard in an arbitral tribunal and latter going to court to resolve the issue of remedies could still be a lengthy and cumbersome process. Their Lordships in *Fulham* failed to provide clear guidance on issue concerning on the extent to which the court could exercise its inherent power of intervention to prevent an arbitral tribunal from granting certain types of remedies.[32] It remains doubtful whether the court would simply give effect to the tribunal's opinion on remedies if such remedies affect the interests of third parties (such as a winding-up order).[33] Arguably, if the court gives effect to the tribunal's views that winding-up order would be appropriate, then this would be 'akin to the arbitral tribunal having the power to award a winding-up order'.[34]

Similarly, the lack of guidance on this point raises the concern of excessive judicial intervention into the arbitral process. This could further undermine the contractual freedom of the parties to use arbitration in resolving shareholder if the court disagrees with any arbitral finding with regard to remedies. Thus, it is still doubtful whether the problems of the excessive length and costs associated with unfair prejudice proceedings could be dealt by the Court of Appeal's two-stage process.

Second, in the absence of an express provision in relation to the duty of confidentiality in the UK Arbitration Act 1996, there could be much uncertainty with regard to the extent to which the materials disclosed

---

[31] Ibid., 346.

[32] Ibid., 344. In *Fulham Football Club (1987) Ltd v. Richards* [2011] Ch 208, 224, Vos J stated that 'Members of companies and the companies themselves can agree to refer disputes that might otherwise support unfair prejudice petitions to arbitration, provided that third parties are not to be bound by the award (as they will not be in this case), and provided that the other kinds of relief mentioned by *Mustill & Boyd on The Law and Practice of Commercial Arbitration in England*, 2nd ed. are not sought (as again they are not in this case). It is beyond the scope of this judgement to consider what might happen if one or more such features were to be present, since they are not in this case.'

[33] Harry McVea, 'Cases: Section 994 of the Companies Act 2006 and the Primacy of Contract', *The Modern Law Review*, 75:6 (2012), 1123–1149 at 1132. See also the *obiter* comments made by Patten LJ in *Fulham Football Club (1987) Limited v. Richards* [2012] Ch 333, 358, '[the arbitrator could] decide whether the complaint of unfair prejudice was made out and whether it would be appropriate for winding-up proceedings to take place or whether the complaint should be limited to some lesser remedy'.

[34] See Yeo Li-Hui Beatrice Mathilda and Chew Yan-Bei Fiona, 'Case Note on *Tomolugen Holdings Ltd v. Silica Investors Ltd* [2016] 1 SLR 373: The Arbitration and Litigation of Minority Shareholder Disputes', *Singapore Academic Law Journal*, 28 (2016), 382–407, 400.

either in an arbitral proceeding can then be disclosed subsequently for the purpose of a later court action. This is particularly so if the court takes a narrower approach with respect to the confidentiality of documents disclosed in the arbitral proceedings. The petitioner has to bear the burden to prove that the materials disclosed in the arbitral proceeding are 'reasonably necessary either for disposing fairly of the action or for saving costs'.[35]

c. An Implied Waiver of the Right of Access to Courts

There is the possibility that the inclusion of an arbitration clause into the company's constitution or a shareholders' agreement to exclude the jurisdiction of the court to grant judicial remedies can undermine the consensual and private nature of arbitration in two ways.

First, a strong policy approach by the UK courts in permitting greater freedom for the shareholders in a private company to contract out some of the statutory unfair prejudice relief could threaten the statutory right of the minority shareholder to bring proceedings under Section 994. At present, the new UK Companies Act provides a high level of freedom and flexibility to the parties to contract out some of the mandatory provisions through the inclusion of a valid arbitration agreement into the company's constitution, or a shareholders' agreement could lead to the inevitable consequence of compelling the shareholders to engage in the arbitration process. This compulsion is largely driven by the fact that shareholders are required to arbitrate their differences before resorting to litigation under the company's constitution or a shareholders' agreement. Particularly, a growing recognition of settlements in the Post-Woolf Reform creates an additional danger of blurring the line between settlement and judgement. Settlement would become the real substitute for court adjudication if the parties have to first submit the unfair prejudice issues to arbitration for settlement.

---

[35] In *Ali Shipping Corporation v. Shipyard Trogir* [1999] 1 WLR 314 at 326–327, Potter LJ sets out the exceptions to the parties' duty of disclosure as follows: (1) Consent. This means that where disclosure is made with the express or implied consent of party who originally produced the material; (2) order of the court, an obvious example of which is an order for disclosure of documents generated by an arbitration for the purposes of a later court action; (3) leave of the court; (4) when it is reasonably necessary for the protection of the legitimate interests of an arbitrating party; and (5) when the interest of justice is required. See also Nigel Blackaby, *Refern and Hunter on International Arbitration*, 6th ed. (Oxford; New York: Oxford University Press, 2015), 124–127, Robert Merkin, *Arbitration Act 1996*, 2nd ed. (London: LLP, 2005), 661–664 and Andrew Tweeddale and Keren Tweeddale, *A Practical Approach to Arbitration Law* (London: Blackstone Press, 1999), 259–260.

It has been suggested that certain statutory rights under corporate law are in fact 'inalienable', and these rights cannot be 'diminished or removed by contract or otherwise'.[36] This highlights that the Court of Appeal in *Fulham's* decision had failed to identify clearly that certain categories of cases brought under unfair prejudice petitions (such as breaches of the fiduciary duties of the directors) cannot be removed by an arbitration agreement contained either in the company's constitution or a shareholders' agreement. It remains doubtful whether an arbitrator is capable of adjudicating the unfair prejudice issues, particularly if they are related to serious deceitful and self-serving acts of mismanagement, such as diversion of company assets, which affect the interests of the members. On that basis, the exercise of contractual freedom to contract out some of the mandatory provisions of the Companies Act may amount to an implied waiver of the right to sue at court.

Second, lawyers are more likely to push their clients to submit their disputes to binding arbitration following the decision in *O'Neill v. Phillips* and the introduction of the Civil Procedural Rules 1998 (CPR) in the United Kingdom. The decision in *O'Neill v. Phillips* imposes an obligation on corporate lawyers to provide alternatives and cost-effective solutions to litigation in the drafting of a company's articles and shareholders' agreement.[37] This approach is consistent with overriding objectives of the CPR.[38] Shortly after the enactment of the CPR, the UK courts took a strong policy approach in promoting ADR. The judicial rhetoric of the duties imposed upon lawyers to assist the court in furthering the 'overriding objectives'[39] by advising their clients to consider the possibility of

---

[36] *Exter City AFC Ltd v. The Football Conference Ltd & Anor* [2004] BCC 498 at 502, Judge Week QC admits that '... the statutory rights conferred on shareholders to apply for relief at any stage are, in my judgment, inalienable and cannot be diminished or removed by contract or otherwise'.

[37] See J. Paul Sykes, *The Continuing Paradox: A Critique of Minority Shareholder and Derivative Claims under the Companies Act 2006*, 29:2; Civil Justice Quarterly 205, (2010) at 229.

[38] Rule 1.4 of the CPR.

[39] Final Report of the Working Party on Civil Justice Reform, paras. 23, 88, 91–100. The operation of civil procedure regime in the United Kingdom was based on the 'overriding objectives' by incorporating the concept of 'proportionality' broadly. This produces an inherent tension between the ideas of utility that the public resources should be fairly distributed, and the concept of equality of justice that the citizens should have the right of access to the courts. In Hong Kong, the civil justice's working party on the CJR realized the problems inherent in the application of 'overriding objectives'. Therefore, Hong Kong amended its RHC rather than introducing a new set of procedural rules.

using ADR to resolve disputes is reflected in the judgement of *Dunnett v. Railtrack*:[40]

> It is to be hoped that any publicity given to this part of the judgement of the court will draw the attention of lawyers to their duties to further the overriding objective in the way that is set out in CPR Part 1 and to the possibility that, if they turn down out of hand the chance of alternative dispute resolution when suggested by the court, as happened on this occasion, they may have to face uncomfortable costs consequences.

Although the inclusion of an arbitration clause in the company's constitution or a shareholders' agreement indicates that the parties have taken a serious step to explore the possibility of ADR,[41] a privately created document drafted by the dominant party (e.g., lawyers) can undermine the essential qualities of ADR.[42] In particular, if the law imposes a legal obligation upon lawyers to bring their clients with them to ADR, it is questionable how lawyers can envisage the core value of assisting the parties to engage ADR, as they are mindful of their potential profits and personal liabilities.[43]

Likewise, an arbitration agreement signed by the shareholders cannot be viewed as an indication that parties are willing to take ADR seriously to resolve shareholder disputes, particularly in the event of a dispute arising. First, it may be impossible for the business parties to foresee future contingencies and to make express provision for all possible events in a pre-dispute arbitration clause.[44] Second, each contractual party may place too little weight on possible future disagreements in a pre-dispute arbitration clause if he or she is overly optimistic about the relationship's long-term success and the trustworthiness of the other party when a company was formed.[45] Third, lawyers are more likely to exert their influence on

---

[40] *Dunnett v. Railtrack Ltd* [2002] 1 WLR 2434 at 2437.

[41] Karl Mackie, 'The Future for ADR Clauses after *Cable & Wireless v. IBM*', *Arbitration International*, 19:3 (2003), 345–362 at 351.

[42] Stephan Landsman, 'ADR and the Cost of Compulsion', *Stanford Law Review*, 57 (2005), 1593–1630 at 1599–1608. Landsman notes that a mandatory pre-dispute arbitration agreement posed a serious risk on the parties to resolve their future disputes voluntarily.

[43] Susan Blake et al., *A Practical Approach to Alternative Dispute Resolution* (Oxford: Oxford University Press, 2011), 280–282.

[44] Christopher A. Riley, 'Contracting Out of Company Law: Section 459 of the Companies Act 1985 and the Role of the Courts', *The Modern Law Review*, 55:6 (1992), 782–802 at 786.

[45] Erik P. M. Vermeulen, *The Evolution of Legal Business Forms in Europe and the United States: Venture Capital, Joint Venture and Partnership Structures* (The Hague: Kluwer Law International, 2003), 8.

their clients to persuade them to submit their disputes to binding arbitration, particularly in the post-Woolf era. Hence, lawyers who blindly encourage their clients to submit their disputes to a pre-dispute arbitration agreement irrespective of whether arbitration is appropriate or not for resolving future disagreements may amount to an implied waiver of the right to access the courts.

As a whole, there is a great deal of legal and practical uncertainty regarding the use of contractual dispute resolution methods to contract out some of the mandatory rules of the company regulation. Thus, the inclusion of a mandatory arbitration provision into the corporate law would come into place by clarifying the types of actions and the subject matter of the disputes that may fall within the jurisdiction of an arbitral tribunal.

7.2.2 New Zealand: Incorporating a Mandatory Arbitration Provision into the Companies Act for Improving the Minority Buyout Remedy

This section analyses the benefits of incorporating a mandatory arbitration provision into the company law, focusing on the recent amendment of the New Zealand Companies Act (NZCA) 1993 which provides an exit regime for dissenting shareholders to refer a dispute to arbitration with respect to a disagreement of the purchase price offered by the majority shareholders.[46] First, the Act offers an additional cost-effective mechanism for dissenting shareholders who do not wish to remain in the company whereby they can exercise their minority buyout rights in requiring the company or a neutral third party to purchase their shares.[47]

Second, Section 112A(6) is inserted into the Companies Act which ensures that the provisions of the Arbitration Act (NZAA) 1996 are applied when matters must be referred to arbitration for determination of a fair and reasonable valuation and available remedies for the parties. This adds clarity to the law that certain types of shareholder disputes must fall within the scope of the jurisdiction of an arbitral tribunal. This prevents the danger of the court exercising its wide case management powers to punish a party in costs if the party fails or refuses to engage in ADR processes. Thus, a shareholder's right of access to the court is guaranteed.

---

[46] Sections 110–115 of the NZCA 1993 provide for the appraisal remedy in New Zealand, with amendments introduced by the Companies (Minority Buy-out Rights) Amendment Act 2008.
[47] Sections 110 and 113 of the NZCA 1993.

The following discussion will examine how the inclusion of a mandatory arbitration provision into the minority buyout regime can achieve the following benefits.

a. Offering Cost-Effective Mechanisms for Determination of Share Valuations

From the sociolegal perspective, the decision of individual actor (i.e., citizen) to take legal action depends on whether there are alternatives to formal court processes in dealing with their disputes.[48] This means that he or she will weigh the burdens and benefits of pursuing legal remedies/actions on his or her behalf. This is particularly true when one experiences that certain types of dispute (such as the breakdown of personal relationships of trust between the members) can be resolved only through the high level of individual judgement rather than legal solutions. Thus, if the corporate law provides an option for the minority shareholder to choose an 'exit' remedy, this may reduce the likelihood of a party to seek judicial redress through the litigation process. The inverse relationship between the existence of exit remedies and judicial remedies can be explained by the fact that only a small fraction of legal problems are brought to the attention of lawyers and the court.[49] Thus, the 'exit' remedy as provided by NZCA 1993 has proved to be more cost effective than the court adjudicative process.

First, minority shareholders can exhaust all the possibilities of informal dispute resolution methods to resolve disputes. This helps them to avoid unnecessary costs and delays associated with shareholder litigation. This analysis is also consistent with the legal and economic theory that the existence of an 'exit' remedy such as the appraisal remedy is inversely related to the use of litigation as a tactical weapon by minority shareholders to voice their grievances against the poor decision(s) made by the controlling shareholders.[50]

Second, appraisal of the exit remedy through an arbitral tribunal is more effective than the valuation of shares for a buyout ordered by the court under Section 174(2)(a) of the NZCA 1993. One possible view is that the unfair prejudice remedy and appraisal remedy are not mutually

---

[48] Frances Kahn Zemans, 'Framework for Analysis of Legal Mobilization: A Decision-Making Model', *American Bar Foundation*, 7:4 (1982), 989–1071 at 989.

[49] Marc Galanter, 'A World Without Trial', *Journal of Dispute Resoltuion*, 7 (2006), 7–34 at 16.

[50] See Marc Galanter, *Adjudication, Litigation, and Related Phenomena, in* Law and the Social Sciences 185 (Leon Lipson and Stanton Wheeler eds., 1986) and David C. Donald, *Shareholder Voice and Its Opponents, Journal of Corporate Law Studies*, 5 (2005), 305–361 at 306.

exclusive. For instance, a dissenting shareholder who has been excluded from participation in the management of a private company may choose either an appraisal remedy or a buyout relief ordered by the court (see Figure 7.1). This is particularly so, as a minority shareholder who is acting as a director might possibly be removed by a special resolution (i.e., a resolution approved by a majority of 75 per cent or, if a higher majority is required by the constitution, that higher majority, of the votes of those shareholders entitled to vote) before the expiration of his or her tenure as a director.[51] Perhaps the most significant difference lies in the fact that the appraisal remedy is to give a dissenting shareholder the right to exit at will by selling out his or her shares at fair value to the company, whereas the unfair prejudice remedy does not provide a unilateral right for a disgruntled shareholder to withdraw from the company.

Lastly, the valuation principles in determining the fair price for the dissenting shareholder's shares is subject to arbitration in relation to the appraisal remedy. By contrast, the method of valuation in governing a buyout order under Section 174(2)(a) is subject to judicial decision-making powers.

However, unfair prejudice proceedings provide a greater breadth of protection than the statutory appraisal remedy, as minority shareholders who find themselves subject to unfair, oppressive or discriminatory treatments (such as serious mismanagement) by the controlling shareholders can commence a petition under Section 174(1). This is due to the fact that the statutory appraisal remedy recognizes that there are certain actions that may be 'unfair' to minority shareholders while not being 'unfairly prejudicial' in terms of the unfair prejudicial remedy.[52] In particular, buyout rights are triggered when the dissenting shareholders fail to oppose a special resolution specified in Section 110.[53] In addition, the range of remedies available under the statutory unfair prejudice provision is wider than the statutory appraisal remedy.[54]

---

[51] Susan Watson, 'The Board of Directors', in John Farrar et al. (eds.), *Company and Securities Law in New Zealand* (Wellington, NZ: Thomson Reuters, 2008), 295–296. Watson provides an excellent analysis of the operation of the New Zealand law to remove directors.

[52] Vanessa Mitchell, 'The US Approach Towards the Acquisition of Minority Shares: Have We Anything to Learn?', *Company and Securities Law Journal*, 14:5 (1996), 283–311 at 299.

[53] Section 110 provides that shareholders may require the company to purchase shares where a shareholder is entitled to vote on the exercise of one or more of powers set out in Section 106 (i.e., powers exercised by special resolution). These powers include the alteration of a company's constitution; approval of a major transaction; approval of an amalgamation of the company under Section 221 of the Act; or the company is required to be put into liquidation.

[54] Judicial remedies available under Section 174(2) are as follows: (a) an order to acquire the shareholder's shares; or (b) an order to pay compensation to a person; or (c) an order in

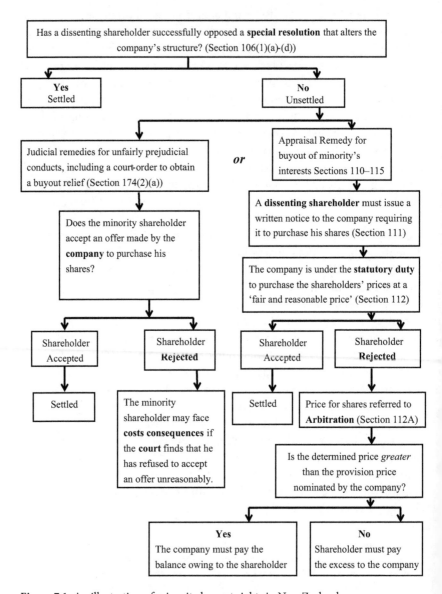

Figure 7.1 An illustration of minority buyout rights in New Zealand.

Nonetheless, the use of arbitration to resolve disputes over value with regard to buyout relief for minority shareholder is surely desirable when a dissenting shareholder objects to the nominated price offered by the company.

First, Lord Justice Jackson in his report on costs highlights that the legal practitioners in New Zealand have expressed their great preference for arbitration instead of litigation in helping their clients to resolve commercial disputes, as the percentage of costs recovered by successful parties is significantly higher in arbitration than what could be obtained in litigation.[55]

Second, dissenting shareholders could make a timely decision with the help of an arbitrator regarding the basis on which the company has calculated the value of its shares.[56] This enhances the timeliness and transparency of information regarding the assessment of the price offered by the company for the dissenting shareholders. Third, the relative bargaining position of the petitioner to negotiate with the controlling shareholders can further be improved, as an arbitrator's neutral role and expertise are crucial to encouraging the parties to compromise on an equal footing for settlement. Finally, the confidential nature of the arbitral process enables family squabbles to be kept out of the public eye, as there are no public records and hearings unless judicial review is sought.[57]

b. Clarifying the Scope of Arbitrability of Specific Types of Disputes under the Company Law

The issue of arbitrability involves determining whether any legal disputes are capable of being settled through the arbitral tribunal instead of a national court.[58] Given that the precise scope of the concept of

---

regulating the future conduct of the company's affairs; or (d) an order to alter the company's constitution; or (e) an order to appoint a receiver of the company; or (f) an order to direct the rectification of the company's records; or (g) an order to put the company into liquidation; or (h) an order to set aside action taken by the company or the board in breach of the Act of the company's constitution.

[55] Lord Justice Jackson, *Review of Civil LItigation Costs: Final Report* (London: The Stationary Office, 2009), 603.

[56] Lynne Taylor, 'Minority Buy-Out Rights in the Company Act 1993', *Canterbury Law Review*, 6 (1997), 539–563 at 555. Taylor notes that although dissenting shareholders could file an application to the court for the request of information held by a company, it is unlikely that this information would be received in sufficient time for them to make a timely decision to either accept or object to the offered price.

[57] In New Zealand, the grounds for setting aside or refusing an arbitration award are rather limited; see Section 34 of the Arbitration Act 1996.

[58] Diederik De Groot, 'Arbitration and Company Law: An Introduction', *European Company Law*, 12:3 (2015), 125–127 at 126.

arbitrabiltiy remains uncertain, the determination of the arbitrability of certain types of shareholder disputes is subject to public interest considerations.[59] Indeed, public policy is generally regarded as a 'judicial control device' that enables the court to exercise its supervisory role to ensure that arbitration meets the minimum standards of fairness in light of the legislative intent and policy of promoting arbitration.[60] However, it has been suggested that a wide interpretation of the concept of public policy poses serious challenges not only to the tribunal's competence in determining the subject matter of the dispute submitted by the parties but also to the freedom of the parties to choose arbitration as an appropriate dispute resolution mechanism to resolve their disputes.[61]

Arguably, the incorporation by reference of the provisions of the arbitration law which are subject to the company legislation not only provides greater certainty with respect to certain types of shareholder disputes which are arbitrable or not. In addition, it specifies every detail of the arbitrator's power in awarding remedies. This prevents the danger of undue interference of the local court to construe the notion of public policy in a broad sense, which contravenes the policy of promoting the greater use of arbitration to resolve shareholder disputes.

The benefits of incorporating a mandatory arbitration provision into the company legislation can be reflected in New Zealand. The Companies (Minority Buy-out) Rights Amendment Bill was introduced into the NZCA 1993 in 2008 which provides that disputes about share valuation are resolved by the arbitral tribunals.[62] Moreover, the new law provides in detail the scope of remedies that may be awarded by an arbitral tribunal in a dispute as to the proposed offer price which is deemed to be unacceptable to the minority shareholders. Essentially, the type of remedy that may be awarded by an arbitral tribunal is not of limited interest.[63] It is possible for an arbitral tribunal to award damages for loss attributable to the shortfall in the initial payment.[64]

---

[59] Choong Yeow-Choy and Warren P. Ganesh, 'Public Policy Consideratoins in Arbitral Proceedings in Selected Common Law Jurisdictions', Hong Kong Law Journal, 44:1 (2014), 179–205 at 188.
[60] Ibid. at 183.
[61] Ibid. at 179.
[62] Section 112A(6) of the NZCA 1993.
[63] Section 112A(4) of the NZCA 1993.
[64] Ibid.

Obviously, the inclusion of the provisions of the NZAA 1996 into the statutory appraisal remedy ensures that arbitral process is conducted in a fair manner under the supervision of the national courts. This is due to the fact that the arbitration law of New Zealand is largely based on the international model of the UNCITRAL International Commercial Arbitration (the Model Law), which guarantees fundamental procedural rights, such as the right to a fair trial and the right of access to the courts.[65] Parties are treated with equality and each party is given a full opportunity to present his or her case to the arbitral tribunals with regard to the statutory appraisal remedy. Despite NZCA1993 making it clear that the power of an arbitrator to making an award of costs cannot be removed or relinquished by a shareholders' agreement, this section does not impose any unacceptable obstruction on the right of the parties to access the court.[66] Instead, a party may file a complaint to the High Court if the amount or allocation of the costs is alleged to be unreasonable, and the court may vary the amount and/or the allocation.[67] It is expected that parties are more willing to accept the arbitral award not only because they rely on the technical knowledge or skills of arbitral tribunals to determine the valuation of minority's shareholding, but also because an arbitrator is bound to act fairly in dealing with the dispute.[68]

Moreover, arbitration as a default method used in dealing with a dispute as to a difference in valuation under the statutory minority buyout regime can protect shareholders against one-sidedness in the making of a pre-dispute arbitration provision.[69] A concern about one-sidedness in a pre-dispute arbitration agreement is that the parties may not be fully aware of the future contingencies that may affect their future business relationship. Hence, the imposition of a mandatory arbitration provision

---

[65] Tómas Kennedy-Grant, 'The New Zealand Experience of the UNCITRAL Model Law: A Review of the Position as at 31 December 2007', *Asian International Arbitration Journal*, 4:1 (2008), 1–63.

[66] Section 112A(7) of the NACA1993 provides that Clause 6 of Schedule 2 of the NZAA 1996 may not be excluded from the arbitration agreement.

[67] Peter Spiller, *Dispute Resolution in New Zealand*, 2nd ed. (Oxford: Oxford University Press, 2007), 161. Two points should be noted relating to the complaint of the unreasonable costs allocation by an arbitrator. First, there is a time limit of three months from the time of receipt of the award for such an application under Clause 6(5) of Schedule 2 of the NZAA. Second, there is no appeal from any decision of the High Court relating to costs under Clause 6(6) of Schedule 2 of the NZAA 1996.

[68] Article 34 of the NZAA 1996.

[69] Ian R. Macneil, *American Arbitration Law: Reformation, Nationalization, Internationalization* (Oxford: Oxford University Press, 1992), 68–70.

into the statutory appraisal remedy can substantially reduce the transaction costs associated with the limitations of drafting a detailed arbitration clause contained in a shareholders' agreement.

7.2.3 South Africa: Recommending the Use of ADR to Deal with Minority Shareholder Disputes through the Issuance of a Voluntary Code of Governance

The inclusion of private informal dispute resolution processes into the voluntary corporate governances in South Africa provides some useful guidelines for Hong Kong to further reform its law on directors' duties. Recently, the King Committee on governance issued the third report on corporate governance in South Africa (King III). The purpose of the King III is to provide a set of codes of governance principles for directors as to how they should make decisions on behalf of the company. Unlike legal authoritative rules devised by the state, the legitimacy of the governance codes derives from a set of business practices established by a group of leading proponents of corporate governance and representatives of significant professional, private and public sector institutions.[70] Compliance tends to be greater, as the recommended practices are presumed to be valid between the members (i.e., the directors) within the same industry.[71]

From the regulator's perspective, the use of voluntary codes for promoting the standard of good corporate governance system is more attractive than the mandatory nature of rules. The advantage of voluntary codes over mandatory rules is that the recommended principles are easy to understand, as they are not rigidly defined as compared with rules.[72] In addition, voluntary principles contained a set of 'normative expectations' of how individual directors are supposed to behave.[73] Ultimately, directors tend to internalize the values of the recommended practices as a matter of routine. By contrast, rules may be specific to a given group at a certain period of time.[74]

---

[70] Lynn McGregor, 'Corporate Governance in South Africa', in Christine A-Mallin (ed.), *Handbook on International Corporate Governance: Country Analysis* (Cheltenham: Edward Elgar, 2011), 397.

[71] Richard W. Scott, *Institutions and Organizations*, 2nd ed. (SAGE, 2001), 54–56.

[72] Adrian Davies, *Best Practice in Corporate Governance: Building Reputation and Sustainable Success* (Surrey: Gower, 2006), 27.

[73] Scott, 'Institutions and Organizations', 56.

[74] Davies, 'Best Practice in Corporate Governance', 27.

The new South African Companies Act has made its rules less pre-scriptive and easier to apply, especially for private enterprises.[75] The rec-ommended practices set out in King III complement the operation of mandatory corporate rules for legal enforcement. The law and the King Codes of corporate governance practices have become inextricable, as the codes provide guidance for the court to determine what is to be generally regarded as an appropriate standard of conduct for a director to comply with the new Companies Act. The interaction between the King Codes and the new corporate law in South Africa provides insights into the develop-ment of a sophisticated ADR programme for shareholder disputes.

a. Director's Duty to Promote the Use of ADR

In South Africa, a director is required to undertake a further duty to apply all the recommended principles of codes as set out in King III. This means that a director owes a duty to his or her company to consider the appro-priate use of ADR to resolve corporate governance disputes.[76] Any failure to comply with the recognized standard of governance in selecting the most appropriate method to resolve disputes in an expedient manner may render an individual director liable at law.

At present, most principles set out in King III, including the appropri-ate use of ADR processes to resolve corporate governance disputes, are applicable to small private companies.[77] The code has made a comprehen-sive coverage of the types of shareholder disputes that originate not purely from a disagreement between the members themselves, but also in dis-putes between the company and a member or a stakeholder. This implies that the code includes corporate governance disputes that mostly involve a company's shareholders, board members, senior executives and other outside stakeholders (e.g., customers, suppliers and creditors). Obviously, the government in South Africa has taken an important step forward in bringing its position more in line with international practice by encour-aging all business entities, including private enterprises, to apply ADR to resolve corporate governance disputes.[78]

---

[75] J. J. Henning, 'Legislative Comment on the South African Close Corporation under the New Companies Act: Part I', *Company Lawyer*, 31:7 (2010), 225–228 at 226.
[76] In Chapter 8 of the King Code Governance for South Africa 2009 covers the range of dir-ectors' duties. Principle 8.6 provides that 'The board should ensure disputes are resolved as effectively, efficiently and expeditiously as possible.'
[77] Francois Le Roux, 'The Applicability of the Third King Report on Corporate Governance to Small and Medium Enterprises', PhD thesis, The University of Stellenbosch (2010), 55.
[78] Louis Bouchez and Alexander Karpf, 'The OECD's Work on Corporate Governance and Dispute Resolution Mechanisms', in Louis Bouchez et al. (eds.), *Topics in*

The downside of the 'hybrid system of governance'[79] in South Africa is that directors are likely to be exposed to the risk of undue interference by litigation initiated by shareholders. This is partly due to the fact that King III endorsed the 'apply or explain' approach in rewriting the governance codes.[80] This approach imposes wide reporting obligations on directors in a private company to include in their annual reports a narrative statement as to how the principles and recommendations can be applied as set out in King III.

Nonetheless, the South African Companies Act 2008 (SACA 2008) (effective from 1 May 2011) provides legal backing for the International Financial Reporting Standards for Small and Medium Enterprises (IFRS for SMEs), and therefore improves the quality of financial reporting and governance in SMEs.[81] This is particularly so as the Act sets out sanctions for non-compliance with the reporting requirements.[82] Obviously, the pressure of legal sanctions for non-compliance with the required reporting standards may create incentive for all SMEs in South Africa to adopt the IFRS for SMEs in preparing their annual reports.

However, it is fair to argue that a recent introduction of the IFRS for SMEs in South Africa is, in fact, a vital counterbalance to the law imposing a series of duties on directors. Directors can discharge their legal responsibilities under the corporate law if they pay close attention to the emanated principles in the Act, and to give reasons to the shareholders for not applying the recommended practices.[83]

b. Facilitating Enforcement of Settlements

The established voluntary code of governance practice facilitates the coordination between the court and the newly established regulatory agency,

---

Corporate Finance: The Quality of Corporate Law and the Role of Corporate Law Judges (Amsterdam: Amsterdam Center for Corporate Finance, 2006).

[79] Mervyn King, 'The Synergies and Interaction between King III and the Companies Act 61 of 2008', *Acta Juridica*, (2010), 446–455 at 447. The hybrid system of governance system in South Africa is that the principles of good governance are being legislated in addition to the voluntary code of governance practice.

[80] McGregor, 'Corporate Governance in South Africa', 397.

[81] The World Bank, *South Africa Report on the Observance of Standards and Codes Accounting and Auditing* at www.worldbank.org (Accessed 8 June 2017), para. 3.3. South Africa is the first country in the world to adopt the IFRS for SMEs (which was issued by the IASB on 9 July 2009) on 13 August 2009.

[82] Ibid., para. 2.1 and Section 29 of the South African Companies Act 2008 (SACA 2008).

[83] Eric Levenstein et al., 'South Africa' in Alexander Loos (ed.), *Directors Liability: A Worldwide Review* (The Hague: Kluwer law International, 2012), 10–13.

called the Companies Tribunal, to establish a relatively inexpensive and informal procedure for enforcing a private settlement. The Companies Tribunal is a new body introduced by the Companies Act which aims to provide expeditious and cost-effective alternatives to court litigation process for the resolution of company disputes.[84] The Companies Tribunal has a dual function.[85] It serves as a forum for voluntary alternative dispute resolution in any matter arising under the Act.[86] It also carries out an adjudicative function in reviewing the administrative decisions made by the Companies and Intellectual Property Commission on an optional basis.[87]

Indeed, the benefits of setting up a specialized court in South Africa are perceived to be more attractive than arbitration process. First, the legal framework for the procedural support on arbitration in South Africa is rather inefficient and unsophisticated as compared with that in its common law counterparts such as the United Kingdom and New Zealand. This is particularly so as its constitutional framework of South Africa provides a legitimate foundation for the Judiciary to exercise a relatively broad supervisory jurisdiction over arbitration processes.[88] Consequently, the involvement of the courts has adversely affected the flexibility of private arbitration.[89] Second, the High Court Rule 37 in South Africa undermines the consensual nature of ADR processes, as parties are obliged to hold a pretrial conference and such an arrangement cannot be waived by shareholder agreements.[90] This means that if parties attempt to resolve shareholder disputes through the court litigation process, they need to follow the procedural rules strictly by considering the possibility of ADR before beginning court proceedings.

By contrast, the Companies Tribunal performs not only a social function of ensuring that the requirements of natural justice are observed in conducting its proceedings; it also facilitates the enforcement of settlements.[91] Once a private settlement is recorded in the form of a consent

---

[84] Section 166 of the SACA 2008.
[85] Henning, 'Legislative Comment on the New South African Companies Act' at 223.
[86] Ibid. and Section 195 of the SACA 2008.
[87] Ibid.
[88] Christa Roodt, 'Autonomy and Due Process in Arbitration: Recalibrating the Balance', *The Comparative and International Law Journal of South Africa*, 41:2 (2011), 311–339 at 312, 318 and 338.
[89] Ibid. at 319–320.
[90] Mohamed Paleker, 'Mediation in South Africa: Here but Not All There' in Nadja Alexander (ed.), *Global Trends in Mediation* (The Hague: Kluwer Law International, 2006), 340–342.
[91] Section 180(1)(a) of the SACA 2008.

order, this makes the settlement relatively easier to enforce in the courts, as a settlement agreement becomes an executor instrument issued by the state.[92] This prevents the courts from applying formal contractual rules in determining whether the parties have complied with the clear terms of their settlement agreement.[93]

In sum, the inclusion of a provision for the resolution of shareholder disputes by ADR into the governance codes is to be welcomed. It assists parties to comply with the rules voluntarily by referring the matter to the Tribunal for resolution by means of mediation, conciliation or arbitration. Also, this provision strikes a proper balance between safeguarding the constitutional rights of disputants to access the courts and judicial remedies,[94] and the need for the parties to resolve their disputes in a cost-effective manner.

7.3 The Future Codification of ADR for Shareholder Disputes in Hong Kong

Along with increasing legislative and judicial activisms in encouraging the greater use of private informal dispute resolution processes for shareholder disputes, it seems promising for Hong Kong to adopt an approach similar to that taken by the United Kingdom, New Zealand and South Africa. However, the views of Hong Kong lawyers should not be ignored, as they can serve as agents of legitimacy supporting ADR development for shareholder disputes.[95] It follows that the author develops three testable series of arguments regarding the conditions under which Hong Kong may learn from the experiences of the United Kingdom, New Zealand and South Africa by incorporating the use of informal dispute resolution methods into the company legislation.

---

[92] Charles Jarrosson, 'Legal Issues Raised by ADR', in Arnold Ingen-Housz (ed.), *ADR in Business: Practice and Issues across Countries and Cultures*, Vol. II (The Hague: Kluwer Law International, 2011).

[93] Mervyn King, 'Mediating Corporate Governance Disputes?', Conference on *The Launch of Southern African IoD Mediation Center* (Paris, 12 February 2007).

[94] In Chapter 2 of the Constitution of South Africa Bill of Right, Section 34 stipulates that everyone has the right to have any legal problem or case developed by a court/independent body. Section 167(3) of the SACA provides that a consent order issued by the court may include an award of damages and it does not preclude a person applying for an award of civil damages unless the consent order includes an award of damages to that person.

[95] See supra note 10.

7.3.1 Building Public Awareness about the Use of Informal Dispute Resolution Processes for Shareholder Disputes through the Code of Corporate Governance

A large proportion of Hong Kong lawyers believe that mediation can be used as a strategic weapon to obtain further information about the other side's interests with no intention to settle through a mediation process (see Figure 7.2). Again, the differences in means among the two groups of legal professionals are not statistically significant ($F = 1.748$, df = 65, n.s.). This raises the question of whether it is possible to introduce a non-legal inducement policy option, such as the publication of guidelines on the corporate use of ADR for SMEs.

In Hong Kong, the level of awareness among local companies' directors with respect to their legal obligations and duties under the corporate law was relatively low, as fewer than half were unaware of the nature and scope of director's duties which have developed from the common law rules and equitable principles.[96] Like in South Africa, the Hong Kong Institute of Directors (HKIoD) published a set of guidelines on corporate governance specifically for SMEs. These guidelines are based on voluntary self-regulation and they cover the standards of ethical behaviour that a company director should owe his or her duties to the company as a whole.[97] Although a voluntary basis for governance compliance may not be effective for ensuring the enforcement of the duties of directors, the uncertainty as to the scope and nature of directors' duties under the common law rules and equitable principles could be supplemented by a code on corporate governance for SMEs. In particular, the company law reform did not go far enough to introduce a comprehensive codification of directors' duties into the new company legislation. Rather, Section 465 of the new Companies Ordinance only clarified the common law duties of care, skill and diligence of directors. Nonetheless, the corporate governance guidelines may serve a vital educational function of raising the awareness of local directors to discharge their duties and responsibilities effectively under the law.

Likewise, the introduction of a voluntary code of corporate governance practice that convinces local directors to consider the possibility

---

[96] Abdul Majid et al., 'Company Directors' Perception of Their Responsibilities and Duties: A Hong Kong Survey', *Hong Kong Law Journal*, 28 (1998), 60–89 at 70.

[97] The Hong Kong Institute of Directors, *Guidelines on Corporate Governance in SMEs in Hong Kong* (2009), 109.

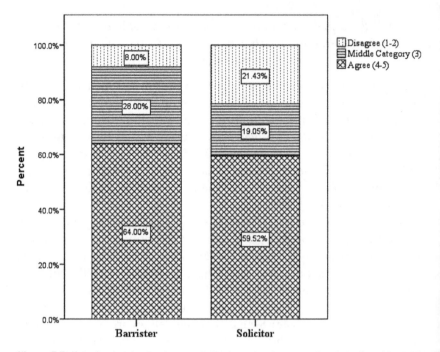

Figure 7.2 Perceived risk of using mediation process to gain advantage for obtaining further information about the other side's information.

of introducing various types of dispute resolution mechanisms for the resolution of shareholder disputes into their corporate policies is to be welcomed. First, compliance tends to be greater, as the inclusion of ADR into the voluntary code of corporate governance for SMEs is in line with the orthodox position in English company law. Specifically, the principle of majority rule, a separation of ownership of control and the degree of managerial freedom to regulate the affairs of the company are three pillars of company law. The code allows the maximum amount of freedom and flexibility for a director to respond more quickly to the recent developments in company law reform and the reform of the civil justice system.

Second, previous empirical research illustrates that companies are much more likely to appreciate the benefits of using ADR to resolve shareholder disputes if directors are more willing to try ADR processes as a matter of corporate policy.[98] Arguably, the proposed code of corporate

[98] Loukas Mistelis, 'International Arbitration – Corporate Attitudes and Practices – 12 Perceptions Tested: Myths, Data and Analysis Research Report', *The American Review of*

governance that supports the greater use of ADR for shareholder disputes could prevent lawyers from putting heavy pressure on their corporate clients to comply with the legal requirement to attend ADR processes (such as mediation) without any intention of settling.[99] On that basis, the inclusion of ADR into the voluntary codes of corporate governance for SMEs would be very helpful in raising the awareness of directors and their lawyers to attend mediation and other alternative processes in a spirit of willingness to negotiate and compromise.

7.3.2 Permissibility of Incorporating an Arbitration Clause in a Shareholders' Agreement

Prior studies believed that the inclusion of a contractual dispute resolution mechanism (such as arbitration) into a shareholder agreement is desirable for small private companies.[100] First, the use of a shareholders' agreement to contract out of the unfair prejudice provision in the corporate law is consistent with the contractarian approach adopted by the House of Lords in *O'Neill v. Phillips*.[101] Second, it has the advantage that it is private, and therefore a shareholder can secretly contract to control the majority voting rights in a company without owning a majority of the shares.[102] Third, a shareholder agreement is one means to reduce the inherent uncertainty arising from the default position in the Act of majority rule.[103] If a shareholders' agreement can be viewed as a means of protecting minority shareholders, lawyers would routinely and persistently act to advise their clients to include a valid arbitration agreement into a shareholders' agreement for the resolution of shareholder disputes.

International Arbitration, 15 (2004), 527–591, 553 and Thomas J. Stipanowich and J. Ryan Lamare, 'Living with ADR: Evolving Perceptions and Use of Mediation, Arbitration, and Conflict Management in Fortune 1000 Corporations', *Harvard Negotiation Law Review*, 19 (2014), 1–68, 32–34.

[99] Order 1A, Rule 3 of the RHC and Rule 5(1)(aa), Order 62 of the RHC.

[100] Note, 'Mandatory Arbitration as a Remedy for Intra-close Corporate Disputes', *Virginia Law Review*, 56 (1970), 271–294 and Lewis D. Solomon and Janet Stern Solomon, 'Using Alternative Dispute Resolution Techniques to Settle Conflicts among Shareholders of Closely Held Corporations', *Wake Forest Law Review*, 22 (1987), 105–126.

[101] McVea, 'Cases', 1133 (quoting from Jennifer Payne, 'Company Law', *All England Annual Review*, 4 (2004), 647–677, paras. 4.8–4.9).

[102] Cally Jordan, 'Family Resemblances: The Family Controlled Company in Asia and Its Implications for Law Reform', *Australian Journal of Corporate Law*, 8 (1997), 89–104 at 102.

[103] Lynne Taylor, 'Shareholder Agreements', in John Farrar et al. (eds.), *Company and Securities Law in New Zealand* (Wellington, NZ: Thomson Reuters, 2008), 67.

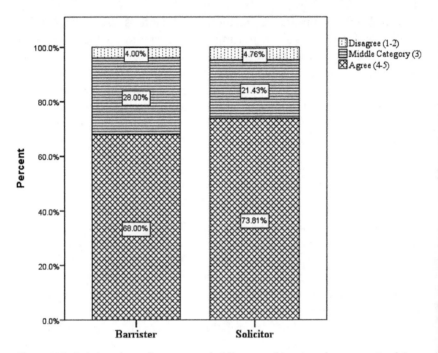

Figure 7.3 Opinion about the courts upholding an arbitration clause contained in a shareholders' agreement.

Approximately more than half of respondents agreed that the Hong Kong Judiciary are willing to enforce a shareholders' agreement containing an arbitration clause for the resolution of minority shareholder disputes (see Figure 7.3). There are no significant differences between the two groups of legal practitioners in their view that the Hong Kong courts were generally in favour of enforcing a shareholders' agreement which allowed the members to resolve their disputes through arbitration proceedings ($F = 0.000$, df = 65, n.s.).

The findings are broadly in line with the approach now taken by the Hong Kong Court of First Instance in *Quiksilver Greater China Ltd v. Quiksilver Glorious Sun JV Ltd*, where it firmly endorsed a pro-arbitration stance of the English Court of Appeal's decision in *Fulham* that parties are free to agree how their dispute are resolved in the context of shareholder disputes.[104]

---

[104] Unreported, HCCW 364 and 365/2013, 25 July 2014 at para. 14.

The permissive nature of the Hong Kong company law that vests a court with considerable discretion to determine the enforceability of a shareholders' agreement which permits minority shareholder disputes to be resolved through arbitration on a case-by-case basis is considered to be more satisfactory and appropriate. This is due to the fact that Section 725 of the new Companies Ordinance gives the court a very wide discretion to make any order that it thinks fit for giving relief. The court may grant the winding-up order despite the 'just and equitable' winding-up remedy is draconian in nature and is likely to be a last resort remedy.[105] The limited fact-finding arbitrator may not be adequate in dealing with the question of statutory unfair prejudice remedies available for minority shareholders.[106]

However, it is uncertain whether an act by the board of directors which is considered as a breach of its fiduciary duties by using its powers for an ulterior motive could be dealt with by means of derivative arbitral proceedings.[107] In particular, unlike in Singapore, there is no statutory provision under the Hong Kong company law that enables minority shareholders to obtain a leave from the court to commence a derivative arbitral proceeding in the name and on behalf of the company.[108] There may remain residual difficulties in case a particular managerial decision amounts to an unfair prejudice to a minority shareholder that cannot be referred directly to arbitration.[109]

In addition, the arbitrability of dispute over minority oppression or unfairly prejudicial conduct remains an open question in Hong Kong.[110] One possible reason for this is that the *Quicksilver* case was focused specifically on winding-up petition, and therefore the parameter of arbitrability was limited to a dispute concerning whether a shareholder's conduct is inconsistent with a shareholders' agreement is arbitrable.[111]

---

[105] Section 177(1)(f) of the Companies (Winding-Up and Miscellaneous Provisions) Ordinance (Cap. 32).

[106] Johnston, 'Arbitrability of Company Law Disputes', 225.

[107] Ibid.

[108] Section 216A of the Companies (Amendment) Act 2014.

[109] Before the Companies (Amendment) Act 2014 came into force, the word 'action' under formerly Section 216A of the Singapore Companies Act 1994 was restrictively interpreted by the Singapore Court; see *Kiyue Co Ltd v. Aquagen International Pte Ltd* [2003] 3 SLR 130 at para. 137.

[110] Koh Swee-Yen, 'Singapore's Highest Court Confirms Pro-arbitration Approach to Shareholder Disputes', *Asian Dispute Review*, (2017), 67–71 at 71.

[111] Ibid.

By contrast, the Singapore Court of Appeal in *Tomolugen Holdings Ltd v. Silica Investor Ltd* held that minority oppression claims were *prima facie* arbitrable.[112] This view was endorsed and followed in the recent decision in *L Capital Jones Ltd and another v. Maniach Pte Ltd.*[113] The reasoning of the Singapore Court of Appeal in the *L Capital Jones* case produces greater certainty on the scope of arbitrability of minority shareholders' claims as the court reaffirmed that minority oppression claims are generally arbitrable. This is in line with the pro-arbitration stance taken by the English, Australian and Canadian courts.[114]

On top of that, the *L Capital Jones* case has taken an important step further in narrowing the potential scope for the aggrieved minority shareholders to rely on the doctrine of public policy to set aside or refuse to enforce the arbitration agreement that covered unfair prejudice claims.[115] In this case, the minority shareholders alleged that the defendants had abused the process of Australian courts in transferring shares in company to a third party at an undervalue. The minority shareholders argued that the issue of abuse of court process was not arbitrable as it would be against public policy within the meaning of Section 11(1) of the International Arbitration Act.[116] The Court of Appeal held that for the application of public policy as a bar to enforcement of arbitral clause contained in a shareholders' agreement, the element of public policy must be directly related to the real question of whether there had been unfairly prejudicial

---

[112] Yeo and Chew, 'Case Note on *Tomolugen Holdings Ltd v. Silica Invetors Ltd* [2016] 1 SLR 373', 388–391.

[113] [2017] SGCA 03, para. 3.

[114] A strong pro-arbitration position in cases involving shareholder disputes was taken by the Australian courts; see, for example, *WDR Delaware Corporation v. Hydrox Holdings Pty Ltd* [2016] FCA 1164 (27 September 2016) and *In the matter of Infinite Plus Pty Ltd* [2017] NSWSC 470 (27 April 2017). The Canadian courts adopt a similar approach preferred in England and Australia. See, for example, *Kints v Kints* [1988] OJ No 3244 and *Acier Leroux Inc v Tremblay* [2004] RJQ 839. The leading case in England on this issue is *Fulham Football Club (1987) Ltd v. Richards* [2012] Ch 333.

[115] *L Capital Jones Ltd and another v Maniach Pte Ltd* [2017] SGCA 3, para. 29. The court held that minority oppression claims were arbitrable because the question of an abuse of the judicial process was neither the essence of the dispute nor a necessary step in proving the claim.

[116] Section 11(1) of the International Arbitration Act provides that ' [a]ny dispute which the parties have agreed to submit to arbitration under an arbitration agreement may be determined by arbitration unless it is contrary to public policy to do so'. Section 11(2) of the International Arbitration Act further states that 'any written law confers jurisdiction in respect of any matter on any court of law but does not refer to the determination of that matter by arbitration shall not, of itself, indicate that a dispute about that matter is not capable of determination by arbitration'.

conducts.[117] Thus, complaints which are incidental to the resolution of the minority oppression disputes would fall outside the realm of public policy.[118]

From the preceding discussion, it can be concluded that the current Companies Ordinance permits a minimum level of judicial intervention with regard to jurisdictional limits of the arbitral tribunals to grant specific kinds of relief such as a winding-up order should be retained. However, much remains to be seen whether the Hong Kong court would follow the recent Singapore decision in the *L Capital Jones* case that minority oppression claims are generally arbitrable unless the fact of a particular case raises public policy considerations.[119]

7.3.3 Expanding the Powers of the Arbitrator to Determine the Share Price in the Proposed Statutory Minority Buyout Regime

There is no statutory appraisal remedy in Hong Kong. This means that the Hong Kong company legislation does not provide a statutory minority buyout regime that enables minority shareholders who disagree with certain fundamental changes to the company structure or certain alternations to shareholders' rights to demand the company to buy back at a fair and reasonable price of the shares they hold.[120] Moreover, the Hong Kong courts do not recognize a right of unilateral withdrawal on the basis that the relationship between the parties has irretrievably broken.[121] As such, the fact that there is no statutory remedy in situations in which there is no fault despite exclusion of members from management is one of the most common allegations in petitions under Section 724 of the Companies Ordinance.[122] Thus, it should not be surprising that a court order for

---

[117] Ibid., para. 29.

[118] Ibid.

[119] Ibid., paras. 31–32.

[120] Hong Kong Standing Committee on Company Law Reform, *The Report of the Standing Committee on Company Law Reform on the Recommendations of a Consultancy Report of the Review of the Hong Kong Companies Ordinance* (Hong Kong: Printing Department, 2000) at paras. 9.1–9.23.

[121] *Re Ching Hing Construction Co Ltd* (unreported, HCCW 889/1999, 23 November 2001) at paras. 43 and 48; *Re Kam Fai Electroplating Factory Ltd* (unreported, HCCW 534/2000, 8 December 2003) at para. 43; and *Re Yung Kee Holdings Ltd* [2014] 2 HKLRD 313 at 355.

[122] Philip Lawton, 'Modelling the Chinese Family Firm and Minority Shareholder Protection: The Hong Kong Experience 1980–1995', *Managerial Law*, 49:5/6 (2007), 249–271 at 262.

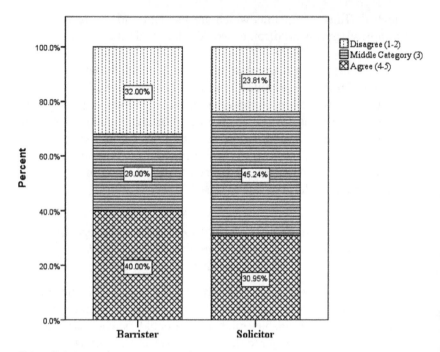

Figure 7.4 Perceived competence of an arbitrator to determine a fair value of shares when a shareholder unreasonably rejects to accept the company's buyout offer.

buyout relief is by far the most commonly sought remedy under Section 725 of the Companies Ordinance .[123]

Consistent with the research finding, the survey finding suggests that fewer than half of respondents believe that the arbitrator is competent in determining the fair value of shares in the event of buyout (see Figure 7.4). The differences in means are not statistically significant ($F = 3.285$, df = 65, n.s.), although the shapes of the distributions are quite different as barristers' responses were more widely dispersed than those of solicitors. The finding illustrated that the majority of the respondents supported the prevailing view that judges are competent in determining the valuation of shares for minority shareholders in the event of a buyout.

Undoubtedly, the court is an appropriate forum to determine the valuation of shares for minority shareholders in the event of a buyout. One possible reason for the survey result may be attributed to the fact that

[123] Lawton, 'Modelling the Chinese Family Firm and Minority Shareholder Protection', 263.

a wealthy corporate user is more likely to act as a 'repeat player' in an arbitral process as he or she has the ability to supply future business to an arbitrator. This poses a potential danger to the minority shareholders, as some arbitrators might decide a much more favourable award to him or her.[124] Therefore, it is less likely for the minority shareholders to achieve a fair outcome, as a wealthy corporate user has the advantage of having more information related to the dispute than the other party does.

Another reason can be attributed to the general perception that a traditional court adjudicative process is the 'most preferable and the fairest mode of dispute resolution' to resolve shareholder disputes.[125] This is in part because judges play important roles in elaborating rules and constructing equitable principles to protect weaker parties.[126] Indeed, a steady stream of judicial decisions handed down by the Hong Kong courts over the past twenty years indicates that the courts display considerable acceptance of court-ordered buyout relief sought by the minority shareholder.[127] The court decision in *Wong Tin Chee Tinly and Others v. Wong To Yick and Another* exemplifies the important role of the court in providing justice between the parties on the issue of valuation of the shares either inside or outside court.[128] On the fact of the case, Justice Yuen noted that[129]

> ... in the absence of an offer for purchase, [it would be reasonable for the Petitioner to seek for the court ordered buy-out relief as] Section 168A provides that a fair value would be assessed under the court order. This is different from the situation in *Virdi v. Abbey Leisure* [1990] BCLC 342 ... where the entire petition was dismissed at first instance, the Judge holding that the petitioner could be left to his remedy for a buy-out, not under statute, but under the articles only. The decision [in *Virdi*] was overturned on appeal ... holding that under the articles, the accountant who was to perform the valuation might value the petitioner's shares at a discount,

---

[124] Darren P. Lindamood, 'Comment: Redressing the Arbitration Process: An Alternative to the Arbitration Fairness Act of 2009', *Wake Forest Law Review*, 45 (2010), 291–318 at 293.

[125] The statistical result is consistent with an experiment study conducted by Thibaut and his colleagues. For details see John Thibaut et al., 'Procedural Justice as Fairness', *Stanford Law Review*, 26 (1974), 1271–1289 at 1288.

[126] Galanter, 'Adjudication, Litigation, and Related Phenomena', 174.

[127] The majority of Hong Kong cases illustrated that Hong Kong courts refused to strike out an unfair prejudice petition on the ground that the respondent had made a reasonable offer to purchase the petitioner's shares at fair price. See, for example, *Ronald Li-kai Chu and Others v. Deacon Te-ken Chiu* [1991] 2 HKLR 572; *Re Prudential Enterprises Ltd* [2002] 3 HKLRD 388 and *Re Ranson Motor Manufacturing Company Limited* [2007] 1 HKLRD 751.

[128] Unreported, HCCW 688/2000, 24 April 2001 at para. 37.

[129] Ibid.

and the petitioner was not acting unreasonably in going to Court to avoid that risk. In the present case, the buy-out order would be pursuant to the provisions of Section 168A.

In sum, it would not be appropriate for Hong Kong to introduce a statutory minority buyout regime for a smaller private company which empowers the arbitrator to value the shares under the exit regime. This is due to the fact that the company law has a contractual character that governs the commercial relationship between the members and the company.[130] An introduction of a statutory minority buyout regime that facilitates dissenting shareholders to exit the company at their own will would contravene the sanctity of contract binding on the company and its members, as there is no infringement of legal or equitable rights or interests under the general law and equitable rules.[131]

7.4 Concluding Comments

ADR policymakers in Hong Kong do not always blindly 'copy' one sophisticated ADR programme from a successful one in another country without considering its own distinctive context. Hong Kong has its own unique features not only because of the high quality of its legal rules and financial reporting standards, but also due to the unique features of shareholder disputes in local small private companies.[132] However, like other common law jurisdictions, Hong Kong is presently considering the use of different policy options in legitimizing the use of ADR for shareholder disputes. At present, the Hong Kong court system is facing enormous pressures not only to alleviate the excessive case-load pressure. In addition, the Judiciary is facing external pressures deriving from the social and economic change.[133] On that basis, this chapter argues that the current policy development on ADR for the resolution of shareholder disputes in Hong Kong can be refined and evolved by gaining comparative insights into other comparable jurisdictions.

From the preceding discussion, one can see that the suggested approaches to the future codification of ADR for shareholder disputes in Hong Kong are best conceived as residing along a continuum from

---

[130] *O'Neill v. Phillips* [1999] BCC 600.

[131] English Law Commission, *Shareholder Remedies Consultation* (Law Commission Consultation Paper No. 142, 1996) at para. 18.10.

[132] See Chapter 1.

[133] Interim Report and Consultative Paper on Civil Justice Reform at para. 9.

principle to rule. At one end of the continuum is the inclusion of the arbitration law into the statutory minority buyout regime. This formal legislative approach empowers the arbitrator to determine the value of the minority's shares where there is a disagreement as to the price offered by the company to purchase the dissenter's shares. The merit of this legislative approach is that it offers greater certainty as to the subject matter of the dispute which falls within the arbitral tribunal's jurisdiction. However, this legislative approach that provides an exit route for dissenting shareholders to leave the company at their own will would undermine the sanctity of the contract binding on the members and the company, as there is no infringement of legal or equitable rights or interests under the general law and equitable rules. Hence, this approach may not be considered as an attractive option for Hong Kong to follow.

At the other end point of the continuum is a more notable form of codification, as this supports a self-regulatory approach to a voluntary basis for ADR compliance which is now available in South Africa. The inclusion of ADR into the voluntary codes of corporate governance for SMEs could possibly be adopted in Hong Kong in the long run, as it provides additional guidelines for the court to determine the appropriate standard of conduct for directors to behave in a manner which is consistent with ADR objectives under the court rules.

The permissive enabling approach of the company law falls between the two ends of this spectrum. This approach permits greater freedom for private companies to contract out some of the members' statutory rights to file a petition to the court through an arbitration agreement, while retaining a certain degree of the court to control over the specific kind of remedies that the arbitral tribunals should not be granted. This approach is widely used in common law jurisdictions such as the United Kingdom, Hong Kong and Singapore, as it is consonant with the traditional role of the court in exercising its gap-filling role to give effect to the objectives of the company legislature and certain business norms. However, it remains unclear whether the Hong Kong courts would follow the robust approach taken by the Singapore Court of Appeal in the *L Capital Jones Ltd* case that unfair prejudice claims are generally arbitrable unless the fact of a particular case raises public policy considerations.

~

Conclusion

C.1 Summary and Contribution of the Study

This book attempts to build up a theoretical framework to examine the key stages of the institutionalization process that may secure the legitimacy of ADR for the resolution of shareholder disputes in Hong Kong. It provides a comprehensive examination of the recent wave of ADR initiatives in Hong Kong with the objective of analysing how the local government, the courts and the legal professions play influential roles in legitimizing the greater use of ADR for shareholder disputes. Apart from the conventional approach of doctrinal analysis used in this book, an interdisciplinary approach was adopted to address the key research questions from different angles, including sociolegal studies, sociology law and economics. The use of pluralist research methods in this book enriches the understanding of how informal out-of-court processes within shareholder disputes evolved since the Civil Justice Reform (CJR) began in 2009.

This book builds on work in new institutional theory from sociology by examining the key stages of institutionalizing ADR practices for shareholder disputes in Hong Kong.[1] According to this model, the institutionalization process was first triggered by a wave of ADR initiatives in responding to the pressures not only within the local court system, but also from interstate competition with regard to the relative attractiveness for doing business (such as the costs of conducting litigation, the availability of non-litigation modes of dispute resolution and similar).[2] These

---

[1] The institutionalization models developed by Tolbert and Zucker in 1999, Greenwood and his colleagues in 2002 were applied and adapted in this present study. See Pamela S. Tolbert and Lynne G. Zucker, 'Studying Organization: Theory & Method', in Stewart R. Clegg and Cynthia Hardy (eds.), *The Institutionalization of Institutional Theory* (Thousand Oaks, CA: SAGE, 1999), 175–178 and Royston Greenwood et al., 'Theorizing Change: The Role of Professional Associations in the Transformation of Institutionalized Fields', *Academy of Management Journal*, 45:1 (2002), 58–80, 59–61.

[2] Hong Kong Judiciary, *Reform of the Civil Justice System in Hong Kong*, Interim Report and Consultative Paper on Civil Justice Reform (Hong Kong Judiciary, 2000) at para. 9.

pressures eventually became a burden on the courts to allocate judicial resources effectively that met the needs and expectations of the disputants. The introduction of procedural innovations (such as mediation) into the Hong Kong courts was partly a response to remove the enormous pressure on the court dockets.[3]

At the beginning stage in the development and promotion of ADR in Hong Kong, foreign policies and initiatives relating to the use of mediation and other alternative processes for shareholder disputes were taken into consideration for implementing a series of reforms. The Hong Kong Judiciary started to experiment with different types of ADR processes to varying degrees; certain types of disputes such as minority shareholder disputes are particularly suitable for mediation and other out-of-court processes.[4] Policy development on ADR for shareholder disputes has been further refined by considering various policy options which could facilitate and encourage a wider use of mediation and other alternative processes to resolve shareholder disputes.[5] Overseas experience in the use of different approaches (legal and non-legal policy instruments) to promote the greater use of ADR to resolve shareholder disputes was taken into consideration in formulating its court rules, company law, judicial directives on ADR and other non-regulatory approaches such as accreditation and training.[6]

However, there is no general consensus about the utility of using ADR to resolve shareholder disputes, as the introduction of ADR into the courts was an attempt to reduce the enormous costs and delays posed by shareholder litigation processes instead of encouraging local lawyers and their clients to appreciate the benefit of ADR.[7] Thus, the early stage in the development and incorporation of ADR into the court system can be described as being at the 'pre-institutionalization stage'. At this stage, lawyers and their clients may have a sense of pressure to use ADR to resolve shareholder disputes despite the fact that court-connected ADR is entirely voluntary. In particular, lawyers in some cases might simply avoid costs penalties and other adverse consequences of failure to encourage their clients to attend mediation sessions with no intention to attempt settlement.[8]

---

[3] See Chapter 2.
[4] Hong Kong Department of Justice, *Report of the Working Group on Mediation* (Hong Kong Department of Justice, 2010) at para. 5.9.
[5] See Chapter 2.
[6] Ibid.
[7] Interim Report and Consultative Paper on Civil Justice Reform, paras. 629–636.
[8] See Chapter 6. Also, the 2015 Survey on the use of mediation in Hong Kong, conducted by Herbert Smith Freehills, revealed that although mediation and other alternative processes

Following the 'pre-institutionalization' stage, the use of informal modes of dispute resolution in resolving shareholder disputes would become more widespread among members of the local legal professions.[9] This stage is generally referred to as the 'semi-institutionalization' stage as it involves the development of some degree of consensus among the local legal professionals in considering the potential benefits of using ADR to assist their clients to resolve shareholder disputes.[10] Informal out-of-court processes often gain moral and/or pragmatic legitimacy at this stage because lawyers are more willing to encourage their clients to attempt ADR not only because they are under both legal and moral obligations to advise their clients to consider the possibility of using ADR.[11] In addition, the change in culture from an adversarial litigation setting to a more cooperative approach to dispute resolution might be seen as an opportunity for local lawyers to make profits on ADR activities.[12] It would not be surprising for local lawyers to be more prepared to offer advice and information to their clients about the proper use of non-adjudicative dispute resolution options to resolve shareholder disputes.[13]

Obviously, mediation and other alternative processes could become widely adopted at the 'semi-institutionalization' stage as theorization develops and becomes more explicit at this stage.[14] Theorization involves the recognition of the problems of court-based shareholder proceedings. For example, excessive length of time and costs associated with unfair prejudice proceedings could be dealt by introducing mediation and other forms of extrajudicial processes into the court's case management

have been introduced under the auspices of the new court rules and practice directions in Hong Kong for more than five years, many litigants and their lawyers were 'paying lip service to the process purely to avoid the adverse costs and other consequences of not mediating.' For a detailed discussion, see 'ADR in Asia Pacific: Spotlight on Mediation in Hong Kong', in *ADR in Asia Pacific Guide*, Vol. 1 (London: Herbert Smith Freehills, 2015), 18. Similarly, Lord Jackson points out that the public and small business were not aware of all the benefits of mediating, which might mean that they were not attempting to participate in the mediation process in good faith. See Lord Justice Jackson, *Review of Civil Litigation Costs: Final Report* (London: The Stationary Office, 2009) at para. 6.3.

[9] See Chapters 4, 5 and 6.
[10] See supra note 1.
[11] Order 1A, Rule 3 of the Rule of High Courts (Cap. 4A) (RHC) and Order 62, Rule 8 of the RHC. See also para. 116A of the Codes of Conduct issued by the Hong Kong Bar Association and para. 10.17(3) of the Hong Kong Solicitors' Guide to Professional Conduct.
[12] Yves Dezalay and Bryant Garth, 'Fussing about the Forum: Categories and Definitions as Stakes in a Professional Competition', *Law and Social Inquiry*, 21 (1996), 285–312 at 288.
[13] See Chapter 6.
[14] See supra note 1.

powers.[15] Alternatively, theorization entails the justification of procedural innovations through judicial interpretation of the court's case management powers to refer cases to some alternative forms of non-litigious
dispute resolution processes.[16] Judges could employ their legal framing
strategies to justify that the application of ADR processes for shareholder
disputes is in line with society's dominant social and economic values,
which are inherent in the Hong Kong Basic Law.[17]

In addition, successful justification of the ADR practices within the
local legal professions is followed by the process of diffusion.[18] This process
considers how the interplay between legal and non-legal policy instruments could contribute to the spread or transmission of ADR practices
among the legal community.[19] ADR practices for shareholder disputes
would be more enduring among members of the local legal professions
as they have already gained a good understanding about the proper use
of ADR through continuing professional development or training.[20]
Corporate clients are properly informed by their lawyers about the benefits of using consensus-oriented dispute resolution methods (such as
mediation) to resolve minority shareholder disputes. ADR practices for
shareholder disputes are thus partially institutionalized through a wave of
ADR initiatives and these include the following:

- The use of extrajudicial processes in conjunction with the court's case
  management powers under the new court rules[21]
- An enactment of a new company law that empowers the court to stay the
  whole or part of the proceedings for the purpose of allowing the matters to be resolved through mediation or other alternative processes[22]
- The introduction of the Mediation Ordinance that provides the basic
  statutory framework for the conduct of mediation
- An enactment of the new Arbitration Ordinance which unifies an
  'international' regime which was based on the UNCITRAL Model Law
  and a 'domestic' regime

---

[15] Rita Cheung, 'The Use of Alternative Dispute Resolution Allied to Active Judicial Case
Management: A New Forum to Deal with Shareholder Disputes in Hong Kong', *Asia
Pacific Law Review*, 16 (2008), 91–104.
[16] See Chapters 4 and 5.
[17] See Chapter 4.
[18] See Chapter 6.
[19] Ibid.
[20] Ibid.
[21] Order 1A, Rule 1(e) of the RHC.
[22] Rule 6(f) of the Companies (Unfair Prejudice Petitions) Proceedings Rules (Cap. 622L).

- Promotion of the 'Mediation First' Pledge within the local business group
- The establishment of the Hong Kong Mediation Accreditation Association Limited (HKMAAL), which is an industry-led body in governing the matters relating to accreditation, training and discipline
- The establishment of the Judiciary's Mediation Information Office, which provides mediation information to the general public
- The Joint Mediation Helpline Office, which was jointly set up by the Hong Kong Bar Association, the Law Society of Hong Kong and other ADR services providers in 2010 to provide one-stop mediation referral services for parties
- The establishment of the Financial Dispute Resolution Centre, which is responsible for administrating an independent Financial Dispute Resolution Scheme to resolve financial disputes between individual customers and financial institutions by adopting the approach of 'mediation first, arbitration next'[23]
- Further development of ADR knowledge and skills in legal education programmes

It is thus suggested that Hong Kong is now somewhere between the stage of semi-institutionalization and the stage of full institutionalization. At this stage, both the Hong Kong government and the Hong Kong Judiciary provide appropriate incentives to encourage lawyers, judges and disputing parties to use ADR more routinely.[24]

Although both the Hong Kong government and the Hong Kong Judiciary have provided supportive and practical steps to institutionalize ADR practices for shareholder disputes in recent years, the utility and benefits of using informal out-of-court processes to resolve shareholder disputes are more vulnerable to challenge by ADR's opponents who might otherwise be unwilling to use ADR. This could be attributed to the fact that a new model of consensus-orientated dispute resolution has not yet been fully institutionalized within the lawyers' normal disputing practice

---

[23] The Financial Dispute Resolution Centre (FDRC) released the consultation paper on the Proposals to Enhance the Financial Dispute Resolution Scheme in October 2016. One of the recommendations made by the FDRC is to enlarge the scope of eligible complainants by including covering small enterprises which have/had a customer relationship with a financial institution or have been provided with a Financial Service. For details, see Financial Dispute Resolution Centre, *Consultation Paper on the Proposals to Enhance the Financial Dispute Resolution Scheme*, 2016, paras 2.21-2.36.

[24] Lynne G. Zucker, 'The Role of Institutionalization Cultural Persistence' in Walter W. Powell and Paul J. DiMaggio (eds.), *The New Institutionalism in Organizational Analysis* (Chicago: University of Chicago Press, 1991), 864–873.

such that ADR could be viewed as a legitimate and fair process supplementing the effective use of court-based shareholder proceedings.[25]

In fact, the persistence of mediation and other extrajudicial processes that become fully institutionalized would depend on the degree of integration of ADR models into the culture of shareholder litigation process.[26] In this way, the utility and benefits of using non-litigation modes of dispute resolution for shareholder disputes would not be questioned or challenged by local legal professions if non-adjudicative dispute resolution processes would become further entrenched and co-opted or assimilated into the traditional, litigation-centred approach to problem solving.[27] ADR would then achieve a taken-for-granted status (cultural-cognitive legitimacy) among the core belief of local lawyers as informal out-of-court processes have become fully incorporated into the legal system.[28] Thus, much more efforts could be made for future reforms in Hong Kong's corporate law, as well as the development of a range of non-legal policy instruments, such as the inclusion of ADR into the voluntary codes of corporate governance practice for SMEs.[29]

This book offers additional policy options for the Hong Kong government and the Hong Kong Judiciary to consider the progress of developing a set of sophisticated ADR policies that might help the local business and legal communities to understand the benefits of using mediation and other alternative processes to resolve shareholder disputes.[30] More specifically, the benefits of using ADR for shareholder disputes would not be questioned or challenged by the local business and legal professional communities at the stage of full institutionalization. At this stage, it is expected that corporate users and their lawyers may consciously or unconsciously adopt ADR processes, as they believe that such an adoption is in conformity with cultural norms, beliefs or rules that are presumed to be acceptable or legitimate in a given society.

---

[25] See Chapter 6.

[26] Jeannette A. Colyvas, 'Ubiquity and Legitimacy: Disentangling Diffusion and Institutionalization', *Sociological Theory*, 29:1 (2011), 27–53 at 43–44. Colyvas notes that 'Institutionalization entails the integration of new practices or structures into sources of reproduction, usually existing ones such as law, the professions, identity categories, and patterns in the life course.'

[27] Thomas O. Main, 'ADR: The New Equity', *University of Cincinnati Law Review*, 74 (2005), 329–404.

[28] Ibid.

[29] See Chapter 7.

[30] Ibid.

Indeed, judges and lawyers are only performing their supervisory roles in either encouraging or assisting the parties to consider the possibility of using out-of-court processes to resolve shareholder disputes. Judges have a duty to exercise their active case management powers to encourage and facilitate the appropriate use of ADR to resolve disputes,[31] whereas lawyers are under a duty, pursuant to Order 1A, Rule 3 of the Rules of the High Court, to provide their clients with information and advice on the application of non-adjudicative processes to resolve shareholder disputes.[32]

At present, corporate users still rely on lawyers to advise them about the legal requirement to consider ADR processes, and on when and how to deploy these processes in resolving shareholder disputes in Hong Kong.[33] Lawyers have taken a more significant role in the post-CJR era by making their clients aware of the benefits and the associated risks for participating in mediation and other alternative processes to resolve shareholder disputes. It is expected that when lawyers representing both the majority and minority shareholders in the mediation process are specialists in both corporate law and ADR, the likelihood of achieving a fair settlement between the parties would be higher.[34] One possible reason for this is that experienced corporate lawyers who are accustomed to ADR processes could reduce some of the information gaps and information asymmetries between shareholders, and at the same time improving the minority shareholders' bargaining strength with the majority shareholders in either settling the claim at mediation or narrowing some of the issues for subsequent court proceedings.[35] On that basis, shareholders would be willing to engage in non-adjudicative processes if lawyers are familiar with corporate law and are experts in ADR.

However, there remain relatively few ADR neutral third parties (such as mediators) with a wide diversity of skill and experiences in the relevant legal, social, economic and other technical fields.[36] The relatively small number of experienced mediators or other neutral third parties

---

[31] Order 1A, Rule 4(2)(e) of the Rules of the High Court (RHC).

[32] See also para. 4 of Practice Direction 31.

[33] ADR in Asia Pacific, 16. In some cases, the court may direct parties to make a joint application to the court for direction pursuant to para. 13 of Practice Direction 31 to provide guidance for the parties on certain proposals in the Mediation Notice and Mediation Response in relation to the mediation (such as disagreement on the choice of mediator).

[34] Oren Gazal-Ayal and Ronen Perry, 'Imbalances of Power in ADR: The Impact of Representation and Dispute Resolution Method on Case Outcomes', *Law & Social Inquiry* (2014), 1–33 at 8.

[35] Ibid., 21.

[36] ADR in Asia Pacific, 10.

in ADR processes (such as expert determination) active in Hong Kong raises suspicion among minority shareholders who are encouraged to use mediation and other non-adjudicative processes as fair and cost-effective alternatives to court litigation process. To improve the role of lawyers in promoting the greater use of ADR within the corporate sector, this book suggests that lawyers should be properly informed about the benefits which ADR could bring through mass media, public education, ADR training and accreditation, as well as the regulative framework within which ADR can be voluntarily used in conjunction with court-based shareholder proceedings.[37] In turn, mediation and other alternative processes would become well-accepted dispute resolution processes for resolution of minority shareholder disputes among the local business community and legal professions.

In addition, this book suggests that the inclusion of mediation and other out-of-court dispute resolution practices into the guidelines on corporate governance for small and medium-sized enterprises (SMEs) may be adopted in Hong Kong, as it provides additional guidelines for the court to determine the appropriate standard of conduct for directors to behave in a manner which is consistent with ADR goals.[38] Following that, it argues that it would not be appropriate for Hong Kong to introduce a statutory minority buyout regime for a smaller private company which empowers the arbitrator to value the shares under the exit regime. This is due to the fact that corporate law is fundamental contractual in nature that governs the commercial relationship between the members and the company.[39] An introduction of a statutory minority buyout regime that facilitates dissenting shareholders to exit the company at their own will would contravene the sanctity of contract binding upon the company and its members as there is no infringement of legal or equitable rights or interests under the general law and equitable rules.[40] On that basis, the current company law that permits members to contract out their statutory right to petition the court for an unfair prejudice remedy is entirely satisfactory.[41] One possible reason for this is that this approach permits greater freedom for members to contract out some of their statutory rights to file

---

[37] See Chapter 6.
[38] See Chapter 7.
[39] *O'Neill v. Phillips* [1999] BCC 600.
[40] English Law Commission, *Shareholder Remedies Consultation* (Law Commission Consultation Paper No. 142, 1996) at para. 18.10.
[41] *Quiksilver Greater China Ltd v. Quiksilver Glorious Sun JV Ltd* (unreported, HCCW 364 and 365/2013, 25 July 2014).

a petition to the court through an arbitration agreement, while retaining a certain degree of court to control over the specific kind of remedies that the arbitral tribunals could grant.

Last but not least, education plays an important role in raising the awareness of legal practitioners and law students in understanding the dispute resolution process of mediation and how to act as conflict dispute resolution advocates in assisting the parties to achieve their best interests.[42] Wilkinson and Burton argue that the success in shifting away from the litigation-centred approach towards a collaborative approach that recognizes the significance of using ADR to resolve civil disputes depends on the role of education.[43] Similarly, Means asserts that corporate lawyers can work effectively in dealing with shareholder disputes if they are experienced in other non-legal disciplines, such as accounting, finance, clinical psychology and social work.[44] Thus, an inter- and intra-disciplinary approach to legal education is necessary, as this may effectively change the role of lawyer from being 'adversarial advocates' for their clients in courtroom litigation to being 'dispute resolvers' in advising their clients to choose the most appropriate process that satisfies the interests of the parties.[45]

As a whole, this book argues that institutionalization of ADR policy depends not only on the efforts of the Judiciary and the government to devise a broad range of policy instruments in supporting the institutionalization process, but also the critical role of legal professions in legitimizing the use of ADR. This argument rests on the assumption that legal professions are affected by 'the set of fundamental political, social and legal ground rules' as they are embedded in an institutional environment (i.e., the legal system).[46] Institution is defined as 'cognitive, normative and

---

[42] It is important to contain this in the context of the current reform of Hong Kong's professional legal education system. See also Julie MacFarlane, 'The Evolution of New Lawyer: How Lawyers Are Reshaping the Practice of Law', *Journal of Dispute Resoltuion*, 1 (2008), 61–81.

[43] Michael Wilkinson and Janet Burton, 'Conclusions' in Michael Wilkinson and Janet Burton (eds.), *Reform of the Civil Process in Hong Kong* (Hong Kong: Butterworths Asia, 2000), 330.

[44] Benjamin Means, 'NonMarket Values in Family Business', *William & Mary Law Review*, 54 (2013), 1185–1250 at 1246–1240.

[45] Traditionally, lawyers concentrate on the 'objective aspects of shareholder disputes' and the applicable law instead of assisting their clients to identify the underlying interests or motivations in the disputes. For a detailed discussion, see Chapter 1.

[46] Douglass C. North, *Institutions, Institutional Change and Economic Performance* (Cambridge: Cambridge University Press, 1990), 143.

regulative structures and actions that provide stability and meaning of social behaviour'.[47] Consequently, institutional frameworks can then be considered as the set of fundamental elements, such as a set of legal rules, norms and beliefs that provide sufficient basis for encouraging the use of private informal dispute resolution processes for shareholder disputes.[48] ADR processes for shareholder disputes can be characterized as 'social fact' if ADR policy has undergone at least three stages of the institutionalization process.

Philip Selznick highlighted the point that a crucial prerequisite for successful institutionalization of policy is how the institutional frameworks are made up.[49] For example, there is less likelihood of gaining sufficient adherence to the objectives of ADR policy if institutional frameworks are made up of a set of authoritative rules. The reasoning is that institutionalization of ADR practices through a set of purely legislative provisions may hamper the flexibility of extrajudicial processes. In particular, consensuality has traditionally been one of the core notions of mediation and other consensus-oriented dispute resolution processes. Individual parties are allowed to use consensus orientated dispute resolution methods to handle their disputes in an ad hoc manner by using a range of non-legal values, such as individual ethics, and cultural and moral norms.[50] Such entirely new and innovative structures for resolving disputes may lose their appealing characteristic of 'voluntariness' if parties are required to undertake non-adjudicative dispute resolution processes compulsorily through a set of legal rules.

Clearly, if formal legislative strategies on the application of private informal dispute resolution methods are backed purely by the threat of costs sanctions, this approach may be counterproductive to motivate the lawyers to behave in a manner which is inconsistent with the original ADR policy goals. This is particularly so as one of the core ADR policy objectives in Hong Kong is to guarantee the fundamental rights and

---

[47] Richard W. Scott, *Institutions and Organizations*, 2nd ed. (Thousand Oaks, CA: SAGE, 2001), 48.

[48] Lance E. Davis and Douglas C. North, *Institutional Change and American Economic Growth* (Cambridge: Cambridge University Press, 1970), 6. According to Davis and North, the term 'institutional frameworks' is defined as 'the set of fundamental political, social, and legal ground rules that establishes the basis for production, exchange, and distribution.'

[49] Philip Selznick, *The Moral Commonwealth: Social Theory and the Promise of Community* (Berkeley: University of California Press, 1992), 280.

[50] Jacqueline M. Nolan-Haley, 'Court Mediation and the Search for Justice through Law', *Washington University Law Quarterly*, 74 (1996), 47–102 at 63–64.

freedoms of the citizens to choose a range of methods of dispute resolution, including both the formal court process and other facilitative, informal and confidential dispute methods.[51] On such a basis, Hong Kong lawyers may reluctantly act in conformity with the original ADR policy goals if they were compelled to encourage their clients to settle at an early stage through ADR processes under the court rules (e.g., costs sanction).

Nonetheless, the current civil procedure rules, corporate law and judicial directives on mediation have encouraged Hong Kong's legal professions and business community to consider the possibility of ADR processes for resolving shareholder disputes. In turn, the courts are induced to apply the court rules and companies legislation in accordance with the objectives of ADR policy.[52] This is due to the fact these policy objectives are designed in line with the core constitutional values of the Basic Law.[53] This may affect the rate of the diffusion of ADR practices for shareholder disputes within the Hong Kong legal profession community.[54] In particular, ADR advocates, such as the Hong Kong Judiciary and the leading legal practitioners, use their intellectual capacities to convince lawyers about the virtues of mediation and other non-adjudicative processes to resolve shareholder disputes.[55] Hence, these findings support the major argument that the spread of ADR practices within Hong Kong's legal professions together with the efforts of both the Judiciary and the government reinforce the institutionalization process of ADR policy for shareholder disputes.[56]

C.2 Extending the Study for Future Research

So far, a wave of ADR initiatives have made mediation an integral part of the dispute resolution landscape since 2009. Although there has been little evidence of mediation and other alternative processes being systematically and effectively used to deal with minority shareholder disputes, the choices of dispute resolution processes that are available to Hong Kong lawyers and their clients to choose in resolving shareholder disputes have been substantially expanded. Parties could choose facilitative-based mediation process in reaching a creative solution (such as an apology)

---

[51] See Chapter 4.
[52] See Chapters 4 and 5.
[53] See Chapter 4.
[54] See Chapter 6.
[55] Ibid.
[56] Ibid.

that goes beyond the types of legal remedies available to members of a company under the shareholder remedies provisions.[57]

Clearly, willingness of a party to apologize would be sufficient to show that he or she has an intention to compromise. To develop a pro-mediation culture, the Department of Justice's Steering Committee conducted two rounds of public consultation on the proposals to enact apology legislation in Hong Kong on June 2015 and February 2016.[58] After the two rounds of public consultations, the Apology Bill was introduced to the Legislative Council on 8 February 2017 for the first reading.[59] The long-awaited Apology Bill have been enacted in an apology law by the Legislative Council on 13 July 2017.[60] With the enactment of this law, Hong Kong becomes the first jurisdiction in Asia with such a law that encourages disputing parties to apologize in legal disputes and bear no legal consequences. In addition, the enactment of apology legislation coupled with the greater use of mediation and other consensus-building processes to resolve shareholder disputes could facilitate amicable settlement, as parties would generally bear no legal consequences if they are willing to say they're sorry in legal disputes.[61] However, the extent to which the proposed apology legislation could effectively achieve the goals of promoting pro-mediation culture and reducing the backlog of civil cases in Hong Kong remains to be seen.[62] In particular, the proposed apology legislation confers a discretionary power on the judge to determine whether the admission of any statement of facts made in the apology could be used in civil, disciplinary and regulatory hearings.[63] The author leaves this topic for further research in the future.

---

[57] Eric M. Runesson and Marie-Laurence Guy, Mediating Corporate Governance Conflict and Disputes: Global Corporate Governance Forum Focus 4 (2007) at www.gcgf.org/ifcext/cgf.nsf/AttachmentsByTitle/Focus+Mediation/$FILE/Focus4_Mediation_12.pdf (Accessed 18 August 2009), 29.

[58] Ibid.

[59] News: Dispute Resolution Legislation, *Asian Dispute Review*, (2017), 95–99 at 96 and Press Release: Final Report and Recommendations on Enactment of Apology Legislation, published 28 November 2016 at www.info.gov.hk/gia/general/201611/28/P2016112800594.htm (Accessed 29 November 2016).

[60] Joyce Ng and Julia Hollingsworth, 'Hong Kong Passes Law Making It Easier to Say "Sorry" Without Legal Consequences', *South China Morning Post* (14 July 2017) at www.scmp.com/news/hong-kong/law-crime/article/20102526/hong-kong/lawmakers-pass-sorry-law(Accessed 18 July 2017).

[61] Chris Lau, '"Sorry Law" Moves a Step Closer', *South China Morning Post*, 29 November 2016, C1.

[62] Ibid. Lawmaker James To Kun-Sun notes that there could be an increasing number of insincere apologies, as in most cases the apologies would not be used as evidence in court to determine legal liability under the proposed Apology Ordinance.

[63] Ibid. and Hong Kong Department of Justice, *Enactment of Apology Legislation in Hong Kong: Final Report and Recommendations* (28 November 2016), 87.

Furthermore, there is a considerable room for the Hong Kong government to develop a specific protocol or rule to reduce some of the problems and difficulties involved in a mixture of mediation and other private dispute resolution processes (such as arbitration, expert determination, early natural evaluation and similar).[64] Although the new Hong Kong Arbitration Ordinance provides a clear statutory framework for conducting a combined arbitration-mediation process (such as med-arb or arb-med), this provision is designed specifically to deal only with issues relating to the confidentiality, natural justice, and other matters relating to the transition from mediation to arbitration, and vice versa. Further discussion surrounding the proper use of a mixture of mediation and other out-of-court processes (such as expert determination, early natural evaluation and similar) should be welcomed and encouraged, as this could maximize the potential use of mediation.

In addition, it is important to examine Hong Kong's lawyers' attitudes about ADR for shareholder disputes instead of their actual use of ADR in resolving shareholder disputes in this empirical legal study. In particular, it was not practical to obtain data regarding Hong Kong lawyers' actual use of ADR in resolving shareholder disputes, as the culture of mediation was relatively novel and had not yet been fully implemented at the time of conducting this empirical legal research.[65]

However, as the CJR has been implemented for a number of years in Hong Kong since 2009, future researchers can adopt a more sophisticated statistical model (such as the Analysis of Variance [ANOVA] technique) to examine whether there are any significant differences in attitudes towards the use of ADR for shareholder disputes among in-house corporate lawyers, corporate directors and minority shareholders. This is particularly true as the CJR has brought significant changes to the role of practicing lawyers in relation to ADR processes. Hong Kong practicing lawyers are now under a duty to assist the court in furthering the underlying objectives by advising their clients to consider the possibility of using ADR processes in resolving disputes.[66] Undoubtedly, the benefits

---

[64] Recently, the Singapore International Mediation Centre established a new 'Arb-Med-Arb' protocol that allows a party to commence arbitration under the auspices of the Singapore International Arbitration Centre. See also Nadja Alexander, How Is Med-Arb Regulated in Hong Kong? (2013) at http://kluwermediationblog.com (Accessed 10 November 2016).

[65] This empirical research began in the early 2012, at a time that the mediation regime was relatively new and had not yet been fully implemented. See *Ansar Mohammad v. Global Legend Transportation Ltd* HKLRD 3 [2010] 273.

[66] See, for example, Order 1A, Rule 3 of the RHC and para. 4 of Practice Direction 31. See, for example, *Kwan Wing Leung v. Fung Chi Leung* [2014] HKDC 1045 (unreported, DCPI

of using mediation and other informal out-of-court processes to resolve shareholder disputes might be widely known not only to those practicing lawyers who offer services to the public. In addition, in-house lawyers, corporate directors and minority shareholders would be more likely to get involved in ADR processes as the CJR has been implemented for a number of years in Hong Kong.[67]

Apart from that, there are several avenues of research that could be further explored in the future, which might enrich the understanding of how the current policies on ADR for shareholder disputes may be refined. First, the relationship between different types of ADR processes requires further exploration in order to understand why Hong Kong lawyers and corporate directors would prefer to choose a particular type of ADR (such as mediation, arbitration, expert determination and similar) in resolving shareholder disputes under any special circumstances.[68] Second, the development of a longitudinal empirical study on the diffusion of ADR practices among local business and legal professional communities is required. A longitudinal model helps to understand how the unfolding changes of an institutional process (such as the relative power and influence of the government, the court and the legal professional organizations on the development of ADR over a period of time) could lead to institutionalization.[69]

In addition, the present empirical study relies primarily on a cross-sectional data to analyse Hong Kong lawyers' attitudes about the use of ADR for shareholder disputes. This analysis is somewhat incomplete, as it includes only a single causal direction instead of an ongoing and multi-directional process in analysing the relationship between the combined set of policy instruments and Hong Kong lawyers' acceptances towards the use of ADR for shareholder disputes. Previous institutional theorists

---

2489/2013 (15 September 2014)) at para. 79. The learned deputy judge Anthony Chow noted that the importance of mediation and the costs consequence of refusing to mediate are well known to the legal profession in the present case as the CJR has been implemented for a period of approximately five years. See also *Wu Yim Kwong Kindwind v. Manhood Development Limited* [2015] HKDC 1431 (unreported, DCCJ 3839/2012 (4 December 2015)) at para. 16, where the court held that legal advisors are under legal obligation to advise their clients about their duty to comply with the CJR's underlying objectives and the practice direction on mediation.

[67] Ibid.

[68] See, for example, David B. Lipsky and Ronald L. Seeber, 'Patterns of ADR used in Corporate Disputes', *Dispute Resolution Journal*, 54:1 (1999), 68–71.

[69] Fariborz Damanpour et al., 'Combinative Effects of Innovation Types and Organizational Performance: A Longitudinal Study of Service Organizations', *Journal of Management Studies*, 46:4 (2009), 650–675 at 652.

such as Walter Powell emphasized the importance of longitudinal studies in understanding how a new practice emerged and has subsequently
earned its legitimacy among members of the local community.[70] His argument rests on the assumption that institutionalized rules, procedures and
other kinds of structural arrangements are 'both dependent variables at
time t [the beginning of the year in which a new practice is adopted] and
independent variables at time t_{+1} [accumulation of the adoption pattern
of a new practice over time].'[71] This means that the process of developing
beliefs and options relating to a new practice among a group of social
actors in a given society presumably occurs through continuous interaction with one's environment rather than as a single and unidirectional
process.[72] Thus, all the conclusions reached in this empirical legal study
remain tentative and require further testing.

Last but most importantly, meta-analysis seems to be the most useful
statistical technique in combining all the relevant empirical literature on
ADR in order to determine whether the average effect size of all empirical work is significant.[73] This innovative approach goes beyond the traditional literature review, as it begins to synthesize the relevant empirical
literature on the same topic, and then statistically summarizes the results
of all individual studies by producing a list of moderator variables, which
help to elucidate aspects of various studies (such as sample size, variables
studies, analytical models used, questionnaire design and similar) that
might have influenced different findings.[74]

In contrast with traditional statistical significance testing, meta-analysis
could be considered as useful statistical tool that provides an objective met-
ric to evaluate the strength of all empirical findings obtained from prior
studies on ADR. It emphasizes effect sizes instead of significance tests (such
as the 0.05 level of significance) which was used in this present study.[75] The

---

[70] Walter W. Powell, 'Expanding the Scope of Institutional Analysis', in Walter W. Powell and
Paul J. DiMaggio (eds.), *The New Institutionalism in Organizational Analysis* (Chicago:
University of Chicago Press, 1991), 201.

[71] Ibid.

[72] John Lande, 'The Diffusion of a Process Pluralist Ideology of Disputing: Factors Affecting
Opinions of Business Lawyers and Executives'. PhD thesis, University of Wisconsin-
Madison, (1995), 63.

[73] Jeremy A. Blumenthal, 'Meta-Analysis: A Primer for Legal Scholars', *Temple Law Review*,
80 (2007), 201–244 at 202.

[74] Ibid., 206.

[75] Ibid., 209–210; Robert Rosenthal, *Meta-Analytical Procedures for Social Research*, rev.
ed. (Thousand Oaks, CA: SAGE, 1991), 17; and Paul G. Nestor and Russell K.Schutt,
Research Methods In Psychology: Investigating Human Behaviour, 2nd ed. (Thousand Oaks,

resulting value of a meta-analysis is thus mostly free of sampling error as compared with traditional statistical significance testing.[76] In particular, the effect size calculation offers 'an index of generalizability of all the empirical findings' on ADR, which enables the Hong Kong government, the Hong Kong Judiciary, judges, lawyers and other major stakeholders to objectively compare a set of studies and to make policy inferences about the future development of ADR in Hong Kong, including issues relating to the ways that lead to full institutionalization of ADR among local business and legal professional communities.

In addition, meta-analysis helps both scholars and policymakers either to reconcile different findings from studies on the same topic or prevent any potential danger of deliberately choosing a particular study from a set of relevant studies in order to advocate particular policies.[77] One possible reason for this is that the empirical evidence regarding the relationship between lawyers' attitudes about informal out-of-court processes and their use of ADR is mixed.[78] It would be extremely difficult for the court to draw reliable general conclusions from the existing empirical research studies if the findings of these studies were either mixed or contradictory.[79] It seems that meta-analysis would be a very attractive avenue of research that could be explored in the future.

Overall, legal empirical research on ADR is under-developed in Hong Kong as compared with the United States, the United Kingdom and Canada. Limited and often inconsistent quantitative data on ADR foreshadow the larger and lively debate about the future development of a list of objective benchmarks for both the Hong Kong government

---

CA: SAGE, 2015), 40. See Chapter 6, where the p-value was used to reject empirical findings that do not reach the 0.05 level of significance.

[76] This argument rests on the assumption that each study in meta-analysis represents a sample taken from a given population. This sample is likely to differ from the population from which it was derived from an unknown amount of sampling error, as sampling errors tend to form a normal distribution with a mean of zero. In other words, when the mean sample-weighted effect is computed across studies in a meta-analysis the resulting value is mostly free of sampling error. For details see Lori Anne Shaw, 'Divorce Mediation Outcome Research: A Meta-Analysis', *Conflict Resolution Quarterly*, 27:4 (2010), 447–467 at 452 (citing Winfred Arthur et al., *Conducting Meta-Analysis Using SAS* (Mahwah, NJ: Lawrence Erlbaum Associates, 2001), 5–6).

[77] Blumenthal, 'Meta-Analysis', 202.

[78] Roselle L. Wissler, 'Court-connected Mediation in General Civil Cases: What We Know from Empirical Research', *Ohio State Journal on Dispute Resolution*, 17 (2002), 641–704 at 469–470.

[79] *Heil v. Rankin* [2001] QB 272 at 304 and Kathy Mack, Court Referral to ADR: Criteria and Research (2003) at www.aija.org.au (Accessed 8 August 2011).

and the Hong Kong Judiciary to evaluate the results of different empirical studies on ADR. It seems clear that further legal empirical research should be conducted to gain deeper insight into the development of a set of objective benchmarks for the Hong Kong government, the Hong Kong Judiciary, lawyers, businesspersons and other key stakeholders, to evaluate the strength of the empirical results from individual studies on ADR.

On the other hand, the reliability or quality of the benchmarks for policy evaluation depends on the number of studies being synthesized by meta-analysis.[80] This means that it would be extremely difficult to draw any firm conclusions from theses comparisons if a small number of studies were included in meta-analysis.[81] Although some of the earliest studies relating to lawyers' attitudes about the use of ADR were conducted almost thirty years ago,[82] the present empirical findings were based primarily on Hong Kong lawyers' attitudes about the use of ADR for shareholder disputes. Thus, more rigorous empirical legal research is needed in analysing the attitudes of lawyers about the use of ADR to resolve shareholder disputes.

Hopefully, future researchers could generate a list of objective indicators that could help the Hong Kong government and the Hong Kong Judiciary to make inference from a set of empirical studies on ADR. It would be expected that ADR could secure its legitimacy as a fair and predominant mode of dispute resolution for shareholder disputes among members of the legal profession group if meta-analysis of all the relevant studies could lend to an overall result that a majority of lawyers had a positive attitude towards the use of ADR for shareholder disputes.

---

[80] Blumenthal, 'Meta-Analysis', 232.
[81] Austin Lawrence et al., 'Report on the Effectiveness of Using Mediation in Selected Civil Law Disputes: A Meta-Analysis,' (2007). The Department of Justice in Canada published a report on the effectiveness of using mediation in selected civil law disputes through a meta-analysis.
[82] Wissler, 'Court-connected Mediation in General Civil Cases', 642–701.

Appendix 1

Measuring the Dependent and Independent Variables

This appendix provides an overview of the hypotheses, operational definitions of variables and anticipated associations among variables for the logistic regression analysis.

A.1 Measuring the Dependent Variable

Rogers defines innovation adoption as the actual utilization of an innovation among individuals.[1] In order to determine the relative spread in which informal out-of-court processes are being adopted by individual lawyers in Hong Kong, the outcome variable of this research has been measured as a dichotomous 'yes' or 'no' answer for ADR adoption among Hong Kong lawyers since the Civil Justice Reform (CJR) started in 2009. The analysis used the following binary dependent variable (variable name is given in capital letters in parentheses):

- Whether or not Hong Kong lawyers were willing to assist their clients to handle shareholder disputes through the adoption of non-adjudicative dispute resolution processes (ADOP)

1	=	If lawyer has chosen to adopt mediation and other resolution alternatives in assisting his or her clients to resolve shareholder disputes more than once
0	=	If otherwise

A.2 Measuring the Independent Variables

The hypotheses, operational definitions of independent variables relating to Hong Kong lawyers' acceptance towards the use of non-adjudicative dispute resolution processes, parameters and hypothesized relationships are summarized as follows (variable names are given in capital letters in parentheses):

---

[1] Rogers, Everett M., *Diffusion of Innovations*, 5th ed. (New York: Free Press, 2003), 221.

Explanation	Operational Definition and Label	Parameter	Predicted Sign	Hypotheses/Theoretical Basis
Compatibility of ADR with court-based shareholder proceedings	The degree to which ADR practice is perceived as being compatible with lawyers' existing legal practices in resolving shareholder disputes (COMPATIBILITY)	β_1	Positive, significant	**H1**: Based on the theories of innovation, diffusion and socio-legal theories
Relative advantage of informal out-of-court processes	The extent to which ADR has its own relative advantage in both aspects of cost-effectiveness and high levels of satisfaction (ADVANTAGES)	β_2	Positive, significant	**H2**: Based on the theories of innovation diffusion and socio-legal theories
Potential barriers to out-of-court settlement	The degree to which ADR settlement is perceived as difficult to enforce in reality (BARRIERS)	β_3	Negative, significant	**H3**: Based on the theories of innovation diffusion and socio-legal theories
Hong Kong lawyers' familiarity with ADR processes	The degree of Hong Kong lawyers' familiarity with ADR processes (FAMILIARITY)	β_4	Positive, significant	**H4**: Based on the theories of innovation diffusion, socio-legal theories and theories of the profession
Relative positions of Hong Kong lawyers in their legal professional networks	The existence of both the Judiciary and legal professional organizations in facilitating the development of shared meanings and values in relation to the operation of ADR (NETWORK)	β_5	Positive, significant	**H5**: Based on the theories of innovation diffusion, social network theory and theories of the profession
Legal culture of early settlements in shareholder disputes	The impact of local legal culture with respect to the way of resolving shareholder disputes (LEGAL CULTURE)	β_6	Positive, significant or no significant association	**H6**: Based on the theories of innovation diffusion and socio-legal theories

BIBLIOGRAPHY

Abel, Richard L. *American Lawyers*. Oxford: Blackwell, 1991.

'England and Wales: A Comparison of the Professional Projects of Barristers and Solicitors'. In Richard Abel and Philips C. Lewis (eds.), *Lawyers in Society*, 39–91. Berkeley: University of California Press, 1995.

'Lawyers and Legal Services'. In Peter Cane and Mark Tushnet (eds.), *The Oxford Handbook of Legal Studies*, 796–816. Oxford: Oxford University Press, 2003.

'ADR in Asia Pacific: Spotlight on Mediation in Hong Kong'. *ADR in Asia Pacific Guide*, Vol. 1. London: Herbert Smith Freehills, 2015.

Ahmed, Masood. 'Implied Compulsory Mediation'. *Civil Justice Quarterly*, 31:2 (2012), 151–175.

Alexander, Nadjia. 'Visualising the ADR Landscape'. *ADR Bulletin*, 7:3 (2004), 1–3.

Alexander, Nadja. 'Global Trends in Mediation: Riding the Third Wave'. In Nadja Alexander (ed.), *Global Trends in Mediation*, 1–36. The Hague: Kluwer Law International, 2006.

International and Comparative Mediation: Legal Perspectives, The Hague: Kluwer Law International, 2009.

The New Hong Kong Mediation Ordinance: Much Ado About Nothing? (2012) at http://kluwermediationblog.com (Accessed 16 April 2012).

How Is Med-Arb Regulated in Hong Kong? (2013) at http://kluwermediation-blog.com (Accessed 10 November 2016).

Anleu, Sharyn L. Roach. *Law and Social Change*. London: SAGE, 2010.

Armour, John. 'Enforcement Strategies in UK Corporate Governance: A Roadmap and Empirical Assessment'. In John Armour and Jennifer Payne (eds.), *Rationality in Company Law: Essays in Honour of D.D. Prentice,* 71–122. Oxford: Hart, 2009.

Armour, John, et al. 'Private Enforcement of Corporate Law: An Empirical Comparison of the United Kingdom and the United States'. *Journal of Empirical Legal Studies*, 6:4 (2009), 687–722.

Arthur, Winfred, et al. *Conducting Meta-Analysis Using SAS*. Mahwah, NJ: Lawrence Erlbaum Associates, 2001.

Astor, Hilary and Chinkin, Christine M. *Dispute Resolution in Australia*. Sydney: Butterworths, 1992.

Auerbach, Jerold S. *Justice without Law?* Oxford: Oxford University Press, 1983.

Babbie, Earl R. *The Practice of Social Research*, 12th ed. Belmont, CA: Thomson Wadsworth, 2007.

Balas, Aron, et al. 'The Divergence of Legal Procedures'. *American Economic Journal: Economic Policy*, 1:2 (2009), 138–162.

Bay, Marvin, et al. 'Note: The Integration of Alternative Dispute Resolution within the Subordinate Courts' Adjudication Process'. *Singapore Academic of Law Journal*, 16 (2004), 501–515.

Bennett, Colin J. 'How States Utilize Foreign Evidence'. *Journal of Public Policy*, 11:1 (1991), 31–54.

Berry, Frances Stokes and Berry, William D. 'Innovation and Diffusion Models in Policy Research'. In Paul A. Sabatier (ed.), *Theories of the Policy Process*, 223–260. Boulder, CO: Westview Press, 2007.

Black, Donald. 'The Elementary Forms of Conflict Management'. *New Directions in the Study of Justice, Law, and Social Control*. New York: Plenum Press, 1990.

Black, Julia. 'What Is Regulatory Innovation?'. In Julia Black et al. (eds.), *Regulatory Innovation: A Comparative Analysis*, 1–15. Cheltenham: Edward Elgar, 2005.

Blackaby, Nigel. *Refern and Hunter on International Arbitration*, 6th ed. Oxford; New York: Oxford University Press, 2015.

Blake, Susan, et al. *A Practical Approach to Alternative Dispute Resolution*. Oxford: Oxford University Press, 2011.

Blumenthal, Jeremy A. 'Meta Analysis: A Primer For Legal Scholars'. *Temple Law Review*, 80 (2007), 201–244.

Bouchez, Louis and Karpf, Alexander. 'The OECD's Work on Corporate Governance and Dispute Resolution Mechanisms'. In Louis Bouchez et al. (eds.), *Topics in Corporate Finance: The Quality of Corporate Law and the Role of Corporate Law Judges*, 3–18 Amsterdam: Amsterdam Center for Corporate Finance, 2006.

Boulle, Lawrence. *Mediation: Principles, Process, Practice*. Sydney: Butterworths, 1996.

Bourdieu, Pierre. 'The Force of Law: Toward a Sociology of the Judicial Field'. *Hastings Law Journal*, 38 (1987), 805–853.

Boyle, A. J. *Minority Shareholders' Remedies*. Cambridge: Cambridge University Press, 2002.

Boyne, George A., et al. 'Explaining the Adoption of Innovation: An Empirical Analysis of Public Management Reform'. *Environment and Planning C: Government and Policy*, 23:4 (2005), 419–435.

Brace, Ian. *Questionnaire Design: How to Plan, Structure and Write Survey Material for Effective Market Research*. London: Kogan Page, 2008.

Brazil-David, Renata. 'Harmonization and Delocalization of International Commercial Arbitration'. *Journal of International Arbitration*, 28:5 (2011), 445–466.

Brekoulakis Stavros L. 'The Notion of the Superiority of Arbitration Agreements Over Jurisdiction Agreements: Time to Abandon It?'. *Journal of International Arbitration*, 24:4 (2007), 341–364.

Brooker, Penny. 'The "Juridification" of Alternative Dispute Resolution'. *Anglo-American Law Review*, 28 (1999), 1–36.

Mediation Law: Journey through Institutionalism to Juridification. London: Routledge, 2013.

Brown, Henry J. and Marriott, Arthur. *ADR Principles and Practice*, 2nd ed. London: Sweet & Maxwell, 2011.

Brunet, Edward. 'Questing the Quality of Alternative Dispute Resolution'. *Tulane Law Review*, 62 (1987), 1–56.

Bühring-Uhle, Christian. *Arbitration and Mediation in International Business*. The Hague: Kluwer Law International, 2006.

Burton, John. *Conflict: Resolution and Provention*. New York: St. Martin's Press, 1993.

Bush, Robert A. Baruch. 'Defining Quality in Dispute Resolution: Taxonomies and Anti-Taxonomies of Quality Arguments'. *Denver University Law Review*, 66 (1989), 335–380.

Bush, Robert A. Baruch and Folger, Joseph P. 'Mediation and Social Justice: Risks and Opportunities'. *Ohio State Journal on Dispute Resolution*, 27 (2012), 1–52.

Cameron, Camille and Kelly, Elsa. 'Litigants in Person in Civil Proceedings: Part I'. *Hong Kong Law Journal*, 32 (2002), 313–342.

Cappelletti, Mauro. 'Alternative Dispute Resolution Processes within the Framework of the World-Wide Access-to-Justice Movement'. *The Modern Law Review*, 56 (1989), 282–296.

Carter, James and Payton, Sophie. 'Arbitration and Company Law in England and Wales'. *European Company Law*, 12:3 (2015), 138–143.

CEDR. CEDR Solve Commercial Mediation Statistics 2001/02 (May 2002) at www.cedr.co.uk (Accessed 4 December 2012).

Cheffins, Brian R. *Company Law: Theory, Structure, and Operation*. Oxford: Clarendon Press, 1997.

Chen Huey-Tsyh and Rossi, Peter H. 'The Multi-Goal, Theory-Driven Approach to Evaluation: A Model Linking Basic and Applied Social Science'. *Social Forces*, 59:1 (1980), 106–122.

'Evaluating with Sense the Theory-Driven Approach'. *Evaluation Review*, 7:3 (1983), 283–302.

Chen-Wishart, Mindy. 'Legal Transplant and Undue Influence: Lost in Translation or a Working Mis-understanding?'. *International and Comparative Law Quarterly*, 62 (2013), 1–30.

Cheung, Rita. 'ADR and Shareholder Disputes: The Anglo-American Experience and Hong Kong Challenges'. *Asian Dispute Review*, (2008), 118–121.

'Corporate Wrongs Litigated in the Context of Unfair Prejudice Claims: Reforming the Unfair Prejudice Remedy for the Redress of Corporate Wrongs'. *Company Lawyer*, 29:4 (2008), 98–104.

'The Use of Alternative Dispute Resolution Allied to Active Judicial Case Management: A New Forum to Deal with Shareholder Disputes in Hong Kong'. *Asia Pacific Law Review*, 16 (2008), 91–104.

Company Law and Shareholders' Rights. Hong Kong: LexisNexis, 2010.

Cheung, Sai-On. 'Construction Mediation in Hong Kong'. In Penny Brooker and Suzanne Wilkinson (eds.), *Mediation in the Construction Industry: An International Review*, 62–81. Oxford: Spon Press, 2010.

Chrisman, P. Oswin, et al. 'Collaborative Practice Mediation: Are We Ready to Serve This Emerging Market?'. *Pepperdine Dispute Resolution Law Journal*, 6:3 (2006), 451–464.

Cohen, Amy J. 'Revisiting Against Settlement: Some Reflections On Dispute Resolution and Public Values'. *Fordham Law Review*, 78 (2009), 1143–1170.

'ADR and Some Thoughts on the Social in Duncan Kennedy's Third Globalization of Legal Thought'. *Comparative Law Review*, 3:1 (2012), 1–11.

Collier, John and Lowe, Vaughan. *The Settlement of Disputes in International Law: Institutions and Procedures*. Oxford: Oxford University Press, 1999.

Colyvas, Jeannette A. 'Ubiquity and Legitimacy: Disentangling Diffusion and Institutionalization'. *Sociological Theory*, 29:1 (2011), 27–53.

Cooley, Linda and Lewkowicz, Jo. *Dissertation Writing in Practice: Turning Ideas into Text*. Hong Kong: Hong Kong University Press, 2003.

Corporate Governance Review by The Standard Committee on Company Law Reform: A Consultation Paper made in Phase I of the Review. Hong Kong: Printing Department, 2001.

Cotterrell, Roger. *The Politics of Jurisprudence: A Critical Introduction to Legal Philosophy*. London: Butterworths, 1989.

Cox, David Roxbee and Snell, E. Joyce. *The Analysis of Binary Data*, 2nd ed. London: Chapman & Hall, 1989.

Creswell, John W. and Clark, Vicki L. Plano. *Designing and Conducting Mixed Methods Research*. Thosand Oaks, CA: SAGE, 2007.

Cronin-Harris, Catherine. 'Mainstreaming: Systematizing Corporate Use of ADR'. *Albany Law Review*, 59 (1995), 847–879.

Damanpour, Fariborz, et al. 'Combinative Effects of Innovation Types and Organizational Performance: A Longitudinal Study of Service Organizations'. *Journal of Management Studies*, 46:4 (2009), 650–675.

Davies, Adrian. *Best Practice in Corporate Governance: Building Reputation and Sustainable Success*. Surrey: Gower, 2006.

Davies, Paul. *Introduction to Company Law*. Oxford: Oxford University Press, 2010.

Davis, Lance E. and North, Douglas C. *Institutional Change and American Economic Growth*. Cambridge: Cambridge University Press, 1970.

Delgado, Richard, et al. 'Fairness and Formality: Minimizing the Risk of Prejudice in Alternative Dispute Resolution'. *Wisconsin Law Review*, (1985), 1359–1404.

Denton, Gavin and Kun, Fan. 'Hong Kong'. In Carlos Esplugues and Silvia Barona (eds.), *Global Perspectives on ADR*, 131–164. Cambridge, UK: Intersentia, 2014.

Dezalay, Yves and Garth, Bryant. 'Fussing about the Forum: Categories and Definitions as Stakes in a Professional Competition'. *Law and Social Inquiry*, 21 (1996), 285–312.

Dignam, Alan J. and Lowry, John. *Company Law*, 8th ed. Oxford: Oxford University Press, 2014.

DiMaggio, Paul. 'Interest and Agency in Institutional Theory'. In Lynne G. Zucker (ed.), *Institutional Patterns and Organizations: Culture and Environment*, 3–22. Cambridge: MA:: Ballinger, 1988.

DiMaggio, Paul J. and Powell, Walter W. 'The Iron Cage Revisited: Institutional Isomorphism and Collective Rationality in Organizational Fields'. *American Sociological Review*, 48:2 (1983), 147–160.

Dobinson, Ian and Johns, Francis. 'Qualitative Legal Research'. In Mike McConville and Chui Wing-Hong (eds.), *Research Methods for Law*, 16–45. Edinburgh: Edinburgh University Press, 2007.

Doidge, Craig G., et al. 'Has New York Become Less Competitive in Global Markets? Evaluating Foreign Listing Choices Over Time'. *Journal of Financial Economics*, 91:3 (2009), 253–277.

Eisenberg, Melvin A. 'The Conception that the Corporation Is a Nexus of Contracts, and the Dual Nature of the Firm'. *The Journal of Corporation Law*, 24 (1998), 819–836.

English Law Commission. *Shareholder Remedies Consultation*. Law Commission Consultation Paper No. 142, 1996.

Shareholder Remedies. London: The Stationary Office, Law Commission Report No. 246, Cm 3769, 1997.

Ewald, William. 'Comparative Jurisprudence (II): The Logic of Legal Transplants'. *The American Journal of Comparative Law*, 43:4 (1995), 489–510.

Fan Kun. 'Mediation and Civil Justice Reform in Hong Kong'. *International Litigation Quartely*, 27:2 (2011), 11–14.

'The New Arbitration Ordinance in Hong Kong'. *Journal of International Arbitration*, 29:6 (2012), 715–722.

Farrar, John H. and Boulle, Laurence J. 'Minority Shareholders Remedies – Shifting Dispute Resolution Paradigms'. *Bond Law Review*, 13 (2001), 1–32.

Farrar, John, et al. 'Dispute Resolution in Family Companies'. *Canterbury Law Review*, 18 (2012), 155–186.

Felstiner, William L. F. 'Avoidance as Dispute Processing: An Elaboration'. *Source: Law & Society Review*, 9:4 (1975), 695–706.

Financial Dispute Resolution Centre. *Consultation Paper on the Proposals to Enhance the Financial Dispute Resolution Scheme*. 2016.

Fiss, Owen M. 'The Supreme Court 1978 Term Forward: The Forms of Justice'. *Harvard Law Review*, 93 (1979), 1–58.

'The Social and Political Foundations of Adjudication'. *Law and Human Behaviour*, 6:2 (1982), 121–128.

'Against Settlement'. *The Yale Law Journal*, 93:6 (1984), 1073–1090.

'Out of Eden'. *The Yale Law Journal*, 94:7 (1985), 1669–1673.

Freidson, Eliot. *Professionalism: The Third Logic*. Cambridge, UK: Polity Press, 2001.

Friedland, Roger and Alford, Robert R. *Powers of Theory: Capitalism, the State, and Democracy*. Cambridge: Cambridge University Press,1985.

Friedman, Lawrence M. 'On Legalistic Reasoning: A Footnote to Weber'. *Wisconsin Law Review*, (1966), 148–171.

'Legal Rules and the Process of Social Change'. *Stanford Law Review*, 19 (1967), 786–840.

'Legal Culture and Social Development'. *Law & Society Review*, 4 (1969), 29–44.

Law and Society: An Introduction. Englewood Cliffs, NJ: Prentice Hall, 1977.

'The Law and Society Movement'. *Stanford Law Review*, 38 (1986), 763–780.

'Some Comments on Legal Interpretation'. *Poetics Today*, 9:1 (1988), 95–102.

'Law, Lawyers, and Popular Culture'. *The Yale Law Journal*, 98 (1989), 1579–1606.

'Lawyers in Cross-Cultural Perspective'. In Richard L. Abel and Philips C. Lewis (eds.), *Lawyers in Society. Comparative Theories*, Vol. III, 1–26. Berkeley: University of California Press, 1989.

Fuller, Lon L. 'Mediation – Its Forms and Functions'. *Southern California Law Review*, 44 (1970), 305–339.

Morality of Law. New Haven, CT: Yale University Press, 1977.

'The Lawyer as an Architect of Social Structures'. In Kenneth I. Winston (ed.), *The Principles of Social Order: Selected Essays of Lon L. Fuller*, 285–292. Oxford: Hart, 2001.

Fung, the Honourable Justice. 'Mediator's Qualifications and Skills', Conference on *Mediation Conference*, Hong Kong, 21 March 2014.

Galanter, Marc. 'Litigation and Dispute Processing: Part One'. *Law & Society Review*, 9:1 (1974), 95–160.

'Adjudication, Litigation, and Related Phenomena'. In Leon Lipson and Stanton Wheeler (eds.), *Law and the Social Sciences*, 151–257. New York: Russell Sage Foundation, 1986.

'A World Without Trial'. *Journal of Dispute Resolution*, 7 (2006), 7–34.

Galanter, Marc and Lande, John. 'Private Courts and Public Authority'. *Studies in Law, Politics, and Society*, 12 (1992), 393–415.

Gazal-Ayal, Oren and Perry, Ronen. 'Imbalances of Power in ADR: The Impact of Representation and Dispute Resolution Method on Case Outcomes'. *Law & Social Inquiry*, (2014), 1–33.

Gelter, Martin. 'The Dark Side of Shareholder Influence: Managerial Autonomy and Stakeholder Orientation in Comparative Corporate Governance'. *Harvard Internationa Law Journal*, 50 (2009), 129–194.

Genn, Hazel. Department for Constitutional Affairs. *Central London Pilot Mediation Scheme, Evaluation Report* (1998).

Paths to Justice: What People Think and Do about Going to Law. Oxford: Hart Publishing 1999.

Court Based ADR initiatives for Non-Family Civil Cases. Department for Constitutional Affairs, Research series1/02, 2002.

'Civil Justice Reform and ADR', Conference on *Civil Justice Reform: What has It Achieved?* Hong Kong, 15 April 2010.

Judging Civil Justice. The Hamlyn Lectures 59th Series. Cambridge University Press, 2010.

'What Is Civil Justice For? Reform, ADR, and Access to Justice'. *Yale Journal of Law and the Humanities*, 24:1 (2012), 397–417.

Genn, Hazel, et al. *Twisting Arms: Court Referred and Court Linked Mediation Under Judicial Pressure.* Ministry of Justice Research Series, Series 1/07, 2007.

Ghai Yash. 'The Rule of Law and Capitalism: Reflections on the Basic Law'. In Raymond Wacks (ed.), *Hong Kong, China and 1997: Essays in Legal Theory*, 343–366. Hong Kong: Hong Kong University Press, 1997.

Goldberg, Stephen B., et al. 'ADR Problems and Prospects: Looking to the Future'. *Judicature*, 69 (1985), 291–299.

Gordon, Grant and Nicholson, Nigel. *Family Wars: Classic Conflicts in Family Business and How to Deal with Them.* London: Kogan Page, 2008.

Greenhalgh, Trisha, et al. 'Diffusion of Innovations in Service Organizations: Systematic Review and Recommendations'. *The Milbank Quartely*, 82:4 (2004), 581–629.

Greenwood, Royston, et al. 'Theorizing Change: The Role of Professional Associations in the Transformation of Institutionalized Fields'. *Academy of Management Journal*, 45:1 (2002), 58–80.

Groot, Diederik De. 'Arbitration and Company Law: An Introduction'. *European Company Law*, 12:3 (2015), 125–127.

Halsbury's Law of Hong Kong, Vol. 37, 2nd ed. (2011).Hong Kong: Butterworths.

Gujarati, Damodar N. *Basic Econometrics.* 4th ed. New York: McGraw Hill, 2003.

Hardy, Cynthia and Maguire, Steve. 'Institutional Entrepreneurship'. In Royston Greenwood et al. (eds.), *The SAGE Handbook of Organizational Institutionalism*, 198–217. Thousand Oaks, CA: SAGE, 2008.

Hedeen, Timothy. 'Coercion and Self-Determination in Court-Connected Mediation: All Mediations Are Voluntary, but Some Are More Voluntary Than Others'. *The Justice System Journal*, 26:3 (2005), 273–291.

Henning, J. J. 'Legislative Comment on the South African Close Corporation Under the New Companies Act: Part I'. *Company Lawyer*, 31:7 (2010), 225–228.

Hill, Timothy and Damon So. 'Resolving Construction Claims through Mediation'. *Asian Dispute Review*, (2010), 58–60.

Hollington, Robin. *Hollington on Shareholders' Rights*, 7th ed. London: Sweet & Maxwell, 2013.

The Hong Kong Basic Law Promotion Sterring Committee. *Introduction to the Basic Law of the Hong Kong Special Administrative Region*. Hong Kong: Law Press/Joint Publishing, 2000.

Hong Kong Civil Procedure. *The White Book*, Vol. 1. London: Sweet & Maxwell, 2013.

Hong Kong Companies Law Revision Committee. *Company Law: Second Report of the Companies Law Revision Committee*. Hong Kong: Government Printer, 1973.

Hong Kong Department of Justice. *Consultancy Study on the Demand for and Supply of Legal and Related Services*. Hong Kong Department of Justice, 2008.

Report of the Working Group on Mediation. Hong Kong Department of Justice, 2010.

Enactment of Apology Legislation in Hong Kong: Final Report and Recommendations, 28 November 2016.

Hong Kong Financial Services and the Treasury Bureau. *Consultation Paper on the Draft Companies Bill: First Phase Consultation*. Hong Kong Financial Services and the Treasury Bureau, 2009.

New Companies Ordinance: Subsidiary Legislation for Implementation of the New Companies Ordinance (Phase Two Consultation Document). Hong Kong Financial Services and the Treasury Bureau, 2012.

The Hong Kong Institute of Directors. *Guidelines on Corporate Governance in SMEs in Hong Kong*, 2009.

Hong Kong Judiciary. *Reform of the Civil Justice System in Hong Kong*, Interim Report and Consultative Paper on Civil Justice Reform. Hong Kong Judiciary, 2000.

Reform of the Civil Justice System in Hong Kong. Final Report of the Working Party on Civil Justice Reform. Hong Kong Judiciary, 2004.

Hong Kong Legal Aid Department. *Litigation vs. Mediation: An Alternative Way to Settle Disputes*, 2010.

Hong Kong Mediation and Arbitration Centre, Pro Bono Mediation Services. www.hkmaac.org/mediation/pro_bono.php (Accessed 19 September 2016).

The Hong Kong SAR Government. *Press Releases: Companies (Unfair Prejudice Petitions) Proceedings Rules Submitted to LegCo*, 15 May 2013.

Press Releases: Companies (Unfair Prejudice Petitions) Proceedings Rules Submitted to LegCo, 15 May 2013.

Hong Kong Standing Committee on Company Law Reform. *The Report of the Standing Committee on Company Law Reform on the Recommendations of a Consultancy Report of the Review of the Hong Kong Companies Ordinance*, Hong Kong: Printing Department, 2000.

Hopt, Klaus J. and Steffek, Felix. 'Mediation: Comparison of Laws, Regulatory Models, Fundamental Issues'. In Klaus J. Hopt and Felix Steffek (eds.), *Mediation: Principles and Regulation in Comparative Perspective*, 3–130. Oxford: Oxford University Press, 2013.

Hosmer, David W. and Lemeshow, Stanley. *Applied Logistic Regression*, 2nd ed. Hoboken, NJ: John Wiley & Son, 2000.

Hwang Hokyu and Powell, Walter W. 'Institutions and Entrepreneurship'. In Sharon A. Alvarez et al. (eds.), *Handbook of Entrepreneurship Research: Disciplinary Perspectives*, 201–232. New York: Springer, 2005.

Hwang Michael. 'The Prospects for Arbitration and Alternative Dispute Resolution'. In Fianna Jesover (ed.), *Corporate Governance in Emerging Markets Enforcement of Corporate Governance in Asia the Unfinished Agenda*, 97–102. Paris: Organisation for Economic Co-operation and Development, 2007.

Hwang Michael, et al. 'ADR in East Asia'. In J. C. Goldsmith et al. (eds.), *ADR in Business: Practice and Issues across Countries and Cultures*, Vol. I, 147–189. The Hague: Kluwer Law International, 2006.

Jack I. H. Jacob, Sir. *The Fabric of English Civil Justice*. London: Stevens, 1987.

Jackson, Lord Justice. *Review of Civil LItigation Costs: Final Report*. London: The Stationary Office, 2009.

'New Approach to Civil Justice: From Woolf to Jackson'. Conference on *Civil Justice Reform: What Has It Achieved?* Hong Kong, 15 April 2010.

Jacobs, Jack B. 'The Role of Specialized Courts in Resolving Corporate Governance Disputes in the United States and in the EU: An American Judge's Perspective'. In Louis Bouchez et al. (eds.), *Topics in Corporate Finance: The Quality of Corporate Law and the Role of Corporate Law Judges*, 95–106. Amsterdam: Amsterdam Center for Corporate Finance, 2006.

Jarrosson, Charles. 'Legal Issues Raised by ADR'. In Arnold Ingen-Housz (ed.), *ADR in Business: Practice and Issues across Countries and Cultures*, Vol. II, 157–181. The Hague: Kluwer Law International, 2011.

Jennings, P. Devereaux and Zandbergen, Paul A. 'Ecologically Sustainable Organizations: An Institutional Approach'. *Academy of Management Review*, 20:4 (1995), 1015–1052.

Jepperson, Ronald L. 'Institutions, Institutional Effects, and Institutionalism'. In Walter W. Powell and Paul J. DiMaggio (eds.), *The New Institutionalism in Organizational Analysis*, 143–163. Chicago: University of Chicago Press, 1991.

Johnson, Cathryn, et al. 'Legitimacy as a Social Process'. *Annual Review of Sociology*, 32 (2006), 53–78.

Johnston, Andrew. 'Arbitrability of Company Law Disputes'. In Qiao Liu and Wenhua Shan (eds.), *China and International Commercial Dispute Resolution*, 195–227. Leiden: Koninklijke Brill NV, 2016.

Jong Eelke de. 'Cultural Determinants of Ownership Concentration Across Countries'. *International Business Governance and Ethics*, 2 (2006), 145–164.

Jordan, Cally. 'Family Resemblances: The Family Controlled Company in Asia and its Implications for Law Reform'. *Australian Journal of Corporate Law*, 8 (1997), 89–104.

Kennedy, Duncan. 'Three Globalizations of Law and Legal Thought: 1850–2000. In David M. Trubek and Alvaro Santos (eds.), *The New Law and Economic Development: A Critical Appraisal*, 19–73. Cambridge: Cambridge University Press, 2006.

Kennedy-Grant, Tómas. 'The New Zealand Experience of the UNCITRAL Model Law: A Review of the Position as at 31 December 2007'. *Asian International Arbitration Journal*, 4:1 (2008), 1–63.

Koh Swee-Yen. 'Singapore's Highest Court Confirms Pro-arbitration Approach to Shareholder Disputes'. *Asian Dispute Review*, (2017), 67–71.

Kim, Susanna M. 'The Provisional Director Remedy for Corporate Deadlock: A Proposed Model Statute'. *Washington and Lee Law Review*, 60 (2003), 111–181.

King, Mervyn. 'Mediating Corporate Governance Disputes?' In Conference on *The Launch of Southern African IoD Mediation Center*, Paris, 12 February 2007.

'The Synergies and Interaction between King III and the Companies Act 61 of 2008'. *Acta Juridica*, (2010), 446–455.

Lack, Jeremy. 'Appropriate Dispute Resolution (ADR): The Spectrum of Hybrid Techniques Available to the Parties'. In Arnold ingen-Housz (ed.), *ADR in Business: Practice and Issues across Countries and Cultures*, Vol. II, 339–379. The Hague: Kluwer Law International, 2011.

Lam Man-hon, Johnson. 'Mediation in the Context of CJR: The Role of the Judiciary', Conference on *CJR: What Has It Achieved?* Hong Kong, 15 April 2010.

'The Speech of the Honourable Mr Justice Lam, Justice of Appeal', Conference on *'Mediation First' Pledge Reception*, Hong Kong, 18 July 2013.

Lambros, Thomas D. 'The Federal Rules of Civil Procedure: A New Adversarial Model for a New Era'. *University of Pittsburgh Law Review*, 50 (1989), 789–807.

Lande, John. 'The Diffusion of a Process Pluralist Ideology of Disputing: Factors Affecting Opinions of Business Lawyers and Executives'. PhD thesis, University of Wisconsin-Madison, 1995.

'Getting the Faith: Why Business Lawyers and Executives Believe Mediation'. *Harvard Negotiation Law Review*, 5 (2000), 137–231.

'Using Dispute System Design Methods to Promote Good-Faith Participation in Court-Connected Mediation Programs'. *UCLA Law Review*, 50 (2002), 70–141.

'Commentary: Focusing on Program Design Issues in Future Research on Court Connected Mediation'. *Conflict Resolution Quarterly*, 22:1–2 (2004), 89–100.

'A Guide for Policymaking that Emphasizes Principles, and Public Needs'. *Alternatives to High Cost Litigation*, 26:11 (2008), 197–205.

'The Movement Toward Early Case Handling in Courts and Private Dispute Resolution'. *Ohio State Journal on Dispute Resolution*, 24:1 (2008), 81–130.

Landsman, Stephan. 'ADR and the Cost of Compulsion'. *Stanford Law Review*, 57 (2005), 1593–1630.

Lau, Alex, et al. 'In Search of Good Governance for Asian Family Listed Companies: A Case Study on Hong Kong'. *The Company Lawyer*, 28:10 (2007), 306–311.

Lau, Chris. '"Sorry Law" Moves a Step Closer', South China Morning Post, 29 November 2016, C1.

The Law Reform Commission of Hong Kong. *Report on Conditional Fees*, 2007.

The Law Society of Hong Kong. *Working Party on Conditional Fees: Response for the Law Reform Commission's Report on Conditional Fees*, 2007.

Lawrence, Austin, et al. Report on The Effectiveness of Using Mediation in Selected Civil Law Disputes: A Meta-Analysis, 2007.

Lawton, Philip. 'Modeling the Chinese Family Firm and Minority Shareholer Protection: The Hong Kong Experience 1980–1995'. *Managerial Law*, 49:5/6 (2007), 249–271.

Lee, Tin-Yan. 'Introductory Note to the New Arbitration Ordinance of the Hong Kong Special Administrative Region'. *International Legal Materials*, 51 (2012), 133–197.

LegCo Panel on Administration of Justice and Legal Services. *Development of Mediation Services and Mediation Services for Building Management Cases*, 2011.

Legislative Council. *Bills Committee on Mediation Bill: Background Brief prepared by the Legislative Council Secretariat*, 2011.

Paper on Companies Bill Prepared by the Legislative Council Secretariat (Background Brief), 2011.

Legislative Council Brief: Companies Ordinance (Ord. No. 28 of 2012), 2013.

Legislative Council Panel on Administration and Legal Services: Mediation, 2013.

Lempert, Richard and Arbor, Ann. 'The Autonomy of Law: Two Visions Compared'. In Gunther Teubner (ed.), *Autopoietic Law: A New Approach to Law and Society*, 152–190. Berlin: Walter de Gruyter, 1988.

Leung Chun-Ying. The HKSAR Chief Executive, *The 2013 Policy Address: Seek Change, Maintain Stability, Serve the People with Pragmatism*. Hong Kong: Printing Department, 2013.

The HKSAR Chief Executive, Hong Kong Chief Executive, *The Policy Address 2014: Support the Needy Let Youth Flourish Unleash Hong Kong's Potential*. Hong Kong: Printing Department, 2014.

The HKSAR Chief Executive. *The 2016 Policy Address: Innovate for the Economy Improve Livelihood Foster Harmony Share Prosperity*. Hong Kong: Printing Department, 2016.

Leung Elsie. 'Mediation: A Cultural Change'. *Asian Pacific Law Review*, 17 (2009), 39–46.

Levenstein, Eric, et al. 'South Africa'. In Alexander Loos (ed.), *Directors Liability: A Worldwide Review*, 3–10. The Hague: Kluwer Law International, 2012.

Liew, Carol. 'Recent Developments in Mediation in East Asia'. In Arnold Ingen-Housz (ed.), *ADR in Business: Practice and Issues across Countries and Cultures*, Vol. II, 515–557. The Hague: Kluwer Law International, 2011.

Lindamood, Darren P. 'Comment: Redressing the Arbitration Process: An Alternative to the Arbitration Fairness Act of 2009'. *Wake Forest Law Review*, 45 (2010), 291–318.

Lipsky, David B. and Seeber, Ronald L. 'Patterns of ADR used in Corporate Disputes'. *Dispute Resolution Journal*, 54:1 (1999), 68–71.

Lloyd-Bostock, Sally. 'Alternative Dispute Resolution and Civil Justice Reform: Is ADR Being Used to Paper Over Cracks?: Reactions to Judge Jack Weinstein's Article'. *Ohio State Journal on Dispute Resolution*, 11 (1996), 397–402.

Lo Stefan H. C and Charles Z Qu. *Law of Companies in Hong Kong*. Hong Kong: Sweet & Maxwell/Thomson Reuters, 2013.

Lopich Robert. 'Collaborative Law Overview: Towards Collaborative Problem-solving in Business'. *ADR Bulletin*, 10:8 (2009), 161–166.

Lounsbury, Michael. 'Institutional Rationality and Practice Variation: New Directions in the Institutional Analysis of Practice'. *Accounting, Organizations and Society*, 33 (2008), 348–361.

Lowry, John. 'The Pursuit of Effective Minority Shareholder Protection: Section 459 of the Companies Act 1985'. *Company Lawyer*, 17 (1996), 67–72.

'Mapping the Boundaries of Unfair Prejudice'. In John de Lacy (ed.), *The Reform of United Kingdom Company Law*, 229–248. London: Cavendish, 2002.

Lynch, Katherine L. *The Forces of Economic Globalization: Challenges to the Regime of International Commercial Arbitration*. The Hague: Kluwer Law International, 2003.

Ma Ngok. 'Electric Corporatism and State Interventions in Post-Colonial Hong Kong'. In Chiu Wing-Kai Stephen and Wong Siu-lun (eds.), *Repositioning the Hong Kong Government*, 63–90. Hong Kong: Hong Kong University Press, 2012.

Macey, Jonathan R. *Corporate Governance: Promise Kept, Promise Broken*. Princeton, NJ: Princeton University Press, 2008.

MacFarlane, Julie. 'The Evolution of New Lawyer: How Lawyers Are Reshaping the Practice of Law'. *Journal of Dispute Resolution*, (2008), 61–81.

The New Lawyer: How Settlement Is Transforming the Practice of Law. Vancouver, B.C.: UBC Press, 2008.

'ADR and the Courts: Renewing Our Commitment to Innovation'. *Marquette Law Review*, 95 (2012), 927–940.

Mack, Kathy. *Court Referral to ADR: Criteria and Research* (2003) at www.aija.org.au (Accessed 8 August 2011).

Mackie, Karl. 'The Future for ADR Clauses After Cable & Wireless v. IBM'. *Arbitration International*, 19:3 (2003), 345–362.

Mackie, Karl, et al. *The ADR Practice Guide: Commercial Dispute Resolution.* Tottel, 2007.

Macneil, Ian R. 'Contracts: Adjustment of Long-Term Economic Relations under Classical Neoclassical, and Relational Contract Law'. *Northwestern University Law Review*, 72:6 (1978), 854–905.

American Arbitration Law: Reformation, Nationalization, Internationalization. Oxford: Oxford University Press, 1992.

Main, Thomas O. 'Traditional Equity and Contemporary Procedure'. *Washington Law Review Association*, 78 (2003), 429–515.

'ADR: The New Equity'. *University of Cincinnati Law Review*, 74 (2005), 329–404.

Majid, Abdul, et al. 'Company Directors' Perception of Their Responsibilities and Duties: A Hong Kong Survey'. *Hong Kong Law Journal*, 28 (1998), 60–89.

Manning, Peter K. '"Big-Bang" Decisions: Notes on a Naturalistic Approach'. In Keith Hawkins (ed.), *The Uses of Discretion*, 249–286. Oxford: Clarendon Press, 1992.

Mather, Lynn, et al. *Divorce Lawyers at Work: Varieties of Professionalism in Practice.* Oxford: Oxford University Press, 2001.

McAdoo, Bobbi, et al. 'Institutionalization: What Do Empirical Studies Tell Us About Court Mediation?'. *Dispute Resolution Magazine*, 9 (2003), 8–10.

McCrudden, Christopher. 'Legal Research and the Social Sciences'. *Law Quarterly Review*, 122 (2006), 632–650.

McGovern, Francis E. 'Beyond Efficiency: A Bevy of ADR Justifications (An Unfootnoted Summary)'. *Dispute Resolution Magazine*, 3 (1996), 12–13.

McGregor, Lynn. 'Corporate Governance in South Africa'. In Christine A-Mallin (ed.), *Handbook on International Corporate Governance: Country Analysis*, 390–413. Cheltenham: Edward Elgar, 2011.

McVea, Harry. 'Cases: Section 994 of the Companies Act 2006 and the Primacy of Contract'. *The Modern Law Review*, 75:6 (2012), 1123–1149.

Means, Benjamin. 'NonMarket Values in Family Business'. *William & Mary Law Review*, 54 (2013), 1185–1250.

Meggitt, Gary and Aslam, Farzana. 'Civil Justice Reform in Hong Kong – A Critical Appraisal'. *Civil Justice Quarterly*, 28:1 (2009), 111–131.

Menkel-Meadow, Carrie. 'For and Against Settlement: Uses and Abuses of the Mandatory Settlement Conference'. *UCLA Law Review*, 33 (1985), 485–514.

'Pursuing Settlement in an Adversary Culture: A Tale of Innovation Co-opted or "The Law of ADR"'. *Florida State University Law Review*, 19 (1991), 1–46.

'Will Managed Care Give Us Access to Justice?'. In Roger Smith (ed.), *Achieving Civil Justice: Appropriate Dispute Resolution for the 1990s*, 89–118. London: Legal Action Group, 1996.

'When Dispute Resolution Begets Disputes of Its Own: Conflicts Among Dispute Profssionals'. *UCLA Law Review*, 44 (1997), 1871–1933.

'From Legal Disputes to Conflict Resolution and Human Problem Solving: Legal Dispute Resolution in a Multidisciplinary Context'. *Journal of Legal Education*, 54:1 (2004), 7–29.

Merkin, Robert. *Arbitration Act 1996*, 2nd ed. London: LLP, 2005.

Meyer, John W. and Rowan, Brian. 'Institutionalized Organizations: Formal Structure as Myth and Ceremony'. *American Journal of Sociology*, 83:2 (1977), 340–363.

Miller, Sandra K. 'Minority Shareholder Oppression in the Private Company in the European Community: A Comparative Analysis of the German, United Kingdom, and French "Close Corporation Problem"'. *Cornell International Law Journal*, 30 (1997), 381–427.

Milman, David. 'The Rise of the Objective Concept of 'Unfairness' in UK Company Law'. *Company Law Newsletter*, 286 (2010), 1–4.

Milne, Richard. 'Blood Ties Serve Business Well During the Crisis'. *Financial Times*, 28 December 2009, p. 15.

Mistelis, Loukas. 'International Arbitration – Corporate Attitudes and Practices – 12 Perceptions Tested: Myths, Data and Analysis Research Report'. *The American Review of International Arbitration*, 15 (2004), 527–591.

Mitchell, Vanessa. 'The US Approach Towards the Acquisition of Minority Shares: Have We Anything to Learn?'. *Company and Securities Law Journal*, 14:5 (1996), 283–311.

Mnookin, Robert H. and Kornhauser, Lewis. 'Bargaining in the Shadow of the Law: The Case of Divorce'. *Yale Law Journal*, 88:5 (1979), 950–997.

Monroe, Bruce. 'Institutionalization of Alternative Dispute Resolution by the State of California'. *Pepperdine Law Review*, 14:4 (1987), 945–987.

Morse, Janice M. 'Principles of Mixed Methods and Multi-method Research Design'. In Abbas Tashakkori and Charles Teddle (eds.), *Handbook of Mixed Methods in Social & Behavioral Research*, 189–208. Thousand Oaks, CA: SAGE, 2003.

Nestor, Paul G. and K. Schutt, Russell. *Research Methods in Psychology: Investigating Human Behaviour*, 2nd ed. Thousand Oaks, CA: SAGE, 2015.

Neuman, William Lawrence, *Basic of Social Research: Qualitative and Quantitative Approaches*, 3rd ed. Pearson, 2012.

News: Dispute Resolution Legislation, *Asian Dispute Review*, (2017), 95–99.

Ng, Joyce and Hollingsworth, Julia. 'Hong Kong Passes Law Making It Easier to Say "Sorry" Without Legal Consequences', *South China Morning Post* (14 July 2017) at www.scmp.com/news/hong-kong/law-crime/article/20102526/hong-kong/lawmakers-pass-sorry-law (Accessed 18 July 2017).

Nolan-Haley, Jacqueline M. 'Court Mediation and the Search for Justice through Law'. *Washington University Law Quarterly*, 74 (1996), 47–102.

'The Merger of Law and Mediation: Lessons from Equity Jurisprudence and Roscoe Pound'. *Cardozo Journal of Conflict Resolution*, 6 (2005), 57–71.

North, Douglass C. *Institutions, Institutional Change and Economic Performance.* Cambridge: Cambridge University Press, 1990.

Note. 'Mandatory Arbitration as a Remedy for Intra-close Corporate Disputes'. *Virginia Law Review*, 56 (1970), 271–294.

'ADR, the Judiciary, and Justice: Coming to Terms with the Alternatives'. *Harvard Law Review*, 113:7 (2000), 1851–1875.

OECD. *Exploratory Meeting on Resolution of Corporate Governance Related Disputes* at www.oecd.org/dataoecd/48/22/37188704.pdf (Accessed 12 December 2011).

Onyema, Emilia. 'The Use of Med-Arb in International Commercial Dispute Resolution'. *American Review of International Arbitration*, 12 (2001), 411–423.

Paleker, Mohamed. 'Mediation in South Africa: Here but Not All There'. In Nadja Alexander (ed.), *Global Trends in Mediation*, 333–369. The Hague: Kluwer Law International, 2006.

Paredes, Tray A. 'A System Approach to Corporate Governance Reform: Why Importing US Corporate Law Isn't the Answer'. *William and Mary Law Review*, 45 (2003), 1005–1157.

Parkinson, J. E. *Corporate Power and Responsibility.* Oxford: Clarendon Press 1993.

Parkinson, John. 'Inclusive Company Law'. In John de Lacy (ed.), *The Reform of United Kingdom Company Law*, 43–58. London: Cavendish, 2002.

Parsons, Talcott. 'Law as an Intellectual Stepchild'. In Harry M. Johnson (ed.), *Social System and Legal Process: Theory, Comparative Perspectives and Special Studies.* 11–58. San Francisco: Jossey-Bass, 1978.

Partington, Martin. 'Empirical Legal Research and Policy-Making'. In Peter Cane and Herbert M. Kritzer (eds.), *The Oxford Handbook of Empirical Legal Research*, 1025–1044. Oxford: Oxford University Press, 2010.

Pawson, Ray and Tilley, Nick. *Realistic Evaluation.* London: SAGE, 1997.

Payne, Jennifer. 'Company Law'. *All England Annual Review*, 4 (2004), 647–677.

'Sections 459–461 Companies Act 1985 in Flux: The Future of Shareholder Protection'. *Cambridge Law Journal*, 64:3 (2005), 647–677.

Picardi, Carrie A. and Masick, Kevin D. *Research Methods: Designing and Conducting Research with a Real-World Focus.* Thousand Oaks, CA: SAGE, 2014.

Pirie, Andrew J. 'Alternative Dispute Resolution in Thailand and Cambodia: Making Sense on (Un)Common Ground'. In Douglas M. Johnston and Gerry Ferguson (eds.), *Asia-Pacific Legal Development.* pp. 501–547. Vancouver, B.C.: UBC Press, 1998.

Porta, Rafael La, et al. 'Law and Finance'. *Journal of Political Economy*, 106:6 (1998), 1113–1155.

'Corporate Ownership Around the World'. *Journal of Finance*, 54:2 (1999), 471–517.

'Investor Protection and Corporate Governance'. *Journal of Financial Economics*, 58 (2000), 3–27.

Powell, Walter W. 'Expanding the Scope of Institutional Analysis'. In Walter W. Powell and Paul J. DiMaggio (eds.), *The New Institutionalism in Organizational Analysis*, 183–203. Chicago: University of Chicago Press, 1991.

Powell, Walter W. and DiMaggio, Paul J. 'Introduction'. In Paul J. DiMaggio and Walter W. Powell (eds.), *The New Institutionalism in Organizational Analysis*, 1–40. Chicago: University of Chicago Press, 1991.

Prentice, D. D. 'The Theory of the Firm: Minority Shareholder Oppression: Sections 459–461 of the Companies Act 1985'. *Oxford Journal of Legal Studies*, 8:1 (1988), 55–91.

Press Release: Final Report and Recommendations on Enactment of Apology Legislation Published, 28 November 2016 at www.info.gov.hk/gia/general/201611/28/P2016112800594.htm (Accessed 29 November 2016).

Press, Sharon. 'Institutionalization: Savior or Saboteur of Mediation?'. *Florida State University Law Review*, 24 (1997), 903–917.

Purdy, Jill M. and Gary, Barbara. 'Conflicting Logics, Mechanisms of Diffusion, and Multilevel Dynamics in Emerging Institutional Fields'. *Academy of Management Journal*, 52:2 (2009), 355–380.

Pruitt, Dean G. and Kim, Sung Hee. *Social Conflict: Escalation, Stalemate, and Settlement*, 3rd ed. New York: McGraw-Hill Higher Education, 2004.

Quek, Dorcas. 'Mandatory Mediation: An Oxymoron? Examining The Feasibility of Implementing a Court-Mandated Mediation Program'. *Cardozo Journal of Conflict Resolution*, 11 (2010), 479–509.

Raven, Robert D. 'Alternative Dispute Resolution: Expanding Opportunities'. *The Arbitration Journal*, 43:2 (1988), 44–48.

Regan, Francis. 'Dispute Resolution in Australia: Theory, Evidence and Dilemmas'. In Gongyi Wang and Roman Tomasic (eds.), *Alternative Dispute Resolution and Modern Rule of Law: Papers from the Sino-Australian Seminar*, 49–59. Beijing: Law Press, 2003.

Reitz, John C. 'How to Do Comparative Law'. *The American Journal of Comparative Law*, 46:4 (1998), 617–636.

Resnik, Judith. 'Many Doors? Closing Doors? Alternative Dispute Resolution and Adjudication'. *The Ohio State Journal on Dispute Resolution*, 10:2 (1995), 211–265.

Reuben, Richard C. 'Constitutional Gravity: A Unitary Theory of Alternative Dispute Resoltuion and Public Civil Justice'. *UCLA Law Review*, 47 (2000), 949–1104.

Riley, Christopher A. 'Contracting Out of Company Law: Section 459 of the Companies Act 1985 and the Role of the Courts'. *The Modern Law Review*, 55:6 (1992), 782–802.

Riskin, Leonard L. 'Mediation and Lawyers'. *Ohio State Law Journal*, 43 (1992), 29–60.

Riskin, Leonard L., et al. *Dispute Resolution and Lawyers*, 3rd ed. Belmont, CA: Thompson West, 2006.

Roberts, Simon and Palmer, Michael. *Dispute Processes: ADR and the Primary Forms of Decision-Making*, 2nd ed. Cambridge: Cambridge University Press, 2005.

Rogers, Everett M. *Diffusion of Innovations*, 5th ed. New York: Free Press, 2003.

Roodt, Christa. 'Autonomy and Due Process in Arbitration: Recalibrating the Balance'. *The Comparative and International Law Journal of South Africa*, 41:2 (2011), 311–339.

Rose, Richard. 'What Is Lesson Drawing?'. *Journal of Public Policy*, 11:1 (1991), 3–30.

Rosenthal, Robert. *Meta-Analytical Procedures for Social Research*, rev. ed. Thousand Oaks, CA: SAGE, 1991.

Roux, Francois Le. *The Applicability of the Third King Report on Corporate Governance to Small and Medium Enterprises*. PhD thesis, The University of Stellenbosch, 2010.

Rowe, Mary and Bendersky, Corinne. 'Workplace Justice, Zero Tolerance, and Zero Barriers'. In Thomas A. Kochan and David B. Lipsky (eds.), *Negotiaions and Change: From the Workplace to Society*, 117–140. Ithaca, NY:: Cornell University Press, 2003.

Rozdeiczer, Lukasz and Campa, Alejandro Alvarez de la. *Alternative Dispute Resolution Manual: Implementing Commercial Mediation - Small and Medium Enterprise Department* at http://rru.worldbank.org/Documents/Toolkits/adr/adr_fulltoolkit.pdf (Accessed 18 August 2009).

Runesson, Eric M. and Guy, Marie-Laurence. Mediating Corporate Governance Conflict and Disputes: Global Corporate Governance Forum Focus 4 (2007) at www.gcgf.org/ifcext/cgf.nsf/AttachmentsByTitle/Focus+Mediation/$FILE/Focus4_Mediation_12.pdf (Accessed 18 August 2009).

Sandborg, David. 'Dispatch From Hong Kong'. *Dispute Resolution Magazine*, (2013), 45–47.

'Construction ADR: Multistep ADR Gets Creative at Hong Kong's New Airport'. *Alternatives to High Cost Litigation*, 17:3 (1999), 41–61.

Sander, Frank E. A. 'Another View of Mandatory Mediation'. *Dispute Resolution Journal*, 16 (2007), 16.

Sander, Frank E. A. and Rozdiczer, Lukasz. 'Matching Cases and Dispute Resolution Procedures: Detailed Analysis Leading to a Mediation-Centered Approach'. *Harvard Negotiation Law Review*, 11 (2006), 1–41.

Schultz, Thomas. 'Secondary Rules of Recognition and Relative Legality in Transnational Regimes'. *The American Journal of Jurisprudence*, 56 (2011), 59–88.

SCMP. Mediation Isn't Being Taken Seriously, 29 July 2011 at www.scmp.com/article/974803/mediation-isnt-being-taken-seriously (Accessed 10 January 2014).

Scott, Richard W. *Institutions and Organizations*, 2nd ed. Thousand Oaks, CA: SAGE, 2001.

Scott, William R. *Financial Accounting Theory*, 3rd ed. Toronto: Prentice Hall, 2003.

Selznick, Philip. *The Moral Commonwealth: Social Theory and the Promise of Community*. Berkeley: University of California Press, 1992.

Shapiro, Martin. *Courts: A Comparative and Political Analysis*. Chicago: University of Chicago Press, 1986.

Shaw, Lori Anne. 'Divorce Mediation Outcome Research: A Meta-Analysis'. *Conflict Resolution Quarterly*, 27:4 (2010), 447–467.

Shipman, Shirley. 'Compulsory Mediation: The Elephant in the Room'. *Civil Justice Quarterly*, 30:2 (2011), 163–191.

Singer, Linda R. *Settling Disputes: Conflict Resolution in Business, Families, and the Legal System*, 2nd ed. Boulder, CO: Westview Press, 1994.

Solomon, Lewis D. and Solomon, Janet Stern. 'Using Alternative Dispute Resolution Techniques to Settle Conflicts among Shareholders of Closely Held Corporations'. *Wake Forest Law Review*, 22 (1987), 105–126.

Spamann, Holger. 'Contemporary Legal Transplants: Legal Families and the Diffusion of (Corporate) Law'. *Brigham Young University Law Review*, 11:6 (2009), 1813–1878.

Spiller, Peter. *Dispute Resolution in New Zealand*, 2nd ed. Oxford: Oxford University Press, 2007.

Statistics Relating to the Number of Local Companies Incorporated in Hong Kong at www.cr.gov.hk/en/statistics/statistics_02.htm (Accessed 10 May 2016).

Sternlight, Jean R. 'Is Alternative Dispute Resolution Consistent with the Rule of Law? Lessons from Abroad'. *DePaul Law Review*, 56 (2006), 569–592.

Stipanowich, Thomas J. and Lamare, J. Ryan. 'Living with ADR: Evolving Perceptions and Use of Mediation, Arbitration, and Conflict Management in Fortune 1000 Corporations'. *Harvard Negotiation Law Review*, 19 (2014), 1–68.

Suchman, Mark C. 'Managing Legitimacy: Strategic and Institutional Approaches'. *Academy of Management Review*, 20:3 (1995), 571–610.

Suddaby, Roy and Greenwood, Royston. 'Rhetorical Strategies of Legitimacy'. *Administrative Science Quartely*, 50 (2005), 35–67.

Sugarman, David. 'Reconceptualising Company Law: Reflections on the Law Commission's Consultation Paper on Shareholder Remedies: Part 1'. *The Company Lawyer*, 18:8 (1997), 226–247.

'Reconceptualising Company Law: Reflections on the Law Commission's Consultation Paper on Shareholder Remedies: Part 2'. *Company Lawyer*, 18:9 (1997), 274–282.

Susskind, Richard. *The End of Lawyer: Rethinking the Nature of Legal Services*, rev ed. Oxford: Oxford University Press, 2010.

Tan, Karen. HKIAC Tops Prestigious Global Arbitration Survey at www.hkiac.org/news/hkiac-tops-prestigious-global-arbitration-survey (Accessed 4 May 2016).

Taylor, Lynne. 'Minority Buy-Out Rights in the Company Act 1993'. *Canterbury Law Review*, 6 (1997), 539–563.

'Shareholder Agreements'. In John Farrar et al. (eds.), *Company and Securities Law in New Zealand*, 65–68. New Zealand: Thomson Reuters, 2008.

Teubner, Gunther. 'Introduction to Autopoietic Law'. In Gunther Teubner (ed.), *Autopoietic Law: A New Approach to Law and Society*, 1–11. Berlin: Walter de Gruyter, 1988.

'"And God Laughed..." Indeterminacy, Self-Reference and Paradox in Law'. *German Law Journal*, 12:1 (2011), 376–406.

Thibaut, John, et al. 'Procedural Justice as Fairness'. *Stanford Law Review*, 26 (1974), 1271–1289.

Tolbert, Pamela S. and Zucker, Lynne G. 'Studying Organization: Theory & Method'. In Stewart R. Clegg and Cynthia Hardy (eds.), *The Institutionalization of Institutional Theory*, 169–184. Thousand Oaks, CA: SAGE, 1999.

Trubek, David. 'Max Weber on Law and the Rise of Capitalism'. *Wisconsin Law Review*, (1972), 720–753.

Tsang, Donald. The HKSAR Chief Executive, *The 2006–07 Policy Address: Proactive Pragmatic Always People First*, 2006.

The HKSAR Chief Executive, *The 2007 Policy Address: A New Direction for Hong Kong*. Hong Kong: Publishing Department, 2007.

Tweeddale, Andrew and Tweeddale, Keren. *A Practical Approach to Arbitration Law*. London: Blackstone Press, 1999.

Twining, William. 'Social Science and Diffusion of Law'. *Journal of Law and Society*, 32:2 (2005), 203–240.

Unger, Roberto Magabeira. *Law in Modern Society: Toward a Criticism of Social Theory*. New York: Free Press, 1976.

Ury, William L., et al. *Getting Disputes Resolved: Designing Systems to Cut the Costs of Conflict*, 1st ed. San Francisco: Jossey-Bass, 1988.

Velasco, Julian. 'The Fundamental Rights of the Shareholder'. *University of California, Davis*, 40:2 (2006), 407–467.

Vermeulen, Erik P. M. *The Evolution of Legal Business Forms in Europe and the United States: Venture Capital, Joint Venture and Partnership Structures*. The Hague: Kluwer Law International, 2003.

Walker, Richard M. 'Innovation Type and Diffusion: An Empirical Analysis of Local Government'. *Public Administration*, 84:2 (2006), 311–335.

Walker, Richard M., et al. *Managing Public Services Innovation: The Experience of English Housing Associations*. Bristol: Policy Press, 2001.

Wallgren, Carita. 'ADR and Business'. In J. C. Goldsmith et al. (eds.), *ADR in Business: Practice and Issues across Countries and Cultures*, Vol. I, 3–19. The Hague: Kluwer Law International, 2006.

Ward, Ettie. 'Mandatory Court-annexed Alternative Dispute Resolution in The United States Federal Courts: Panacea or Pandemic?'. *St. John's Law Review*, 81 (2007), 77–98.

Warner, Rebecca M. *Applied Statistics: From Bivariate through Multivariate Techniques*. Thousand Oaks, CA: SAGE, 2008.

Watson, Alan. *Legal Transplants: An Approach to Comparative Law*. Lake Mary, FL: Vandeplas, 1974.

Watson, Garry D. 'From an Adversarial to a Managed System of Litigation: A Comparative Critique of Law Woolf's Interim Report'. In Roger Smith (ed.), *Achieving Civil Justice: Appropriate Dispute Resolution for the 1990s*, 63–88. London: Legal Action Group, 1996.

Watson, Susan. 'The Board of Directors'. In John Farrar et al. (eds.), *Company and Securities Law in New Zealand*, 269–329. New Zealand: Thomson Reuters 2008.

Wedderburn, K. W. 'Shareholders' Rights and the Rule in *Foss v Harbottle*'. *Cambridge Law Journal*, (1957), 194–215.

Weiss, Carol H. *Evaluation: Methods for Studying Programs and Policies*, 2nd ed. Englewood Cliffs, NJ: Prentice Hall, 1998.

Wejnert, Barbara. 'Integration Models of Diffusion of Innovations: A Conceptual Framework'. *Annual Review of Sociology*, 28 (2002), 297–326.

Westphal, James E. 'The Social Construction of Market Value: Institutionalization and Learning Perspectives on Stock Market Reactions'. *American Sociological Review*, 69 (2004), 433–457.

Wilkinson, Michael. 'Introduction'. In Michael Wilkinson and Janet Burton (eds.), *Reform of the Civil Process in Hong Kong*, 1–62. Hong Kong: Butterworths Asia, 2000.

Wilkinson, Michael and Burton, Janet. 'Conclusions'. In Michael Wilkinson and Janet Burton (eds.), *Reform of the Civil Process in Hong Kong*, 323. Hong Kong: Butterworths Asia, 2000.

Wilkinson, Michael and Sandor, Michael. *The Professional Conduct of Lawyers in Hong Kong*. Hong Kong: Butterworths, Asia, 2008.

Williamson, Oliver E. 'Transaction-Cost Economics: The Governance of Contractual Relations'. In Peter J. Buckley and Jonathan Michie (eds.), *Firms, Organizations and Contract: A Reader in Industrial Organization*, 168–198. Oxford: Oxford University Press, 1996.

Wilson, Claire. *Hong Kong Mediation Ordinance: Commentary and Annotations*. Hong Kong: Sweet & Maxwell/Thomson Reuters, 2013.

Wissler, Roselle L. 'Court-connected Mediation in General Civil Cases: What We Know from Empirical Research'. *Ohio State Journal on Dispute Resolution*, 17 (2002), 641–704.

'Barriers to Attorneys' Discussion and Use of ADR'. *Ohio State Journal on Dispute Resolution*, 19:2 (2004), 459–508.

Wolfe, Richard A. 'Organizational Innovation: Review, Critique and Suggested Research Directions'. *Journal of Management Studies*, 31:3 (1994), 405–431.

Wong, Albert. 'Bar Chief Backs Reforms on Financial Checks'. *The Standard*, 13 January 2009, A3.

Wong, Hung. 'Changes in Social Policy in Hong Kong since 1997: Old Wine in New Bottles?' In Lam Wai-man et al. (eds.), *Contemporary Hong Kong Government and Politics*, 277–296. Hong Kong: Hong Kong University Press, 2012.

Wong, Wilson and Yuen, Raymond. 'Economic Policy'. In Lam Wai-man et al. (eds.), *Contemporary Hong Kong Government and Politics*. Hong Kong: Hong Kong University Press, 2012.

Wong Yan-Lung. 'The Benefits of Mediation'. In Conference on *Hong Kong Mediation Council Annual Dinner*, Hong Kong, 17 March 2006.

'The Use and Development of Mediation in Hong Kong'. *Asian Dispute Reivew*, (2008), 54–56.

The World Bank. *South Africa Report on the Observance of Standards and Codes Accounting and Auditing* at www.worldbank.org (Accessed 8 June 2017).

World Bank Group. *Doing Business 2016: Measuring Regulatory Quality and Efficiency* at www.doingbusiness.org (Accessed 10 September 2016).

Yeo Li-Hui, Beatrice Mathilda and Chew, Fiona. 'Case Note on *Tomolugen Holdings Ltd v. Silica Invetors Ltd* [2016] 1 SLR 373: The Arbitration and Litigation of Minority Shareholder Disputes'. *Singapore Academic Law Journal*, 28 (2016), 382–407.

Yeow-Choy Choong and Ganesh, Warren P. 'Public Policy Consideratoins in Arbitral Proceedings in Selected Common Law Jurisdictions'. *Hong Kong Law Journal*, 44:1 (2014), 179–205.

Young, Angus. 'Reforming Directors' Duties in Hong Kong: The Journey, Stakeholders and Oversights'. *International Company and Commercial Law Review*, 23:4 (2012), 142–154.

Yuen, Rimsky, 'HK a Perfect Partner in Mediation'. In Conference on *Asia Pacific International Mediation Summit*, India, 15 February 2015.

Yuen, Rimsky. 'Secretary Justice's Speech'. In Conference on *19th International Congress of Maritime Arbitration*, 11 May 2015.

Yun Zhao. 'Revisiting the Issue of Enforceability of Mediation Agreements in Hong Kong'. *China-EU Law Journal*, 1(2013), 115–133.

Zemans, Frances Kahn. 'Framework for Analysis of Legal Mobilization: A Decision-Making Model'. *American Bar Foundation*, 7:4 (1982), 989–1071.

Zucker, Lynne G. 'Organizations as Institutions'. In Samuel B. Bacharach (ed.), *Research in the Sociology of Organizations: A Research Annual*, 83–107. Greenwich, CT: JAI Press, 1983.

'The Role of Institutionalization Cultural Persistence'. In Walter W. Powell and Paul J. DiMaggio (eds.), *The New Institutionalism in Organizational Analysis*, 169–184. Chicago: University of Chicago Press, 1991.

Zuckerman, A. A. S. 'Reform in the Shadow of Lawyers' Interests'. In A. A. S. Zuckerman and Ross Cranston (eds.), *Reform of Civil Procedure: Essay on "Access to Justice"*, 61–78. Oxford: Clarendon Press, 1995.

Zuckerman, Adrian. 'The Challenge of Civil Justice Reform: Effective Court Management of Litigation'. *City University of Hong Kong Law Review*, 1:1 (2009), 49–71.

Zuckerman, Adrian A. S. *Civil Procedure* London: LexisNexis UK, 2003.

Zweigert, Konrad and Käotz, Hein. *Introduction to Comparative Law*, 3rd rev. ed. Oxford: Clarendon Press, 1998.

INDEX

arbitrator powers, share price determination, proposed statutory buy-out regime, 211–212

Basic Law, 38

Civil Justice Reform (CJR), 15–16, 30, 42–43, 72–73
context-mechanisms-outcome (CMO) pattern configurations, 49, 63
corporate governance code, informal dispute resolution public awareness, 205–206
Cotterrell, Roger, 25
court-connected initiatives legitimacy, 71–75
Ansar Mohammad v. Global Legend Transportation Ltd, 87
Chu Chung Ming v. Lam Wai Dan, 96
Civil Justice Reform (CJR) and, 72–73
dispute resolution forums, access opportunities, 100–102
Golden Eagle International (Group) Ltd v. GR Investment Holdings, 87–88
Good Try Investments Ltd v. Easily Development Ltd, 99
judicial acceptance, ADR policy evaluation, 81–102
judicial case management, 83–89
Kwan Wing Leung v. Fung Chi Leung, 98, 99–100
O'Neill v. Philips, 80
Order 22, 97–98

Pacific Long Distance Telephone v. New World Telecommunications Ltd, 88, 92–93
policy objectives, 75–77
Practice Direction 3.3, 94–95
proportionality, cost penalties, 96–100
proportionality, court referrals, 92–96
proportionality, dispute resolution processes choice, 89–102
proportionality, private ADR processes *vs.* public adjudicative courts, 90–100
Re NTK Technology (HK) Ltd, 98–99
Re Sun Light Elastic Ltd, 92–93, 94
cultural-cognitive legitimacy, 54–55

development pathway, 30–31
Arbitration Ordinance (Cap. 609), 34–35
Basic Law and, 38
Gao Haiyan v. Keeneye Holdings Ltd, 35
government policy, 38–39
in Hong Kong, 31–37
Hong Kong Airport Core Programme (ACP), 32
Hong Kong International Arbitration Centre (HKIAC), 32–33
hybrid forms, med-arb, 35–36
judicial support, shareholder disputes early/informal resolution, 39–43
mediation *vs.* arbitration, 38–39
mediation pilot processes, 36–37

257